LIMITATION
OF ACTIONS

AUSTRALIA
The Law Book Company
Brisbane • Sydney • Melbourne • Perth

CANADA
Carswell
Ottawa • Toronto • Calgary • Montreal • Vancouver

Agents:
Steimatzky's Agency Ltd., Tel Aviv;
N.M. Tripathi (Private) Ltd., Bombay;
Eastern Law House (Private) Ltd., Calcutta;
M.P.P. House, Bangalore;
Universal Book Traders, Delhi;
Aditya Books, Delhi;
MacMillan Shuppan KK, Tokyo;
Pakistan Law House, Karachi, Lahore

LIMITATION OF ACTIONS

RUTH REDMOND-COOPER

B.A. (Kent), Licence en Droit (Paris XI), LL.M. (Bristol)
Lecturer in Law, University of Leicester
Director of Education, Rubinstein Callingham Polden
and Gale, Solicitors

LONDON   SWEET & MAXWELL   1992

Published in 1992 by
Sweet & Maxwell Limited of
South Quay Plaza, 183 Marsh Wall, London E14 9FT
Phototypeset by MFK Typesetting Ltd., Hitchin, Herts
Printed and bound in Great Britain
by Hartnolls Ltd., Bodmin

British Library Cataloguing in Publication Data

A CIP catalogue record for
this book is available
from The British Library

ISBN 0–421–45260–9

Acknowledgment
Statutory material used
in this publication is
Crown copyright

For Marjorie and James

PREFACE

My aim in writing this book has been to provide a succinct, but comprehensive account of the law governing limitation periods throughout a wide range of relationships and causes of action. I was encouraged in this enterprise by frequent reminders from colleagues in the professions of the need for a text which is both readily accessible to the non-specialist practitioner and also capable of yielding further authority for those whose needs require them to explore the subject more fully.

It is well known that problems of limitation can arise at short notice in any species of action, and the practitioner may find him or herself called upon to advise speedily but with relative certainty.

The recent avalanche of case law in this area, much of it unreported, and the complexity of the relevant statutes have reinforced my belief that an authoritative but concise treatment of the law is much needed.

I should like to thank Kirsty Keywood, postgraduate student at Leicester University, for her help in tracking down elusive materials. My greatest debt, however, is owed to Caroline Forder of the Faculteit der Rechtsgeleerheid, Rijksuniversiteit Limburg, both for her unflagging encouragement during the course of this project and for her invaluable criticisms of the chapter on Adverse Possession; any errors which may remain, are of course, my entire responsibility.

The law as stated is up-to-date to July 6, 1992.

Ruth Redmond-Cooper   September 1992

CONTENTS

Preface **vii**
Table of Cases **xi**
Table of Statutes **xxv**
Table of E.C. and International Treaties and Conventions **xxviii**

1 NATURE AND PURPOSE OF LIMITATION
   PERIODS **1**

   The legislation **3**

2 GENERAL ISSUES RELATING TO LIMITATION
   PERIODS **8**

   Accrual of the cause of action **8**
   The calculation of time **10**
   Expiry of limitation period prior to issue of writ **11**
   Determination of limitation issue: final or
   interlocutory **11**
   Onus of proving validity or expiry of writ **11**
   Calculation of the period of validity of the writ **12**
   Extension of the writ **12**
   Amendment of the writ and of pleadings **13**
   Addition of a new party **16**
   Third party proceedings **16**
   Contribution **17**
   Counter-claims/set-off **17**
   Dismissal for want of prosecution **18**
   Disability **19**

3 FRAUD, CONCEALMENT AND MISTAKE **21**

   Extinction of title and the fraud provisions **21**
   Discoverable with reasonable diligence **25**
   Third parties and postponement of limitations **29**
   Relevance of the Latent Damage Act 1986 **30**

4 PERIODS OF LIMITATION IN CONTRACT **31**

   Accrual of the cause of action **33**
   Availability of a concurrent action in tort **36**
   Action for money had and received **37**
   Contracts of loan **37**
   Insurance contracts **41**
   Limitation periods in contracts of carriage **41**
   Contracts and the Latent Damage Act 1986 **42**

5 TORT **44**

   Accrual of the cause of action **44**
   Negligence **44**
   The Latent Damage Act 1986 **52**
   Trespass and false imprisonment **56**
   Defamation **56**
   Nuisance **58**
   Conversion **58**
   Breach of statutory duty **61**
   Limitation periods imposed by statutes other than the
   Limitation Act **61**

6 PERSONAL INJURY ACTIONS 64

Definition of personal injury 64
The running of time 66
Criminal injuries compensation 74

7 JUDICIAL DISCRETION TO EXCLUDE THE
LIMITATION PERIOD 75

Discretion of the court 75
Relevance of principles established in Birkett v. James 77
Prejudice to the defendant 78
Prejudice to the plaintiff 79
Relevant circumstances 80
Application of section 33 in multi-partite claims 84

8 ADVERSE POSSESSION 86

General matters 86
Requirements for acquisition of title by limitation 88
When is possession adverse? 91
The intention of the squatter: animus possidendi 94
The intention of the owner 95
Accrual of the cause of action 95
Effect of expiry of time 97

9 PRESCRIPTION 100

Common conditions of acquisition 101
Common law prescription 104
The lost modern grant 104
The Prescription Act 1832 104
Easements of light 106

10 ADMINISTRATIVE AND EUROPEAN COMMUNITY
LAW 108

English administrative law 108
European Community law 109

11 EQUITY, TRUSTS AND DEATH 114

Equity 114
Trusts 115
Death 116

APPENDIX 1 121

Table of limitation periods 121

APPENDIX 2 127

Limitation Act 1980 (as amended) 127
Foreign Limitation Periods Act 1984 156
Prescription Act 1832 158

Index 161

TABLE OF CASES

Ackbar v. Green (C.F.) & Co. Ltd. [1975] Q.B. 582; [1975] 2 W.L.R. 773; 119 S.J. 219;
     [1975] 2 All E.R. 65; :[1975] 1 Lloyd's Rep. 673 66
A'Court v. Cross (1825) 3 Bing. 329; 11 Moore C.P. 198; 4 L.J.O. S.C.P. 79; 130 E.R.
     540 .... 1, 2
Acsim (Southern) Ltd. v. Danish Contracting and Development Co. Ltd. (1989) 47 B.L.R.
     55; (1990) B.L.M., July p. 1 17
Adams Holden & Pearson v. Trent Regional Health Authority (1989) 47 B.L.R. 34 ..... 10, 78
Agromet Motoimport Ltd. v. Maulden Engineering Co. (Beds.) Ltd. [1985] 1 W.L.R. 762;
     (1985) 129 S.J. 400; [1985] 2 All E.R. 436; (1985) 82 L.S.Gaz. 1937. 10
Aikman v. Hallett & Co., March 20, 1987, unreported 50
Allen v. Sir Alfred McAlpine & Sons Ltd. See Allen v. McAlpine (Sir Alfred) & Sons.
—— v. McAlpine (Sir Alfred) & Sons; Bostic v. Bermondsey and Southwark Group Hospital
     Management Committee; Sternberg v. Hammond [1968] 2 Q.B. 229; [1968] 2 W.L.R.
     366; [1968] 1 All E.R. 543; sub nom. Allen v. McAlpine (Sir Alfred) & Sons; Bostic v.
     Bermondsey & Southwark Hospital Management Committee; Sternberg v. Hammond
     (1968) 112 S.J. 49, C.A. 19
—— v. Waters [1935] 1 K.B. 200, C.A. 2
Amalgamated Investment and Property Co. Ltd. (in liquidation) v. Texas Commerce Inter-
     national Bank Ltd. [1982] Q.B. 84; [1981] 3 W.L.R. 565; (1981) 125 S.J. 623; [1981] 3
     All E.R. 577; [1981] Com.L.R. 236, C.A.; affirming [1981] 2 W.L.R. 554; (1980) 125
     S.J. 133; [1981] 1 All E.R. 923; [1981] Com.L.R. 37 96
Amantilla Ltd. v. Telefusion plc (1987) 9 ConLR 139 39
Angus v. Dalton (1877) 3 Q.B.D. 85; 42 J.P. 452; 47 L.J.Q.B. 163; 38 L.T. 510; reversed on
     other grounds (1878) 4 Q.B.D. 162; 43 J.P. 412; 48 L.J.Q.B. 225; 40 L.T. 605; 27
     W.R. 623, C.A.; on appeal sub nom. Dalton v. Angus (1881) 6 App. Cas. 740; 46 J.P.
     132; 30 W.R. 191; sub nom. Public Works Com'rs v. Angus & Co., Dalton v. Angus &
     Co. [1881–1885] All E.R. Rep. 1; 50 L.J.Q.B. 689; 44 L.T. 844, H.L. 102, 104
Anns v. Merton London Borough Council [1978] A.C. 728; [1977] 2 W.L.R. 1024; (1977) 121
     S.J. 377; (1977) 75 L.G.R. 555; [1977] J.P.L. 514; (1977) 243 E.C. 523, 591; sub nom.
     Anns v. London Borough of Merton [1977] 2 All E.R. 492, H.L.; affirming sub nom.
     Anns v. Walcroft Property Co. (1976) 241 E.G. 311, C.A. 46
Applegate v. Moss; Archer v. Moss [1971] 1 Q.B. 406; [1971] 2 W.L.R. 541; sub nom. Archer
     v. Moss; Applegate v. Moss (1970) 114 S.J. 971; [1971] 1 All E.R. 747, C.A. 22, 27
Arab Bank v. Barclays Bank (Dominion, Colonial and Overseas) [1954] A.C. 495; [1954] 2
     W.L.R. 1022; 98 S.J. 350; [1954] 2 All E.R. 226, H.L.; affirming [1953] 2 Q.B. 527;
     [1953] 3 W.L.R. 67; 97 S.J. 420; [1953] 2 All E.R. 263; [1953] C.L.Y. 248, C.A.;
     affirming [1952] W.N. 529; [1952] 2 T.L.R. 920; 96 S.J. 851; [1952] C.L.Y. 236. .. 38
Archer v. Brown [1985] Q.B. 401; [1984] 3 W.L.R. 350; (1984) 128 S.J. 532; [1984] 2 All E.R.
     267; (1984) 134 New L.J. 235; (1984) 81 L.S.Gaz. 2770 65
—— v. Catton & Co. Ltd. [1954] 1 W.L.R. 775; 98 S.J. 337; [1954] 1 All E.R. 896 .. 8, 41, 67
—— v. Moss, Applegate v. Moss. See Applegate v. Moss; Archer v. Moss.
Aries Tanker Corporation v. Total Transport Ltd.; Aries, The [1977] 1 W.L.R. 185; (1977)
     121 S.J. 117; [1977] 1 All E.R. 398; [1977] 1 Lloyd's Rep. 334, H.L.; affirming [1976]
     2 Lloyd's Rep. 256, C.A. 17, 42
Aries Tanker, The. See Aries Tanker Corporation v. Total Transport; Aries, The
Armitage, dec'd, Re; Ellam v. Norwich Corporation [1972] Ch. 438; [1972] 2 W.L.R. 503;
     (1971) 116 S.J. 62; 70 L.G.R. 305; sub nom. Armitage's Will Trusts, Re; Ellam v. City
     and County of Norwich [1972] 1 all E.R. 708. 87
Arnold v. Central Electricity Generating Board [1988] A.C. 228; [1987] 3 W.L.R. 1009;
     (1987) 131 S.J. 1487; [1987] 3 All E.R. 694; (1987) 84 L.S.Gaz. 3416, H.L.; affirming
     [1987] 2 W.L.R. 245; (1987) 84 L.S.Gaz. 743; (1987) 131 S.J. 167, C.A.; reversing
     [1968] 3 W.L.R. 171; (1986) 130 S.J. 484; (1986) 83 L.S.Gaz 2090 5
Artisan's Land and Mortgage Corpn., Re [1904] 1 Ch. 796; 73 L.J.Ch. 581; 52 W.R. 330; 48
     S.J. 222; 12 Mans. 98 32
Atkinson v. Bradford Third Equitable Benefit Building Society (1890) 25 Q.B.D. 377; 59
     L.J.Q.B. 360; 62 L.T. 857; 38 W.R. 630, C.A. 38

Att.-Gen. v. Cocke [1988] Ch. 414; [1988] 2 W.L.R. 542; (1988) 132 S.J. 418; [1988] 2 All
E.R. 391; [1988] L.S.Gaz., April 1, 1988 115
Autocephalus Greek Othodox Church of Cyprus v. Goldberg 171, F. Supp. 1374 (5 D.Ind.
1989) (District Court) Trans. No. 89–2809 of the U.S.C.A. for the Seventh Circuit 30
Aylott v. West Ham Corporation [1927] 1 Ch. 30; 90 J.P. 165; 95 L.J. Ch. 533; 135 L.T. 424,
427; 42 T.L.R. 516; 24 L.G.R. 429, C.A. 32

B.P. Properties v. Buckler (1988) 5 P. & C.R. 337; (1987) 284 E.G. 375; [1987] 2 E.G.L.R.
168; (1987) 137 New L.J. 899, C.A. 5, 89, 91, 97
Bagot v. Stevens Scanlan & Co. Ltd. [1966] 1 Q.B. 197; [1964] 3 W.L.R. 1162; 108 S.J. 604;
[1964] 3 All E.R. 577; [1964] 2 Lloyd's Rep. 353 36
Baker v. Courage & Co. [1910] 1 K.B. 56; [1908–1910] All E.R. Rep. 65; 79 L.J.K.B. 313:
101 L.T. 854 25
—— v. Ollard & Bentley (a firm) (1982) 126 S.J. 593 .... 50, 52
—— (G.L.) v. Medway Building and Supplies [1958] 1 W.L.R. 1216; 102 S.J. 877; [1958] 3
All E.R. 540; [1958] C.L.Y. 2095, C.A.; reversing [1958] 2 All E.R. 532. Petition for
leave to appeal to House of Lords dismissed [1959] 1 W.L.R. 492, H.L. . 13, 22, 27, 115
Balfour Beatty Construction Ltd. v. Parsons Brown & Newton Ltd., The Financial Times,
November 7, 1990, C.A. 14
Bank of America National Trust and Savings Association v. Epidavros Gulf Shipping Co.
S.A.; Cape Sounion, The [1990] 2 Lloyd's Rep. 329 6
Bank of Boston Connecticut (formerly Colonial Bank) v. European Grain and Shipping;
Dominique, The [1988] A.C. 1056; [1989] 2 W.L.R. 440; (1989) 133 S.J. 219; [1989] 1
All E.R. 545; [1989] 1 Lloyd's Rep. 431; [1989] L.S.Gaz. March 8, 43, H.L.;
reversing Colonial Bank v. European Grain and Shipping; Dominique, The [1988] 3
W.L.R. 60; (1988) 132 S.J. 896; [1988] 1 F.T.L.R. 327; [1988] 3 All E.R. 233; [1988]
1 Lloyd's Rep. 215; (1988) L.S.Gaz. February 17, 1988, C.A.; reversing [1987] 1
Lloyd's Rep. 239 42
Banks v. CBS Songs, The Times, January 30, 1992, C.A. 15
Basildon District Council v. Manning (1975) 237 E.G. 878 91
Battersby v. Anglo American Oil Co. Ltd. [1945] K.B. 23, C.A. 12, 13
Beaman v. A.R.T.S. Ltd. [1949] 1 K.B. 550; 65 T.L.R. 389; 93 S.J. 236; [1949] 1 All E.R.
465, C.A.; reversing [1948] W.N. 224; 64 T.L.R. 285; [1948] 2 All E.R. 89 ..... 21, 22
Beer v. London Borough of Waltham Forest, December 16, 1987, unreported 84
Bell v. Peter Brown & Co. [1990] 2 Q.B. 495; [1990] 3 W.L.R. 510; [1990] 3 All E.R. 124;
(1990) 140 New L.J. 701, C.A. 33, 34, 35, 36, 43, 49, 50, 53
Bentley v. Bristol & Western Health Authority, The Times, December 6, 1990 70
Berg v. Glentworth Bulb Co. Ltd., July 25, 1988, C.A., unreported 43, 53, 56
Berry v. Stone Manganese Marine Ltd. [1971] 115, S.J. 966; (1971) 12 K.I.R. 13; [1972] 1
Lloyd's Rep. 182 .... 58, 65
Beswick v. Beswick [1968] A.C. 58; [1967] 3 W.L.R. 932; 111 S.J. 540; [1967] 2 All E.R.
1197, H.L.; affirming [1966] Ch. 538; [1966] 3 W.L.R. 396; 110 S.J. 507; [1966] 3 All
E.R. 1; [1966] C.L.Y. 1915, C.A.; reversing [1965] 3 All E.R. 858; [1965] C.L.Y. 632 14
Billings v. Reed [1945] K.B. 11; [1944] 2 All E.R. 415 64
Bills v. Fernandez-Gonzalez (1982) 132 New L.J. 66 91
Birkett v. James [1978] A.C. 297; [1977] 3 W.L.R. 38; (1977) 121 S.J. 444; [1977] 2 All E.R.
801, H.L. 18, 19, 77
Biss v. Lambeth, Southwark and Lewisham Health Authority (Teaching) [1978] 1 W.L.R.
382; (1978) 122 S.J. 32; [1978] 2 All E.R. 125, C.A. 78
Bliss v. South East Thames Regional Health Authority [1978] I.C.R. 700; [1985] I.R.L.R.
308, C.A.; reversing (1984) 134 New L.J. 121 65
Blow, Re, St. Bartholomew's Hospital (Governors) v. Cambden [1914] 1 Ch. 233; 58 S.J. 136;
83 L.J.Ch. 185; 109 L.T. 913; 30 T.L.R. 117, C.A. 119
Bosma v. Larsen [1966] 1 Lloyd's Rep. 22 40
Bowring-Hanbury's Trustee v. Bowring-Hanbury [1943] Ch. 104; 87 S.J. 39; [1943] 1 All
E.R. 48; 112 L.J.Ch. 37; 168 L.T. 72; 59 T.L.R. 121, C.A. 118
Bradley v. Eagle Star Insurance Co. Ltd. [1989] A.C. 957; [1989] 2 W.L.R. 568; [1989] 1 All
E.R. 961; [1989] I.C.R. 301; (1989) 133 S.J. 359; [1989] 1 Lloyd's Rep. 465; [1989]
BCLC 496; (1989) New L.J. 330; 1989 Fin.LR 253; [1989] L.S.Gaz. May 3, 38, H.L.;
affirming 1988 Fin.LR 238; [1988] 2 Lloyd's Rep. 233 40
—— v. Hanseatic Shipping Co. Ltd. [1986] 2 Lloyd's Rep. 34, C.A. 76
Bray v. Stuart A. West & Co. (1989) 139 New L.J. 753 3

Brickfield Properties Ltd. *v*. Newton; Rosebell Holdings *v*. Newton [1971] 1 W.L.R. 862;
    115 S.J. 307; [1971] 3 All E.R. 328, C.A. 35
Bridges *v*. Mees [1957] Ch. 475; [1957] 3 W.L.R. 215; 101 S.J. 555; [1957] 2 All E.R. 577   97
Bridle *v*. Ruby [1988] 3 W.L.R. 191; (1988) 132 S.J. 897; [1988] 3 All E.R. 64; (1988) 56 P. &
    C.R. 155; [1988] L.S.Gaz. May 18, 42, C.A. 103
British Anzani (Felixstowe) Ltd. *v*. International Marine Management (U.K.) Ltd. [1980]
    Q.B. 637; [1979] 3 W.L.R. 451; (1978) 123 S.J. 64; [1979] 2 All E.R. 1063; (1978) 39
    P. & C.R. 189; (1978) 250 E.G. 1183 18
British Steel Corp. *v*. Cleveland Bridge & Engineering Co. Ltd. [1984] 1 All E.R. 504; (1983)
    Build. L.R. 94; [1982] Com. L.R. 54 37
Brueton *v*. Woodward [1941] 1 K.B. 680; 85 S.J. 154; [1941] 1 All E.R. 470; 110 L.J.K.B.
    645; 165 L.T. 348; 57 T.L.R. 349 33
Brunswick (Duke) *v*. Harmer (1849) 14 Q.B. 185; 19 L.J.Q.B. 20; 14 L.T.O.S. 198; 14 Jur.
    110; 117 E.R. 75; subsequent proceedings (1850) 1 L.M. & P. 505; 19 L.J.Q.B. 456;
    15 L.T.O.S. 248; 14 Jur. 620 57
Buck *v*. English Electric Co. Ltd. [1977] I.C.R. 629; [1977] 1 W.L.R. 806; [1978] 1 All E.R.
    271 83
Buckinghamshire County Council *v*. Moran [1990] Ch. 623; [1989] 3 W.L.R. 152; (1989) 133
    S.J. 849; [1989] 2 All E.R. 225; 88 L.G.R. 145; (1989) 58 P. & C.R. 236; (1989) New
    L.J. 257; C.A.; affirming (1988) 86 L.G.R. 472; (1988) 56 P. & C.R. 372 .... 86, 88,
                                                    89, 90, 94, 95
Bulli Coal Mining Co. *v*. Osborne [1899] A.C. 351; [1895–1899] All E.R. Rep. 506; 68
    L.J.P.C. 49; 80 L.T. 430; 47 W.R. 545; 15 T.L.R. 257, P.C. 22
Bumper Development Corp. Ltd. *v*. Commissioner for Police for the Metropolis [1991] 1
    W.L.R. 1362; [1991] 4 All E.R. 638; (1991) 135 S.J. 382; *The Times*, February 14,
    1991; *The Guardian*, March 5, 1991, C.A. 59

Cadija Umma *v*. S. Don Manis Appu [1939] A.C. 136; 108 L.J.P.C. 13, P.C. 90
Cannon *v*. Barnsley Metropolitan Borough Council, *The Times*, June 24, 1992, E.A.T. 110
Caparo Industries plc *v*. Dickman [1990] 2 A.C. 605; [1990] 2 W.L.R. 358; [1990] 1 All E.R.
    568; (1990) 134 S.J. 494; [1990] BCC 164; [1990] BCLC 273; [1990] E.C.C. 313;
    [1990] L.S.Gaz. March 28, 42; (1990) 140 New L.J. 248, H.L.; reversing [1989] Q.B.
    653; [1989] 2 W.L.R. 316; (1989) 133 S.J. 221; [1989] 1 All E.R. 798; (1989) 5 BCC
    105; [1989] BCLC 154; 1989 PCC 125; (1988) 138 New L.J. 289, C.A.; reversing in
    part (1988) 4 BCC 144; [1988] BCLC 387, D.C. 37, 46
Cargill *v*. Gotts [1981] 1 W.L.R. 441; (1980) 125 S.J. 99; [1981] 1 All E.R. 682; (1980) 41 P. &
    C.R. 300; [1981] J.P.L. 515, C.A.; reversing [1980] 1 W.L.R. 521; [1980] 2 All E.R.
    49; (1979) 40 P. & C.R. 122; [1980] J.P.L. 602 102
Carr-Saunders *v*. McNeil (Dick) Associates [1986] 1 W.L.R. 922; (1986) 130 S.J. 525; [1986]
    1 all E.R. 888; (1987) 53 P. & C.R. 14; [1986] 2 E.G.L.R. 181; (1986) 279 E.G. 1359;
    (1986) 83 L.S.Gaz. 2331 .... 106, 107
Cartledge *v*. Jopling (E.) & Sons Ltd. [1963] A.C. 758; [1963] 2 W.L.R. 210; 107 S.J. 73;
    [1963] 1 All E.R. 341; [1963] 1 Lloyd's Rep. 1, H.L.; affirming [1962] 1 Q.B. 189;
    [1961] 3 W.L.R. 838; 105 S.J. 884; [1961] 3 All E.R. 482, [1961] 2 Lloyd's Rep. 61,
    C.A.; [1961] C.L.Y. 5055 .... 4, 8, 44, 45, 67
Central Abestos Co. *v*. Dodd [1973] A.C. 518; [1972] 3 W.L.R. 333; 116 S.J. 584; [1972] 2 All
    E.R. 1135; [1972] 2 Lloyd's Rep. 413; 13 K.I.R. 75, H.L.; affirming *sub nom*. Smith *v*.
    Central Asbestos Co. [1972] 1 Q.B. 244; [1971] 3 W.L.R. 206; 115 S.J. 443; [1971] 3
    All E.R. 204; [1971] 2 Lloyd's Rep. 151, 11 K.I.R. 239, C.A. 4, 68, 84
Central Electricity Board *v*. Halifax Corporation [1963] A.C. 785; [1962] 3 W.L.R. 1313; 106
    S.J. 936; [1962] 3 All E.R. 915; 61 L.G.R. 125, H.L. 10
Central Insurance Co. *v*. Seacalf Shipping Corp.; Aiolos, The [1985] 2 Lloyd's Rep. 25,
    L.A. 39
Chandris *v*. Argo Insurance Co., 107 S.J. 575; [1963] 2 Lloyd's Rep. 65 41
Chaplin *v*. Boys [1971] A.C. 356; [1969] 3 W.L.R. 322; 113 S.J. 608; [1969] 2 All E.R. 1085,
    H.L., affirming *sub nom*. Boys *v*. Chaplin [1968] 2 Q.B. 1; [1968] 2 W.L.R. 328; 111
    S.J. 968; [1968] 1 All E.R. 283, C.A.; affirming [1967] 3 W.L.R. 266; 11 S.J. 297;
    [1967] 2 All E.R. 665 7
Chappell *v*. Cooper; Player *v*. Brugiere [1980] 1 W.L.R. 958; (1979) 124 S.J. 544; [1980] 2 All
    E.R. 463, C.A. 77, 79
Chatsworth Investments Ltd. *v*. Cussins (Contractors) Ltd. [1969] 1 W.L.R. 1; (1968) 112
    S.J. 843; [1969] 1 All E.R. 143, C.A. 39

Chelmsford District Council v. Evers (T.J.) (1983) 25 B.L.R. 99; (1984) 1 Const. L.J.
65 .... 16, 35, 45
Chesworth v. Farrar [1967] 1 Q.B. 407; [1966] 2 W.L.R. 1073; 110 S.J. 307; [1966] 2 All E.R.
107 37
China v. Harrow Urban District Council [1954] 1 Q.B. 178; [1953] 3 W.L.R. 885; 118 J.P.41;
97 S.J. 797; [1953] 2 All E.R. 1296; 51 L.G.R. 681; 46 R & I.T. 750, D.C. 3
Cladakis v. Commission of the European Communities (No. 276/85) [1987] E.C.R. 495 ... 111
Clark v. Woor [1965] 1 W.L.R. 650; 109 S.J. 251; [1965] 2 All E.R. 253 23
Clarkson v. Modern Foundries Ltd. [1957] 1 W.L.R. 1210; 101 S.J. 960; [1958] 1 All E.R.
33 61
Coburn v. Colledge [1897] 1 Q.B. 702; 41 S.J. 408; [1895–1899] All E.R. Rep. 539; 66
L.J.Q.B. 462; 76 L.T. 608; 45 W.R. 488; 13 L.T.R. 321, C.A. 8, 44
Cockerill-Sambre S.A. v. Commission of the European Communities (No. 42/85) [1987] 1
C.M.L.R. 325; [1985] 9 E.C.R. 3749, European Ct. 111, 112
Colchester Borough Council v. Smith [1992] 2 W.L.R. 728; [1992] 2 All E.R. 561, C.A.;
affirming [1991] Ch. 448; [1991] 2 W.L.R. 540; [1991] 2 All E.R. 29; (1990) 62 P. &
C.R. 242 .... 5, 94, 95, 96
Collin v. Westminster (Duke) [1985] Q.B. 581; [1985] 2 W.L.R. 553; (1985) 129 S.J. 116;
[1985] 1 All E.R. 465; (1985) 50 P. & C.R. 380; (1984) 17 H.L.R. 246; [1985] 1
E.G.L.R. 109; (1985) 273 E.G. 881; (1984) 25 R.V.R. 4; (1985) 82 L.S.Gaz. 767,
C.A. 3, 31, 32, 33
Collinge v. Heywood (1839) 9 A. & E. 633; 1 Per. & Dav. 502; 2 Will. Woll. & H. 107; 8
L.J.Q.B. 98; 112 E.R. 1352 40
Colls v. Home and Colonial Stores Ltd. [1904] A.C. 179; [1904–1907] All E.R. Rep. 5; 73 L.J.
Ch. 484; 90 L.T. 687; 53 W.R. 30; 20 T.L.R. 475, H.L.; reversing sub nom. Home and
Colonial Stores Ltd. v. Colls [1902] 1 Ch. 302, C.A. 107
Compania de Electricidad de la Provincia de Buenos Aires Ltd., Re [1980] Ch. 146; [1979] 2
W.L.R. 316; (1978) 122 S.J. 145; [1978] 3 All E.R. 668 32
Conquer v. Boot [1928] 2 K.B. 336 15
Conry v. Simpson [1983] 3 All E.R. 369, C.A. 75, 81
Cork and Brandon Rly. Co. v. Goode (1853) 13 C.B. 826; 1 C.L.R. 345; 22 L.J.C.P. 198; 21
L.T.O.S. 141; 17 Jur. 555; 1 W.R. 410; 138 E.R. 1427 32
Cornish, Re, ex p. Board of Trade [1896] 1 Q.B. 99; 40 S.J. 100; 65 L.J.Q.B. 106; 73 L.T.
602; 44 W.R. 161; 12 T.L.R. 69; 3 Mans. 48, C.A. 115
County and District Properties v. Jenner (C.) & Son [1976] 2 Lloyd's Rep. 728; (1974) 230
E.G. 1589 40
Curtis v. Wild [1991] 4 All E.R. 172 63

D.W. Moore & Co. v. Ferrier. See Moore (D.W.) & Co. v. Ferrier.
D. & F. Estates v. Church Commissioners for England [1988] 3 W.L.R. 368; (1988) 132 S.J.
1092; [1988] 2 All E.R. 992; (1988) 41 B.L.R. 1; (1988) 138 New L.J. 210; [1988]
L.S.Gaz. September 14, 46, H.L.; affirming [1987] 1 FTLR 405; (1987) Const.L.J.
110; (1987) 36 Build.L.R. 72; (1988) ConLR 12, C.A.; affirming in part (1987) 7
ConLR 40 .... 37, 46, 47, 61
Dale v. British Coal Corporation (No.1), The Times, June 25, 1992, C.A. 11
Dalton v. Angus. See Angus v. Dalton.
Dance v. Triplow, The Times, December 4, 1991, C.A. 105, 106
Davis v. City & Hackney Health Authority, The Times, January 27, 1989 .... 70, 72, 73, 83
—— v. Ministry of Defence, The Times, August 7, 1985, C.A. 68, 69
Dawson v. Norfolk (Duke) (1815) 1 Price 246; 145 E.R. 1391 102
—— v. Spain-Gower, October 18, 1988, C.A., unreported 20, 83
Department of Transport v. Smaller (Chris) (Transport) [1989] A.C. 1197; [1989] 2 W.L.R.
578; (1989) 133 S.J. 361; [1989] 1 All E.R. 897; (1989) 139 New L.J. 363, H.L. .. 19
Derry v. Sanders [1919] 1 K.B. 233; 63 S.J. 115; 88 L.J.K.B. 410; 120 L.T. 194; 35 T.L.R.
105, C.A. 103
Diment v. Foot (N.H.) Ltd. [1974] 1 W.L.R. 1427; 118 S.J. 180; [1974] 2 All E.R. 785; 28 P.
& C.R. 163 .... 101, 102
Diplock, Re, Diplock v. Wintle. See Ministry of Health v. Simpson.
Donovan v. Gwentoys Ltd. [1990] 1 W.L.R. 472; [1990] 1 All E.R. 1018; (1990) 134 S.J. 910;
[1990] L.S.Gaz. April 25, 40, H.L. 1, 74, 78, 80, 84
Driscoll-Varley v. Parkside Health Authority, January 15, 1990, unreported 70
Duke of Brunswick v. Harmer. See Brunswick (Duke) v.Harmer.

Duke of Leeds v. Earl of Amherst. *See* Leeds (Duke) v. Amherst (Earl).
Dulieu v. White [1901] 2 K.B. 669; 45 S.J. 578; [1900–1903] All E.R. Rep. 353; 70 L.J.K.B.
    837; 85 L.T. 126; 50 W.R. 76; 17 T.L.R. 555 65

Earle v. Bellingham (No. 2) (1857) 24 Bear. 448; 27 L.J.Ch. 545; 30 L.T.O.S. 162; 3 Jur.
    N.S. 1237; 6 W.R. 45; 53 E.R. 430. 119
Easy v. Universal Anchorage Co. Ltd. [1974] 1 W.L.R. 899; 118 S.J. 464; [1974] 2 All E.R.
    1105, C.A. 78
Eaton v. Swansea Waterworks Co. (1851) 17 Q.B. 267; 20 L.J.Q.B. 482; 17 L.T.O.S. 154; 15
    Jur. 675; 117 E.R. 1282 102
Eckersley v. Binnie and Partners (1988) 18 ConLR 1; (1988) B.L.M. April, p. 7, C.A. ... 35, 36
Eddis v. Chichester Constable [1969] 2 Ch. 345; [1969] 3 W.L.R. 48; 113 S.J. 386; [1969] 2
    All E.R. 912, C.A.; affirming [1969] 1 W.L.R. 385; (1968) 113 S.J. 146; [1969] 1 All
    E.R. 546. Petition of leave to appeal to the House of Lords refused 4, 21, 27, 29, 61
Edgington v. Clark [1964] 1 Q.B. 367; [1963] 3 W.L.R. 721; 107 S.J. 617; [1963] 3 All E.R.
    468, C.A. 96
Ellett-Brown v. Tallishire Ltd., March 29, 1990, C.A., unreported 91
Emmott v. Minister for Social Welfare and Att.-Gen. (Case 208/90) [1991] I.R.L.R. 387,
    European Ct. 110
Esso Petroleum Co. Ltd. v. Marsdon [1976] Q.B. 801; [1976] 2 W.L.R. 583; 120 S.J. 131;
    [1976] 2 All E.R. 5; [1976] 2 Lloyd's Rep. 305, C.A.; reversing in part [1975] Q.B.
    819; [1975] W.L.R. 147; (1974) 119 S.J. 81; [1975] 1 All E.R. 203 36

Fairweather v. St. Marylebone Property Co. [1963] A.C. 510; [1962] 2 W.L.R. 1020; 106 S.J.
    368; [1962] 2 All E.R. 288, H.L.; affirming *sub nom.* St. Marylebone Property Co. v.
    Fairweather [1962] 1 Q.B. 498; [1961] 3 W.L.R. 1083; 105 S.J. 947; [1961] 3 All E.R.
    560; [1961] C.L.Y. 4967, C.A. 98, 99
Fannon v. Backhouse, *The Times*, August 22, 1987, C.A.; (1988) B.L.M. February, p. 8 . 14
Ferriera Valsabbia SpA v. Commission of the European Communities (No. 209/83) [1984]
    E.C.R. 3089 111
Firma C-Trade S.A. v. Newcastle Protection and Indemnity Association; Fanti, The; Socony
    Mobil Oil Inc. v. West of England Shipowners Mutual Insurance Association; Padre
    Island, The (No. 2) [1991] 2 A.C. 1; [1990] 3 W.L.R. 78; [1990] 2 All E.R. 705; (1990)
    134 S.J. 833; [1990] BCLC 625; [1990] 2 Lloyd's Rep. 191, H.L.; reversing [1989] 1
    Lloyd's Rep. 239, C.A. 40
Firman v. Ellis; Ince v. Rogers; Down v. Harvey; Pheasant v. Smith (S.T.H.) (Tyres) [1978]
    Q.B. 886; [1978] 3 W.L.R. 1; [1978] 122 S.J. 147; [1978] 2 All E.R. 851, C.A.;
    affirming (1977) 121 S.J. 606; *The Times*, July 8, 1977 .... 75, 77, 78, 79, 81
Flight v. Thomas (1840) 11 A. & E. 688; 3 Per. & Dav. 442; 113 E.R. 575, Ex.Ch.; on appeal
    (1841) 8 Cl. & Fin. 231, H.L. 105
Florida Hotels Pty. Ltd. v. Mayo (1965) 113 C.L.R. 588 26
Forster v. Outred & Co. [1982] W.L.R. 86; [1981] 125 S.J. 309; [1982] 2 All E.R. 753,
    C.A. 33, 44, 49, 50, 52
Foster v. South Glamorgan Health Authority [1988] I.C.R. 526; [1988] I.R.L.R. 277,
    E.A.T. 84
Fowell v. N.C.B. *See* Fowell v. National Coal Board.
——— v. National Coal Board, *The Times*, May 28, 1986, C.A. 73
Fowley Marine (Elmsworth) Ltd. v. Gafford [1968] 2 Q.B. 618; [1968] 1 W.L.R. 842; 112
    S.J. 114; [1968] 1 All E.R. 979; [1968] 1 Lloyd's Rep. 343, C.A. 87

G.L. Baker v. Meadway Building and Supplies. *See* Baker (G.L.) v. Medway Building and
    Supplies.
Gale, *Re*, Blake v. Gale (1885) 31 Ch.D. 196; (1886) 32 Ch.D. 571, C.A.; (1883) 22 Ch.D.
    820; 53 L.J.Ch. 694; 48 L.T. 101; 31 W.R. 538 119
Gardner v. Hodgson's Kingston Brewery Co. Ltd. [1903] A.C. 229; 72 L.J.Ch. 558; 88 L.T.
    698; 52 W.R. 16; 19 T.L.R. 458, H.L. 102
George Wimpey & Co. v. Sohn. *See* Wimpey (George) & Co. v. Sohn.
Gilbert-Ash (Northern) v. Modern Engineering (Bristol) [1974] A.C. 689; [1973] 3 W.L.R.
    421; 117 S.J. 745; [1973] 3 All E.R. 195; 72 L.G.R. 1, H.L.; reversing *sub nom.*
    Modern Engineering (Bristol) v. Gilbert-Ash (Northern) (1973) 71 L.G.R. 162,
    C.A. 17
Good v. Parry [1963] 2 Q.B. 418; [1963] 2 W.L.R. 846; 107 S.J. 194; [1963] 2 All E.R. 59,
    C.A. 38

Graham v. Voigt, 89 A.C.T.R. 11 65
Gray v. T.P. Bennett & Son (1987) 43 B.L.R. 63; 13 Con.L.R. 22 .... 23, 26, 28
—— v. Wykeham-Martin January 17, 1977 (S.C. Library, Transcript No. 10A), unreported   93
Greater Nottingham Co-operative Society Ltd. v. Cementation Piling and Foundations Ltd.
    [1988] 3 W.L.R. 396; (1988) 132 S.J. 754; [1988] 2 All E.R. 971; (1988) 41 BLR 43;
    (1988) 4 Const.L.J. 216; (1988) 138 New L.J. 112, C.A.; reversing [1985] C.I.L.L.
    160 .... 36, 49
Green (R. & H.) & Silley Weir v. British Railways Board [1985] 1 W.L.R. 570; [1985] 1 All
    E.R. 237; (1980) 17 Build. L.R. 94 40
Guidera v. NEI Projects (India), January 30, 1990, C.A., unreported 69
Gunnella (Monique) v. Commission of the European Communities (No. 33/72) [1973] E.C.R.
    475, European Ct. 110
Gutsell v. Reeve [1936] 1 K.B. 272; 79 S.J. 796; [1935] All E.R.Rep. 117; 105 L.J.K.B. 213;
    154 L.T. 1; 52 T.L.R. 55, C.A. 32

Halford v. Brookes [1991] 1 W.L.R. 428; [1991] 3 All E.R. 559, C.A.; reversing *The
    Independent*, November 27, 1990, C.A. 82, 117
Halls v. O'Dell (1991) 135 S.J. (LB) 204; *The Times*, November 5, 1991; *The Independent*,
    November 6, 1991; *Financial Times*, November 20, 1991, C.A. 19
Hardy v. Ryle (1829) 9 B. & C. 603; 2 Man. & Ry. M.C. 301; 4 Man. & Ry. K.B. 295; 7
    L.J.O.S. M.C. 118; 109 E.R. 224 56
Harris v. Lombard (New Zealand) [1974] 2 N.Z.L.R. 161 65
Hartley v. Birmingham City D.C. [1992] 2 All E.R. 213; *The Independent*, August 16, 1991,
    C.A. 10, 78, 79, 80
Hayes v. Dodd (James and Charles) (a firm) [1990] 2 All E.R. 815, C.A. 65
Hayward v. Challoner. *See* Hayward v. Chaloner.
—— v. Chaloner [1968] 1 Q.B. 107; [1967] 3 W.L.R. 1068; *sub nom.* Hayward v. Challoner,
    111 S.J. 519; [1967] 3 All E.R. 122, C.A. 92–93, 97
Healey v. Hawkins [1968] 1 W.L.R. 1967; (1968) 112 S.J. 965; [1968] 3 All E.R. 836; 20 P. &
    C.R. 69 104
Hedley Byrne & Co. v. Heller & Partners [1964] A.C. 465; [1963] 3 W.L.R. 101; 107 S.J. 454;
    [1963] 2 All E.R. 575; [1963] 1 Lloyd's Rep. 485, H.L.; affirming [1962] 1 Q.B. 396;
    [1961] 3 W.L.R. 1225; 105 S.J. 910; [1961] 3 All E.R. 891; [1961] C.L.Y. 518, C.A.;
    affirming *The Times*, December 21, 1960; [1960] C.L.Y. 168 .... 15, 37, 46, 47
Hellenic Steel v. Svolmar Shipping Co.; Komninos S, The [1991] 1 Lloyd's Rep. 370;
    Financial Times, January 16, 1991, C.A.; reversing [1990] 1 Lloyd's Rep. 541;
    Financial Times, January 16, 1990 6
Henriksens Rederi A/S v. T.H.Z. Rolimpex; Brede, The [1974] Q.B. 233; [1973] 3 W.L.R.
    556; [1973] 2 Lloyd's Rep. 333; 117 S.J. 600; [1973] 3 All E.R. 589, C.A.; affirming
    [1972] 2 Lloyd's Rep. 511 .... 17, 18
Hermine, The. *See* Unitramp v. Garnac Grain Co. Ltd.
Hetton Victory Club Ltd. v. Swainston [1983] I.C.R. 341; (1983) 127 S.J. 171; [1983] 1 All
    E.R. 1179; [1983] I.R.L.R. 164, C.A.; affirming [1983] I.R.L.R. 139; (1982) 126 S.J.
    673; [1983] 1 All E.R. 1179, E.A.T. 11
Heywood v. Wellers (a firm) [1976] Q.B. 445; [1976] 2 W.L.R. 101; (1975) 120 S.J. 9; [1976]
    1 All E.R. 300; [1976] 2 Lloyd's Rep, 88, C.A. 65
Higgins v. Betts [1905] 2 Ch. 210; 49 S.J. 535; 74 L.J.Ch. 621; 92 T. 850; 53 W.R. 549; 21
    T.L.R. 552 106
Hill (William) Organisation v. Sunley (Bernard) & Sons (1982) 22 B.L.R. 1, C.A. ... 23, 28, 36
Hinz v. Berry [1970] 2 Q.B. 40; [1970] 2 W.L.R. 684; 114 S.J. 111; [1970] 1 All E.R. 1074,
    C.A. 65
Hochster v. de la Tour (1853) 2 E. & B. 678; 1 C.L.R. 846; 22 L.J.Q.B. 455; 22 L.T.O.S.
    171; 17 Jur. 972; 1 W.R. 469; 118 E.R. 922 34
Hollins v. Verney (1884) 13 Q.B.D. 304; 48 J.P. 580; 53 L.J.Q.B. 430; 51 L.T. 753; 33 W.R.
    5, C.A. 101
Horbury v. Craig Hall & Rutley (1991) C.I.L.L. 692 .... 15, 54, 55
Hornsey Local Board v. Monarch Investment Building Society (1889) 24 Q.B.D. 1; [1886–
    1890] All E.R. Rep. 992; 59 L.J.Q.B. 105; 61 L.T. 867; 54 J.P. 391, 38 W.R. 85; 6
    T.L.R. 30, L.A. 119
Howard E. Perry & Co. v. British Railways Board. *See* Perry (Howard E.) & Co. v. British
    Railways Board.

Howe v. David Brown Tractors (Retail) (Rustons Engineering Co., Third Party) [1991] 4 All
    E.R. 30, C.A. 14, 16, 66
Howlett, Re, Howlett v. Howlett [1949] Ch. 767; [1949] L.J.R. 1632; 65 T.L.R. 569; 93 S.J.
    632; [1949] 2 All E.R. 490 116
Huber v. Steiner (1835) 2 Bing. N.C. 202; 1 Hodg. 206; 6 Scott 304; [1835–1842] All E.R.
    Rep. 159; 132 E.R. 80 6
Hughes v. Griffin [1969] 1 W.L.L. 23; 112 S.J. 907; [1969] 1 All E.R. 460; 20 P & C.R. 113,
    C.A. 91–92
Hyde v. Pearce [1982] 1 W.L.R. 560; (1982) 125 S.J. 119; [1982] 1 All E.R. 1029, C.A. ... 92
Hydrocarbons Great Britain Ltd. v. Cammel Laird Shipbuilders Ltd. (1991) 25 ConLR 131;
    (1992) B.L.M. 5 .... 14, 15
Hyman v. Van den Bergh [1908] 1 Ch. 167; 52 S.J. 114; 77 L.J.Ch. 154; 98 L.T. 478, C.A. 106
Hyundai Heavy Industries Co. Ltd. v. Papadopoulos [1980] 1 W.L.R. 1129; (1980) 124 S.J.
    592; [1980] 2 All E.R. 29; [1980] 2 Lloyd's Rep. 1, H.L.; affirming [1979] 1 Lloyd's
    Rep. 130, C.A. 39

Ichard v. Frangoulis [1977] 1 W.L.R. 556; (1976) 121 S.J. 287; [1977] 2 All E.R. 461 65
Imperial Chemical Industries v. Commission of the European Communities (No. 48/69)
    [1972] E.C.R. 619; [1972] C.M.L.R. 557, European Ct. 111
Internationale Handelsgesellschaft GmbH v. Einfuhr-und Vorratsstelle Für Getreide und
    Futtermittel (No. 11/70); Einfuhr-und Vorratsstelle für Getreide und Futtermittel v.
    Firma Köster, Berodt & Co. (Case 25/70); Einfuhr-und Vorratsstelle Für Getreide und
    Futtermittel v. Firma Günther Henck (case 26/70); Firma Ottscheer v. Einfuhr-und
    Vorratsstelle Für Getreide-und Futtermittel (Case 30/70) [1970] E.C.R. 1125; [1972]
    C.M.L.R. 155, European Ct. 111
Iron Trade Mutual Insurance Co. Ltd. v. Buckenham (J.K.) Ltd. [1990] 1 All E.R. 808;
    [1989] 2 Lloyd's Rep. 85; (1990) B.L.M., May, pp. 1–4, D.C. 9, 30, 37, 42, 51, 53
Islander Trucking Ltd. (in liquidation) v. Hogg Robinson & Gardner Mountain (Marine)
    Ltd. [1990] 1 All E.R. 826 .... 9, 30, 51

Jackson v. Horizon Holidays Ltd. [1975] 1 W.L.R. 1468; 119 S.J. 759; [1975] 3 All E.R. 92,
    C.A. 65
James McNaughton Paper Group v. Hicks Anderson [1991] 2 Q.B. 113; [1991] 2 W.L.R.
    641; [1991] 1 All E.R. 134; (1990) 140 New L.J. 1311; (1990) BCC 891; [1991] BCLC
    235; The Independent, September 11, 1990, C.A. 15
Jarvis v. Swans Tours Ltd. [1973] Q.B. 233; [1972] 3 W.L.R. 954; 116 S.J. 822; [1973] 1 All
    E.R. 71, C.A. 65
Jessamine Investment Co. v. Schwartz [1977] 2 W.L.R. 145; 120 S.J. 384, [1976] 3 All E.R.
    521, C.A. 91, 92, 96
Joachimson v. Swiss Bank Corp. [1921] 3 K.B. 110; 65 S.J. 434; [1921] All E.R. 92; 90
    L.J.K.B. 973; 125 L.T. 338; 37 T.L.R. 534; 26 Com. Cas. 196, C.A. 38
Jolly, Re, Gatherole v. Norfolk [1900] 2 Ch. 616; 44 S.J. 642; [1900–1903] All E.R. Rep. 286,
    69 L.J.Ch. 661; 83 L.T. 118; 48 W.R. 657; 16 T.L.R. 521, C.A. 97, 98
Jones v. Bellgrove Properties [1949] 2 K.B. 700; 65 T.L.R. 451; sub nom. Jones v. Bellgrove
    Properties, 93 S.J. 512; [1949] 2 All E.R. 198; C.A.; affirming 65 T.L.R. 166 38
—— v. Jones [1970] 2 Q.B. 576; [1970] 3 W.L.R. 20; 114 S.J. 374; [1970] 3 All E.R. 47,
    C.A. 10, 13, 78
—— v. Price, The Independent, January 16, 1992, C.A. 102
—— v. Trollope Colls Cementation Overseas Ltd., The Times, January 26, 1990, C.A. ... 6, 7
Junior Books Ltd. v. Veitchi Co. Ltd., The [1983] 1 A.C. 520; [1982] 3 W.L.R. 477; (1982)
    126 S.J. 538; [1982] 3 All E.R. 201; [1982] Com.L.R. 221; (1982) 79 L.S.Gaz. 1413;
    (1981) 21 Build. L.R. 66, H.L. 46

Kaliszewska v. John Clague & Partners [1984] C.I.L.L. 131; (1984) Const. L.J. 137; (1984) 5
    ConLR 62 .... 21, 23–24
Kamouh v. Associated Electrical Industries International [1980] Q.B. 199; [1979] 2 W.L.R.
    795; (1978) 122 S.J. 714 38
Katzenstein Adler Industries v. Borchard Lines Ltd.; Gladys, The [1988] 2 Lloyd's Rep. 274;
    [1988] 138 New L.J. 94 13
Kaur (Pritam) v. Russel (S.) & Sons [1973] 1 Q.B. 336; [1973] 2 W.L.R. 147; (1972) 117 S.J.
    91; sub nom. Kaur (Pritam) (Administratix of Bikar Singh) v. Russell (S.) & Sons
    [1973] 1 All E.R. 617, C.A.; reversing [1972] 3 W.L.R. 663; 116 S.J. 446; [1972] 3 All
    E.R. 305 10

Kennett *v.* Brown [1988] 1 W.L.R. 582; (1988) 132 S.J. 752; [1988] 2 All E.R. 600; [1988] L.S.Gaz. May 18, 43, C.A. 16

Ketteman *v.* Hansel Properties [1987] A.C. 189; [1987] 2 W.L.R. 313; (1987) 131 S.J. 134; [1988] 1 All E.R. 38; [1987] 1 FTLR 284; (1987) 85 L.G.R. 409; (1987) 36 Build. L.R. 1; [1987] 1 E.G.L.R. 237; (1987) 84 L.S.Gaz. 657; (1987) 137 New L.J. 100, H.L.; affirming 1 W.L.R. 1274; (1984) 128 S.J. 800; [1985] 1 All E.R. 352; (1985) 49 P. & C.R. 257; (1985) 27 Build. L.R. 1; [1984] C.I.L.L. 109; (1984) 271 E.G. 1099; (1984) 81 L.S.Gaz. 3018, C.A. 15, 16, 45

Kilgour *v.* Gaddes [1904] 1 K.B. 457; [1904–1907] All E.R. Rep. 679; 73 L.J.K.B. 233; 90 L.T. 604; 52 W.R. 438; 20 T.L.R. 240, C.A. 103

King *v.* Victor Parsons & Co. [1973] 1 W.L.R. 29; 116 S.J. 901; [1973] 1 All E.R. 206; [1973] 1 Lloyd's Rep. 189, C.A.; affirming [1972] 1 W.L.R. 801; (1971) 116 S.J. 239; [1972] 2 All E.R. 625; [1972] 1 Lloyd's Rep. 213 23

Kirby *v.* Leather [1965] 2 Q.B. 367; (1965) 2 W.L.R. 1318; 109 S.J. 357; (1965) 2 All E.R. 441, C.A. 20

Kitchen *v.* Royal Air Force Association [1958] 1 W.L.R. 563; 102 S.J. 363; [1958] 3 All E.R. 241, C.A. 22

Kleinwort Benson *v.* Barbrak; Same *v.* Choithram (T.) & Sons (London): Same *v.* Chemical Importation and Distribution State Enterprises; Same *v.* Shell Markets (M.E.); Myrto, The (No. 3) (1987) A.C. 597; [1987] 2 W.L.R. 1053; (1987) 131 S.J. 594; [1987] 2 All E.R. 289; [1987] 1 FTLR 43; [1987] 2 Lloyd's Rep. 1; (1987) 84 L.S.Gaz. 1651; (1987) 137 New L.J. 388, H.L.; [1985] 2 Lloyd's Rep. 567 .... 12, 13

Komninos S., The. *See* Hellenic Steel Co. *v.* Svolmar Shipping Co.; Komninos S., The.

Lacey (William) (Hounslow) Ltd. *v.* Davis [1957] 1 W.L.R. 932; 101 S.J. 629; [1957] 2 All E.R. 712 37

Lambert *v.* Lewis [1982] A.C. 225; [1981] 2 W.L.R. 713; [1981] 1 All E.R. 1185; [1981] Lloyd's Rep. 17; *sub nom.* Lexmead (Basingstoke) *v.* Lewis (1981) 125 S.J. 310; [1981] R.T.R. 346, H.L.; reversing [1980] 2 W.L.R. 299; (1979) 124 S.J. 50; [1980] 1 All E.R. 978; [1980] R.T.R. 152; [1980] 1 Lloyd's Rep. 311, C.A.; reversing in part *sub nom.* Lambert *v.* Lewis; Lexmead (Basingstoke), Third Party; Dixon-Bate (B.), Fourth Party [1979] R.T.R. 61; [1978] 1 Lloyd's Rep. 610 34

Lampitt *v.* Poole Borough Council, Taylor (Third Party) [1991] 2 Q.B. 545; [1990] 3 W.L.R. 179; [1990] 2 All E.R. 887, C.A. 4

Lands Allotment Co., *Re* [1894] 1 Ch. 616; 38 S.J. 235; [1891–1894] All E.R. Rep. 1032; 63 L.J.Ch. 291; 70 L.T. 286; 42 W.R. 404; 10 T.L.R. 234; 1 Mans 107; 7 R. 115, C.A.   115

Leeds (Duke) *v.* Amherst (Earl) (1846) 2 Ph. 117; 16 L.J.Ch. 5; 10 Jur. 956; 41 E.R. 886, L.C. 114

Leicester Wholesale Fruit Market Ltd. *v.* Grundy (D.H.) (No. 1) [1990] 1 W.L.R. 107; [1990] 1 All E.R. 442; (1990) 134 S.J. 374; (1989) 5 Const.L.J. 282, C.A. 11

—— *v.* —— (No. 2) (1990) 53 B.L.R. 1 .... 15, 25

Leigh *v.* Jack (1879) 5 Ex. D. 264; 49 L.J.Q.B. 220; 42 L.T. 463; 44 J.P. 488; 28 W.R. 452, C.A. 88, 89, 90, 93, 95

Leivers *v.* Barber, Walker & Co. [1943] 1 K.B. 385, C.A. 31, 33

Letang *v.* Cooper [1964] 1 Q.B. 232; [1964] 3 W.L.R. 573; 108 S.J. 519; [1964] 2 All E.R. 929; [1964] 2 Lloyd's Rep. 339, C.A.; reversing [1964] 2 Q.B. 53; [1956] 2 W.L.R. 642; 108 S.J. 180; [1964] 1 All E.R. 669; [1964] 1 Lloyd's Rep. 188 .... 56, 64

Limpgrange *v.* Bank of Commerce and Credit International S.A.; Bank of Credit and Commerce International S.A. *v.* Smith [1986] FLR 36 38

Littledale *v.* Liverpool College [1900] 1 Ch. 19; [1895–1899] All E.R. Rep. Ext. 1329; 69 L.J.Ch. 87; 81 L.T. 564; 48 W.R. 177; 16 T.L.R. 44 C.A. 94

Liverpool Corp. *v.* Coghill (H.) & Son [1918] 1 Ch. 307; 82 J.P. 129; 87 L.J.Ch. 186; 118 L.T. 336; 34 T.L.R. 159; 16 L.G.R. 91 102

Lloyd's Bank Ltd. *v.* Margolis [1954] 1 W.L.R. 644; 98 S.J. 250; [1954] 1 All E.R. 734 . 37, 38

London Borough of Lewisham *v.* Leslie & Co. Ltd. (1978) 250 E.G. 1289; (1978) 12 Build. L.R. 22, C.A. 28

London Borough of Merton *v.* Lowe (1981) 18 B.L.R. 130, C.A. 35

London Congregational Union Inc. *v.* Harriss & Harriss [1988] 1 All E.R. 15; (1986) 280 E.G. 1342; (1987) 3 Const.L.J. 37; (1987) 35 Build. L.R. 58; (1987) 8 ConLR 52; [1986] 2 E.G.L.R. 155, C.A.; reversing in part [1985] 1 All E.R. 335; [1984] C.I.L.L. 85; (1984) 1 Const.L.J. 54 .... 11, 45

Long *v.* Hepworth [1968] 1 W.L.R. 1299; (1968) 112 S.J. 485; [1968] 3 All E.R. 248   64
Lord St. John *v.* Boughton. *See* St. John (Lord) *v.* Boughton.
Lye *v.* Marks and Spencer plc, *The Times*, February 15, 1988, C.A.   84
Lynn *v.* Bamber [1930] 2 K.B. 72; 74 S.J. 298; 99 L.J.K.B. 504; 143 L.T. 231; 46 T.L.R.
     367 ....   9, 33

McCafferty *v.* Metropolitan Police District Receiver [1977] 1 W.L.R. 1073; [1977] I.C.R.
     799; (1977) 121 S.J. 678; [1977] 2 All E.R. 756, C.A. 71, 83, 84
McGahie *v.* Union of Shop, Distributive and Allied Workers, 1966 S.L.T. 74   66
McNaughton *v.* Hicks Anderson. *See* James McNaughton Paper Group *v.* Hicks Anderson.
Marren *v.* Dawson Bentley & Co. Ltd. [1961] 2 Q.B. 135; [1961] 2 W.L.R. 679; 105 S.J. 383;
     [1961] 2 All E.R. 270   10
Marsden *v.* Miller, *The Times*, January 23, 1992, C.A.   94
Marshall *v.* Martin, June 10, 1987, C.A., unreported   82
—— *v.* Southampton & South-West Hampshire Health Authority (Teaching) (No. 152/84)
     [1986] Q.B. 401; [1986] 2 W.L.R. 780; [1986] I.C.R. 335; (1986) 130 S.J. 340; [1986] 2
     All E.R. 584; [1986] 1 C.M.L.R. 688; [1986] 2 E.C.R. 723; [1986] I.R.L.R. 140;
     (1986) 83 L.S.Gaz. 1720, European Ct.   84
Marston *v.* British Railways Board [1976] I.C.R. 124   82
Masters *v.* Brent London Borough Council [1978] 1 Q.B. 841; [1978] 2 W.L.R. 768; (1977)
     122 S.J. 300; [1978] 2 All E.R. 664; (1977) 76 L.G.R. 379; (1977) 245 E.G. 483 ...   58
Maxwell *v.* Murphy (1957) 96 C.L.R. 261, High Ct. of Australia   5
Melton *v.* Walker & Stanger (1981) 125 S.J. 861   50
Metall und Rohstoff AG *v.* Donaldson Lufkin & Jenrette Inc. [1990] 1 Q.B. 391; [1989] 3
     W.L.R. 563; (1989) 133 S.J. 1200; [1989] 3 All E.R. 14, C.A.; reversing in part [1988]
     3 W.L.R. 548; [1988] 3 All E.R. 116; [1988] 2 FTLR 93; [1988] L.S.Gaz., September
     14, 46   7
Midland Bank Trust Co. *v.* Hett, Stubbs and Kemp (a firm) [1979] Ch. 384; [1978] 3 W.L.R.
     167; (1977) 121 S.J. 830; [1978] 3 All E.R. 571 ....   2, 33, 35, 36, 49, 50
Miller *v.* Jackson [1977] Q.B. 966; [1977] 3 W.L.R. 20; (1977) 121 S.J. 287; [1977] 3 All E.R.
     338, C.A.   100
—— *v.* London Electrical Manufacturing Co., 120 S.J. 80; [1976] 2 Lloyd's Rep. 284,
     C.A.   84
Mills *v.* Silver [1991] Fam. 217; [1991] 2 W.L.R. 324; [1991] 1 All E.R. 449; (1990) 61 P. &
     C.R. 366; (1990) 134 S.J. 1402; *The Independent*, July 11, 1990, C.A. 102, 103,
                                                         104, 105
Ministry of Health *v.* Simpson [1051] A.C. 251; 66 T.L.R. (Pt. 2) 1915; [1950] 2 All E.R.
     1137; *sub nom. Re* Diplock, Minister of Health *v.* Simpson, 94 S.J. 777, H.L.;
     affirming *sub nom. Re* Diplock, Diplock *v.* Wintle [1984] Ch. 465; [1984] L.J.R. 1670;
     92 S.J. 484; *sub nom. Re* Diplock's Estate; Diplock *v.* Wintle [1984] 2 All E.R. 318,
     C.A.; reversing [1947] Ch. 716; [1947] L.J.R. 1158; 177 L.T. 40; 91 S.J. 248; [1947] 1
     All E.R. 522 ....   24, 25, 37, 119
Misset *v.* Council of the European Communities (Case No. 152/85) [1987] E.C.R. 223; *The*
     Times, March 23, 1987, European Ct.   112
Mitchell *v.* Harris Engineering Co. Ltd. [1967] 2 Q.B. 703; [1967] 3 W.L.R. 447; 111 S.J.
     355; [1967] 2 All E.R. 682, C.A.   13
Modern Engineering (Bristol) *v.* Gilbert-Ash (Northern). See Gilbert-Ash (Northern) *v.*
     Modern Engineering (Bristol).
Mondel *v.* Steel (1841) 8 M. & W. 858; 1 Dowl. N.S. 1; 10 L.J. Ex. 426; 151 E.R. 1288 ..   17
Moore (D.W.) & Co. *v.* Ferrier [1988] 1 W.L.R. 267; (1988) 132 S.J. 227; [1988] 1 All E.R.
     400, C.A. 49, 50–51
Moschi *v.* Lep Air Services Ltd. [1973] A.C. 331; [1972] 2 W.L.R. 1175; 116 S.J. 372; [1972]
     2 All E.R. 393, H.L.; affirming *sub nom.* Lep Air Services *v.* Rolloswin Investments
     [1971] 3 All E.R. 45, C.A.   39
Moses *v.* Lovegrove [1952] 2 Q.B. 533; [1952] 1 T.L.R. 1324; 96 S.J. 344; [1952] 1 All E.R.
     1279, C.A. 91, 92, 96
Mouna, The [1991] 2 Lloyd's Rep. 221; *The Times*, May 7, 1991, C.A.; reversing [1990] 2
     Lloyd's Rep. 7; *The Times*, March 24, 1990.   13
Mount Carmel Investments Ltd. *v.* Peter Thurlow Ltd. [1988] 1 W.L.R. 1078; [1988] 3 All
     E.R. 129; (1988) 57 P. & C.R. 396, C.A.   98

Murphy v. Brentwood District Council [1991] 1 A.C. 398; [1990] 3 W.L.R. 414; [1990] 2 All
    E.R. 908; (1990) 22 H.L.R. 502; (1990) 134 S.J. 1076; 21 Con.L.R. 1; 89 L.G.R. 24;
    (1990) 6 Const.L.J. 304; (1990) 54 L.G. Rev. 1010; [1990] L.S.Gaz. August 29, 15;
    (1990) 134 S.J. 1058; (1990) 134 S.J. 1974; 50 B.L.R. 1; (1990) 3 Admin.L.R. 37,
    H.L.; reversing [1990] 2 W.L.R. 944; [1990] 2 All E.R. 269; 88 L.G.R. 333; (1990)
    134 S.J. 458; [1990] L.S.Gaz. February 7, 42, C.A.; affirming 13 Con.L.R. 96 .. 15, 37,
                                                       46, 47–48, 61
Murray v. East India Co. (1821) 5 B. & Ald. 204; [1814–1823] All E.R. Rep. 227; 106 E.R.
    1167 2
Musurus Bey v. Gadban [1894] 2 Q.B. 352; 38 S.J. 511; [1893–1894] All E.R. Rep. 761; 63
    L.J.Q.B. 621; 71 L.T. 51; 42 W.R. 545; 10 T.L.R. 493; 9 R. 519, C.A. 8

Napper v. National Coal Board, March 1, 1990, C.A., unreported 80, 81, 84
Nash v. Eli Lilly [1991] 2 Med.L.R. 169; The Times, January 31, 1991 ... 69, 70, 80, 81, 84–85
National Bank of Commerce v. National Westminster Bank [1990] 2 Lloyd's Rep. 514;
    Financial Times, March 18, 1990 38
National Geographical Association v. Peter Thimbleby [1984] 25 B.L.R. 94 11
Nebe v. Commission of the European Communities (No. 24/69) [1970] E.C.R. 145 110
Newham v. Lawson (1971) 115 S.J. 446; (1971) 22 P. & C.R. 852 .... 103, 107
Newman v. Bevan Funnell Ltd., October 29, 1990, C.A., unreported 74, 83
Newton v. Cammell Laird & Co. (Shipbuilders and Engineers) [1969] 1 W.L.R. 415; 113 S.J.
    89; [1969] 1 All E.R. 708; 6 K.I.R. 195; [1969] 1 Lloyd's Rep. 224, C.A. 68, 72
Nicholson v. England [1926] 2 K.B. 93; [1925] All E.R. Rep. 335; 95 L.J.K.B. 505; 134 L.T.
    702, D.C. 96
Nisbet and Potts' Contract, Re [1906] 1 Ch. 386; 50 S.J. 191; [1904–1907] All E.R. Rep. 865;
    75 L.J.Ch. 238; 94 L.T. 297; 54 W.R. 286; 22 T.L.R. 233, C.A. 99
Nitrigin Eireann Teoranta v. Inco Alloys Ltd. [1992] 1 All E.R. 854 47

Ocean Estates Ltd. v. Pinder (Norman) [1969] 2 A.C. 19; [1969] 2 W.L.R. 1359; sub nom.
    Ocean Estates v. Pinder (1969) 113 S.J. 71, P.C. 94
Oliver, Re, Theobald v. Oliver [1927] 2 Ch. 323; 71 S.J. 710; 96 L.J.Ch. 496; 137 L.T.
    788 119
O'Reilly v. Mackman; Millbanks v. Secretary of State for the Home Department [1983] 2
    A.C. 237; [1982] 3 W.L.R. 1096; (1982) 126 S.J. 820; [1982] 3 All E.R. 1124, H.L.;
    affirming O'Reilly v. Mackman; Derbyshire v. Same; Dougan v. Same; Millbanks v.
    Home Office [1982] 3 W.L.R. 604; (1982) 126 S.J. 578; [1982] 3 All E.R. 680; (1982)
    79 L.S.Gaz. 1176, C.A.; reversing (1982) 126 S.J. 312 108

Paradise Beach and Transportation Company Ltd. v. Price-Robinson (Cyril) [1968] A.C.
    1072; [1968] 2 W.L.R. 873; sub nom. Paradise Beach and Transportation Co. v.
    Robinson (1968) 112 S.J. 113; sub nom. Paradise Beach and Transportation Co. v.
    Price-Robinson [1968] 1 All E.R. 530, P.C. 94
Parker (William C.) v. Harn (F.J.) & Son [1972] 1 W.L.R. 1583; 116 S.J. 903; [1972] 3 All
    E.R. 1051, C.A. 19
Peco Arts Inc. v. Hazlitt Gallery Ltd. (1983) 1 W.L.R. 1315; (1983) 127 S.J. 806; [1983] 3 All
    E.R. 193; (1984) 81 L.S.Gaz. 203 .... 25, 26, 27, 28
Pegler v. Railway Executive [1948] A.C. 332; [1948] L.J.R. 939; 64 T.L.R. 212; 92 S.J. 296;
    [1948] 1 All E.R. 559, H.L.; affirming sub nom. Pegler v. Great Western Ry., 63
    T.L.R. 178; [1947] 1 All E.R. 355 33
Penny v. Brice (1865) 18 C.B.N.S. 393; 11 L.T. 632; 13 W.L. 342; 144 E.R. 497 118
Perry v. Phillips (Sidney) & Son (a firm) [1982] 1 W.L.R. 1297; (1982) 126 S.J. 626; [1982] 3
    All E.R. 705; (1983) 22 Build. L.R. 120; (1982) E.G. 888; (1982) 79 L.S.Gaz. 1175,
    C.A.; reversing [1982] 1 All E.R. 1005; [1981] 260 E.G. 389 65
—— (Howard E.) & Co. v. British Railways Board [1980] I.C.R. 743; [1980] 1 W.L.R. 1375;
    (1980) 124 S.J. 591; [1980] 2 All E.R. 579 59
—— (Patrick J.) v. Woodfarm Homes Ltd. (1975) I.R. 104, Irish Sup. Ct. 98
Pheasant v. Smith (S.T.H.) (Tyres) Ltd. See Firman v. Ellis.
Phillips v. Eyre (1870) L.R. 6 Q.B. 1; 10 B. & S. 1004; 40 L.J.Q.B. 28; 22 L.T. 869, Ex.
    Ch. 7
Phillips-Higgins v. Harper [1954] 1 Q.B. 411; [1954] 2 W.L.R. 782; 98 S.J. 250; [1954] 2 All
    E.R. 5ln, C.A.; affirming [1954] 2 W.L.R. 117; 98 S.J. 45; [1954] 1 All E.R. 116 .24, 25
Pilmore (Matthew Ernest Martin) v. Northern Trawlers [1986] 1 Lloyd's Rep. 552 ..... 75, 83

Pirelli General Cable Works Ltd. *v.* Faber (Oscar) & Partners [1983] 2 A.C. 1; [1983] 2 W.L.R. 6; (1983) 127 S.J. 16; [1983] 1 All E.R. 65; (1983) 265 E.G. 979; (1983) 133 New L.J. 63, H.L.; reversing (1982) 263 E.G. 879, C.A. . 4, 8, 36, 41, 44, 45, 46–49, 52
Portico Housing Association Ltd. *v.* Moorehead (Brian) and Partners (1985) 1 Const.L.J. 226; [1985] C.I.L.L. 155; (1985) 6 Con.L.R. 1; *The Times*, February 5, 1984, C.A.   12
Post Office *v.* Norwich Union Fire Insurance Society Ltd. [1967] 2 Q.B. 363; [1967] 2 W.L.R. 709; 111 S.J. 71; [1967] 1 All E.R. 577; [1967] 1 Lloyd's Rep. 216, C.A.; reversing, 110 S.J. 867; [1966] 2 Lloyd's Rep. 499; 116 New L.J. 1544; [1966] C.L.Y. 6351; Petition for leave to appeal to the House of Lords dismissed. 40
Powell *v.* McFarlane (1977) 38 P. & C.R. 452 . . . . 90, 92, 94, 95
Pratt *v.* Cook, Son & Co. (St. Paul's) Ltd. [1940] A.C. 437; 104 J.P. 135; 84 S.J. 167; [1940] 1 All E.R. 410; 109 L.J.K.B. 293; 162 L.T. 243; 56 T.L.R. 363; 38 L.G.R. 125, H.L.   32
Presland *v.* Bingham (1888) 41 Ch.D. 268; 53 J.P. 583; 60 L.T. 433; 37 W.R. 385, C.A. . 105
Price *v.* Hilditch [1930] 1 Ch. 500; 99 L.J.Ch. 299; 143 L.T. 33 106
Prideaux *v.* Webber (1661) 1 Lev. 31; 1 Keb. 204; 83 E.R. 282 21
Prior *v.* Horniblow (1836) 2 Y. & C. Ex. 200; 160 E.R. 369 119
Pritam Kaur *v.* S. Russell & Sons Ltd. *See* Kaur (Pritam) *v.* Russell (S.) & Sons.
Pugh *v.* Savage [1970] 2 Q.B. 373; [1970] 2 W.L.R. 634; 114 S.J. 109; [1970] 2 All E.R. 353; 21 P. & C.R. 242, C.A. 102, 103, 104, 105

R. *v.* Dairy Produce Quota Tribunal for England and Wales, *ex p.* Caswell [1990] 2 A.C. 738; [1990] 2 W.L.R. 1320; [1990] 2 All E.R. 434; [1990] C.O.D. 243; (1990) 2 Admin.L.R. 765; (1990) 140 New L.J. 742, H.L.; affirming [1989] 1 W.L.R. 1089; [1990] C.O.D. 44; (1989) 2 Admin.L.R. 55; (1989) 139 New L.J. 901; [1989] L.S.Gaz, November 15, 39, C.A.; affirming [1989] C.O.D. 283; [1989] 26 E.G. 130; [1989] 2 C.M.L.R. 502 109
—— *v.* Secretary of State for the Environment, *ex p.* Davies [1991] 1 P.L.R. 78; (1990) 61 P. & C.R. 487; [1991] J.P.L. 540; [1991] C.O.D. 160; *The Independent*, October 31, 1990, C.A.; affirming (1989) 3 P.L.R. 73; [1989] C.O.D. 569; *The Times*, May 15, 1989 96
—— *v.* Stratford-upon-Avon District Council, *ex p.* Jackson [1985] 1 W.L.R. 1319; (1985) 130 S.J. 854; [1985] 3 All E.R. 769; (1985) 51 P. & C.R. 76; (1985) 84 L.G.R. 287; (1985) 82 L.S.Gaz. 3533, C.A. 108, 109
—— *v.* Williams [1942] A.C. 541 31
R. B. Policies at Lloyds *v.* Butler (1950) 1 K.B. 76; 65 T.L.R. 436; 93 S.J. 553; [1949] 2 All E.R. 226; 82 Ll.L.Rep. 841 . . . . 1, 8, 61
R. & H. Green & Silley Weir *v.* British Railways Board. See Green (R. & H.) & Silley Weir *v.* British Railways Board.
Rains *v.* Buxton (1880) 14 Ch.D. 537; 49 L.J.Ch. 473; 43 L.T. 88; 28 W.R. 954 88
Ramsden *v.* Lee [1992] 2 All E.R. 204, C.A. 76, 79
Randall *v.* Stevens (1853) 2 E. & B. 641; 1 C.L.R. 641; 23 L.J.Q.B. 68; 21 L.T.O.S. 344; 18 Jur. 128; 118 E.R. 907 89
Rath *v.* C.S. Lawrence & Partners (1990) 26 ConLR 16 19
Read *v.* Brown (1888) 22 Q.B.D. 128; 58 L.J.Q.B. 120; 60 L.T. 250; 37 W.R. 131; 5 T.L.R. 97, C.A. 8
Red House Farms (Thorndon) Ltd. *v.* Catchpole (1977) E.G.D. 798, C.A. 90
Rhodes *v.* Smethurst (1846) 6 M. & W. 351; 9 L.J.Ex. 330, 4 Jur. 702; 151 E.R. 447, Ex.Ch. 118
Richardson, *Re, ex p.* St. Thomas's Hospital (Governors) [1911] 2 K.B. 705; 80 L.J.K.B. 1232; 105 L.T. 226; 18 Mans. 327, C.A. 40
Rimmer *v.* Liverpool City Council [1985] Q.B. 1; [1984] 2 W.L.R. 426; (1984) 128 S.J. 225; [1984] 1 All E.R. 930; (1984) 47 P. & C.R. 516; (1984) 269 E.G. 319; (1984) 82 L.G.R. 424; (1984) 12 H.L.R. 23; (1984) 81 L.S.Gaz. 664, C.A. 35
Robinson, *Re*, McLaren *v.* Public Trustee [1911] 1 Ch. 502; 55 S.J. 271; [1911–1913] All E.R. Rep. 296; 80 L.J.Ch. 381; 104 L.T.331 114
Robinson *v.* Unicos Property Corpn. Ltd. [1962] 1 W.L.R. 520; 106 S.J. 193; [1962] 2 All E.R. 24, C.A. 14
Ronex Properties Ltd. *v.* Laing (John) Construction Ltd. [1983] Q.B. 398; [1982] 3 W.L.R. 875; (1982) 126 S.J. 727; [1982] 3 All E.R. 961; (1982) 79 L.S.Gaz. 1413, C.A. . . . 2, 11
Rundell *v.* Murray (1821) Jac. 311; 37 E.R. 868, L.C. 114
Russo-Asiatic Bank, *Re*; Russian Bank for Foreign Trade, *Re* [1934] Ch. 720; 78 S.J. 647; [1934] All E.R. Rep. 558; 103 L.J.Ch. 336; 152 L.T. 142; [1934] B. & C.R. 71 . . .   8

St. John (Lord) v. Boughton (1838) 9 Sim. 219; 7 L.J.Ch. 208; 2 Jur. 413; 59 E.R. 342 .. 38

Schiavo v. Council of European Communities (Nos. 122 and 123/79) [1981] E.C.R. 473 .. 110

Schwarzwaldmilch GmbH v. Einfuhr-und Vorratsstelle Für Fette (No. 4/68) [1968] E.C.R. 377, [1969] C.M.L.R. 406, European Ct. 111

Scott v. Avery (1865) 5 H.L. Cas. 811; [1843–1860] All E.R. Rep. 1; 25 L.J. Ex. 308; 28 L.T.O.S. 207; 2 Jur. N.S. 815; 4 W.R. 746; 10 E.R. 1121, H.L. 10

Seddon v. Smith (1877) 36 L.T. 168 94

Sevcon Ltd. v. Lucas CAV Ltd. [1986] 1 W.L.R. 462; (1986) 130 S.J. 340; [1986] 2 All E.R. 104; [1986] R.P.C. 609; [1986] F.S.R. 338; (1986) 83 L.S.Gaz. 1641, H.L.; affirming [1985] F.S.R. 545, C.A. 8, 9

Shaw v. Shaw [1954] 2 Q.B. 429; [1954] 3 W.L.R. 265; 98 S.J. 509; [1954] 2 All E.R. 638, C.A. 22

Shelley v. Paddock [1980] Q.B. 348; [1980] 2 W.L.R. 647; (1979) 123 S.J. 706; [1980] 1 All E.R. 1009, C.A.; affirming [1979] Q.B. 120; [1978] 2 W.L.R. 877; (1977) 122 S.J. 317; [1978] 3 All E.R. 129 65

Simmons v. Dobson [1991] 1 W.L.R. 720; [1991] 4 All E.R. 25; (1991) 135 S.J. 509; *The Times*, April 16, 1991, C.A. 103

Simpson v. Northwest Holst Southern Ltd. [1980] 1 W.L.R. 968; (1980) 124 S.J. 313; [1980] 2 All E.R. 471, C.A. 71

—— v. Smith, *The Times*, January 19, 1989, C.A. 19

Singer v. Harrison Clark, April 15, 1987, unreported, ... 24

Skingsley v. Cape Asbestos Co. Ltd., 112 S.J. 355; [1968] 2 Lloyd's Rep. 201, C.A. 68

Smith v. Bush (Eric S.); Harris v. Wyre Forest District Council [1990] 1 A.C. 831; [1989] 2 W.L.R. 790; (1989) 133 S.J. 597; (1990) 9 Tr.L.R. 1; 87 L.G.R. 685; (1989) 21 H.L.R. 424, [1989] 2 All E.R. 514; [1989] 17 E.G. 68 and [1989] 18 E.G. 99; (1989) 139 New L.J. 576; (1989) 153 L.G. Rev. 984, H.L.; affirming [1988] Q.B. 743; (1987) 131 S.J. 1423; [1987] 3 All E.R. 179; (1987) 19 H.L.R. 287; [1987] 1 E.G.L.R. 157; [1988] T.L.R. 77; (1987) 84 L.S.Gaz. 3260; (1987) 137 New L.J. 362, C.A. 56

—— v. Central Asbestos Co. Ltd. *See* Central Asbestos Co. v. Dodd.

Società Industriale Metallurgica di Napoli (Simet) SpA & Acciairie e Ferriere de Roma (Feram) v. High Authority of the E.C.S.C. (Nos. 25 and 26/65) [1967] E.C.R. 33 . 112

Société Commerciale de Réassurance v. ERAS (International) (Note) [1992] 2 All E.R. 82, C.A. 9, 30, 36, 42, 49, 53

Société pour l'exportation de sucres SA v. Commission of the European Communities (No. 88/76) [1977] E.C.R. 709, European Court's previous proceedings [1976] E.C.R. 1585, European Ct. 112

Solling v. Broughton [1893] A.C. 556; 63 L.J.P.C. 21, P.C. 89

Sparham-Souter v. Town and Country Developments (Essex) Ltd. [1976] 1 Q.B. 858; [1976] 2 W.L.R. 493; 120 S.J. 216; [1976] 2 All E.R. 65; 74 L.G.R. 355, C.A. 44

Spectrum Investment Co. v. Holmes [1981] 1 W.L.R. 221; (1980) 125 S.J. 47; [1981] 1 All E.R. 6; (1980) 41 P. & C.R. 133 98

Spoor v. Green (1874) L.R. 9 Exch. 99; 43 L.J. Ex. 57; 30 L.T. 393; 22 W.R. 547 35

Steadman v. Scholfield, *The Times*, April 15, 1992 63

Steamship Mutual Underwriting Association Ltd. v. Trollope & Colls (City) Ltd. (1986) 33 Build. L.R. 77; (1986) 6 ConLR 11; (1986) 2 Const.L.J. 224, C.A.; affirming (1985) 6 ConLR 11; (1985) 2 Const.L.J. 75 .... 14, 15, 19

Stephen v. Riverside Health Authority, *The Times*, November 29 and November 24, 1989 68

Stile v. Finch (1634) Cro. Car. 384; 79 E.R. 932 2

Stubbings v. Webb [1991] 3 W.L.R. 383; [1991] 3 All E.R. 949; *The Times*, April 3, 1991; *The Daily Telegraph*, May 14, 1991, C.A. 56, 65, 72

Sturges v. Bridgman (1879) 11 Ch.D. 852; 43 J.P. 716; 48 L.J.Ch. 785; 41 L.T. 219; 28 W.R. 200, C.A. 100, 102

Surrendra Overseas v. Government of Sri Lanka [1977] 1 W.L.R. 565; [1977] 2 All E.R. 481; [1977] 1 Lloyd's Rep. 653 38

Swainston v. Hetton Victory Club Ltd. *See* Hetton Victory Club Ltd. v. Swainston.

Tai Hing Cotton Mill Ltd. v. Lin Chong Hing Bank Ltd. [1986] A.C. 80; [1985] 3 W.L.R. 317; (1985) 129 S.J. 503; [1985] 2 All E.R. 947; [1986] FLR 14; [1985] 2 Lloyd's Rep. 313; (1985) 135 New L.J. 680; (1985) 82 L.S.Gaz. 2995, P.C. 36, 49

Taylor v. Taylor, *the Times*, April 14, 1984, C.A. 76

—— v. Whitehead (1781) 2 Doug. K.B. 744; [1775–1802] All E.R. Rep. 332; 99 E.R. 475 103

Tecbild Ltd. *v.* Chamberlain (1969) 20 P. & C.R. 683; (1969) 209 E.G. 1069, C.A. 88, 89, 91, 94

Tehidy Minerals Ltd. *v.* Norman [1971] 2 Q.B. 528; [1971] 2 W.L.R. 711; (1970) 115 S.J. 59; [1971] 2 All E.R. 475; 22 P. & C.R. 371, C.A. 101

Telfair Shipping Corporation *v.* Inersea S.A.; Caroline P, The [1985] 1 W.L.R. 553; (1985) 129 S.J. 283; [1985] 1 All E.R. 243; [1984] 2 Lloyd's Rep. 466; (1985) 82 L.S.Gaz. 1781 .... 39, 40

Thompson *v.* Brown Construction (Ebbw Vale). See Thompson *v.* Brown (Trading as Brown (George Albert) (Builders) & Co.).

——— *v.* Brown (Trading as Brown (George Albert) (Builders) & Co.) [1981] 1 W.L.R. 744; [1981] 125 S.J. 377; *sub nom.* Thompson *v.* Brown Construction (Ebbw Vale) [1981] 2 All E.R. 296, H.L. 75, 76, 78, 79, 80, 81, 82

Thorne *v.* Heard & Marsh [1895] A.C. 495; 64 L.J.Ch. 652; 73 L.T. 291; 44 W.R. 155; 11 T.L.R. 464; 11 R. 254, H.L. 115, 116

Thursby *v.* Warren (1628) Cro. Car. 159; 79 E.R. 738 2

Tichborne *v.* Weir [1891–1894] All E.R. Rep. 449; 67 L.T. 735; 8 T.L.R. 713; 4 R. 26, C.A. 99

Tickner *v.* Buzzacott [1965] Ch. 426; [1965] 2 W.L.R. 154; 109 S.J. 74; [1964] 1 All E.R. 131 99

Tilcon Ltd. *v.* Land and Real Estate Investments Ltd. [1987] 1 W.L.R. 46; [1987] 1 All E.R. 615; (1987) 131 S.J. 76; (1986) L.S.Gaz. 3673, C.A. 18

Tito *v.* Waddell (No. 2;) Tito *v.* Att.-Gen. [1977] Ch. 106; [1977] 2 W.L.R. 496; [1977] 3 All E.R. 129; judgment on damages [1977] 3 W.L.R. 972(N.) 21, 24, 115

Tottenham Hotspur Football and Athletic Co. Ltd. *v.* Princegrove Publishers Ltd. [1974] 1 W.L.R. 113; (1973) 118 S.J. 35; [1974] 1 All E.R. 17; (1973) 27 P. & C.R. 101 ... 114

Tozer Kelmsley & Milbourn (Holdings) Ltd. *v.* Jarvis (J.) & Sons Ltd. (1983) 1 Const.L.J. 79 45

Transoceanic Petroleum Carriers *v.* Cook Industries Inc.; Mary Lou, The [1981] 2 Lloyd's Rep. 272; [1982] Com.L.R. 173 34

Treloar *v.* Nute [1977] 1 W.L.R. 1295; [1977] 1 All E.R. 230, C.A. 88, 89, 93

Trow *v.* Ind Coope (West Midlands) Ltd. [1967] 2 Q.B. 899; [1967] W.L.R. 633; 111 S.J. 375; [1967] 2 All E.R. 900, C.A.; affirming *sub nom.* Trow *v.* Ind Coope; Trow *v.* Ind Coope (West Midlands) [1966] 3 W.L.R. 1300; 110 S.J. 964; [1967] 1 All E.R. 19 .... 10, 12

UBAF Ltd. *v.* European American Banking Corp; Pacific Colcotronis, The [1984] Q.B. 713; [1984] 2 W.L.R. 508; (1984) 128 S.J. 243; [1984] 2 All E.R. 226; [1984] 1 Lloyd's Rep. 258; (1984) 81 L.S.Gaz. 429, C.A. 44, 51–52

Union Lighterage Co. *v.* London Graving Dock Co. [1902] Ch. 557; [1900–1903] All E.R. Rep. 234; 71 L.J.Ch. 791; 87 L.T. 381; 18 T.L.R. 754, C.A. 102

Unitramp *v.* Garnac Grain Co. Inc.; Hermine, The [1979] 1 Lloyd's Rep. 212, C.A.; reversing [1978] 2 Lloyd's Rep. 37 34

Vane *v.* Vane (1873) 8 Ch. App. 383; 42 L.J. Ch. 299; 28 L.T. 320; 21 W.R. 252 29

Waddon *v.* Whitecroft-Scovill [1988] 1 W.L.R. 309; (1988) 132 S.J. 263; [1988] 1 All E.R. 996; (1988) L.S.Gaz. March 16, 43, H.L. 13

Waghorn *v.* Lewisham & North Southwark Health Authority, June 23, 1987, Q.B.D., unreported 84

Walkley *v.* Precision Forgings Ltd [1979] 1 W.L.R. 606; (1979) 123 S.J. 354, [1979] 2 All E.R. 548, H.L.; reversing [1978] 1 W.L.R. 1228; (1978) 122 S.J. 645; [1979] 1 All E.R. 102, C.A. 19, 76, 77, 79

Wallis's Cayton Bay Holiday Camp Ltd. *v.* Shell-Mex and B.P. Ltd. [1975] Q.B. 94; [1974] 3 W.L.R. 387; 118 S.J. 680; [1974] 3 All E.R. 575; 29 P. & C.R. 214, C.A. 91, 93

Ward (Helston) Ltd. *v.* Kerrier District Council (Ref. 218/1980) (1984) 24 R.V.R. 18; [1981] J.P.L. 519, Lands Tribunal 105

Warren *v.* Murray [1894] 2 Q.B. 648; 64 L.J.Q.B. 42; 71 L.T. 458; 48 W.R. 3; 10 T.L.R. 573; 9 R. 793, C.A. 96

Wassell *v.* Leggatt [1986] 1 Ch. 554; 65 L.J.Ch. 240; *sub nom.* Wassell, *Re*, Wassell *v.* Leggatt, 40 S.J. 276; 74 L.T. 99; 44 W.R. 298; 12 T.L.R. 208 116

Watts v. Morrow [1991] 1 W.L.R. 1421; [1991] 4 All E.R. 937; (1991) 23 H.L.R. 608; [1991]
    EGCS 88; (1991) 141 New L.J. 1331; [1991] NPC 98; *The Independent*, August 20,
    1991; *The Guardian*, September 4, 1991, C.A.; reversing [1991] 14 E.G. 111; [1991] 15
    E.G. 113; 24 ConLR 125   65
West Bank Estates Ltd. v. Arthur (Shakespeare Cornelius) [1967] A.C. 665; [1966] 3 W.L.R.
    750; 110 S.J. 602, P.C. 90, 94
Westminster City Council v. Clifford Culpin & Partners (a firm) (1987) 137 New L.J. 736,
    C.A. 2, 18
Wham-O Manufacturing Co. v. Lincoln Industries Ltd. [1985] R.P.C. 127, C.A. (New
    Zealand)   59
Wilkinson v. Ancliff (BLT) Ltd. [1986] 1 W.L.R. 1352; [1986] 3 All E.R. 427; (1986) 130 S.J.
    766; (1986) L.S.Gaz. 3248, C.A. 69, 70
William C. Parker v. F.J. Ham & Son Ltd. *See* Parker (William C.) v. Ham (F.J.) & Son.
William Hill Organisation v. Bernard Sunley & Sons. *See* Hill (William) Organisation v.
    Sunley (Bernard) & Sons.
William Lacey (Hounslow) v. Davis. *See* Lacey (William) (Hounslow) v. Davis.
Williams v. Usherwood (1983) 45 P. & C.R. 235, C.A. 89, 81, 94
Williams Bros. Direct Supply Ltd. v. Raftery [1958] 1 Q.B. 159; [1957] 3 W.L.R. 931; 101
    S.J. 921; [1957] 3 All E.R. 593; C.A. 88, 89, 96
Willis v. Howe (Earl of) [1893] 2 Ch. 545; 62 L.J.Ch. 690; 69 L.T. 358; 41 W.R. 433; 9
    T.L.R. 415; 2 R. 427, C.A.   95
Wimbledon and Putney Commons Conservators v. Dixon (1875) 1 Ch.D. 362; 40 J.P. 102;
    [1874–1880] All E.R. Rep. 1218; 45 L.J.Ch. 353; 33 L.T. 679; 24 W.R. 466, C.A.   103
Wimpey (George) & Co. v. Sohn [1967] Ch. 487; [1966] 2 W.L.R. 414; 110 S.J. 15; [1966] 1
    All E.R. 232; [1965] C.L.Y. 4000, C.A.   94
Windsor Steam Coal Co. [1929] 1 Ch. 151; 98 L.J.Ch. 147; 140 L.T. 80, C.A.; affirming on
    other grounds [1928] Ch. 609; 72 S.J. 335: 97 L.J.Ch. 238; [1928] B. & C.R. 36 ..   115
Woods v. Att.-Gen, July 18, 1990, unreported 71, 80, 81
Workvale, *Re* (in dissolution), *sub nom.* Workvale (No. 2) *Re* [1992] 1 W.L.R. 416; [1992] 2
    All E.R. 627; C.A.; affirming [1991] 1 W.L.R. 294 .... 8, 72
Wright v. Pepin [1954] 1 W.L.R. 635; 985 S.J. 252; [1954] 2 All E.R. 52   38

Ydun, The [1899] P. 236; 68 L.J.P. 101; 81 L.T. 10; 15 T.L.R. 361; 8 Asp.M.L.C. 551,
    C.A.   5
Yew Bon Tew alias Yong Boon Tiew v. Kenderaan Bas Mara [1983] 1 A.C. 553; [1982] 3
    W.L.R. 1026; (1982) 126 S.J. 729; [1982] 3 All E.R. 833, P.C. 1, 5
Yorkshire Electricity Board v. British Telecommunications [1986] 1 W.L.R. 1029; (1986) 130
    S.J. 613; [1986] 2 All E.R. 961; (1986) 34 Build. L.R. 9; (1986) 84 L.G.R. 857; (1986)
    83 L.S.Gaz. 2661, H.L.; reversing (1985) 129 S.J. 468; (1985) 82 L.S.Gaz. 2663;
    (1985) 83 L.G.R. 760, C.A. 40, 41
Young v. G.L.C. and Massey, December 19, 1986, reported 71, 74

TABLE OF STATUTES

1832 Prescription Act (2 & 3 Will. 4, c. 71) 4, 100, 102, 103, 104, 105, 106
s. 2 .... 105, 106
s. 3 .... 101, 106
s. 4 .... 105, 106
s. 7 105
1888 Trustee Act (51 & 52 Vict., c. 59)—
s. 8(1) 115
1911 Maritime Conventions Act (1 & 2 Geo. 5, c. 57) 63
1925 Trustee Act (15 & 16 Geo. 5, c. 19)—
s. 68(17) 115, 119
Land Registration Act (15 & 16 Geo. 5, c. 21) 98, 99
s. 75 98
(1) 97, 98
Administration of Estates Act (15 & 16 Geo. 5, c. 23)—
s. 44 119
1934 Law Reform (Miscellaneous Provisions) Act (24 & 25 Geo. 5, c. 41) 117
s. 1 118
1937 Factories Act (1 Edw. 8 & 1 Geo. 6, c. 67) 67
1939 Limitation Act (2 & 3 Geo. 6, c. 21) . 1, 4, 5, 15, 31, 61, 64, 67, 97
s. 13 89
s. 26 29
1946 Coal Industry Nationalisation Act (9 & 10 Geo. 6)—
s. 49(3) 87
1950 Arbitration Act (14 Geo. 6, c. 27)—
s. 13A 18
Public Utilities Street Works Act (14 Geo. 6, c. 39) 41
s. 26 40
1954 Law Reform (Limitation of Action etc.) Act (2 & 3 Eliz. 2, c. 36) 64
1956 Copyright Act (4 & 5 Eliz. 2, c. 74)—
s. 18 59
1959 Rights of Light Act (7 & 8 Eliz. 2, c. 56) 106
Mental Health Act (7 & 8 Eliz. 2, c. 72) 20
1961 Carriage by Air Act (9 & 10 Eliz. 2, c. 27) 42
s. 5(1) 42
Sched. I
art. 29(1) 64

1963 Limitation Act (c. 47) 4, 67
1965 Carriage of Goods by Road Act (c. 37) 42
1967 Leasehold Reform Act (c. 88) .. 32, 33
1968 Theft Act (c. 60) 59
s. 15(1) 59
1969 Family Law Reform Act (c. 46)—
s. 1 20
1970 Proceedings Against Estates Act (c. 17)—
s. 1 118
Equal Pay Act (c. 41) 5
1971 Carriage of Goods by Sea Act (c. 19) 41
1972 Defective Premises Act (c. 35) .. 5, 61
s. 1(1) 61
1973 Matrimonial Causes Act (c. 18) . 5
1975 Limitation Act (c. 54) 4
Sex Discrimination Act (c. 65) .. 5
1976 Fatal Accidents Act (c. 30) ... 23, 117
s. 1(3) 117
Race Relations Act (c. 74) 5
1977 Torts (Interference with Goods) Act (c. 32) 58, 59
s. 1(a) 58
Unfair Contract Terms Act (c. 50) 31, 73
s. 13(1)(a) 31
1978 Employment Protection (Consolidation) Act (c. 44) 5
s. 67(2) 3, 11
Civil Liability (Contribution) Act (c. 47) 17
1979 Sale of Goods Act (c. 54)—
s. 14(3) 34
s. 53(1) 17
1980 Limitation Amendment Act (c. 24) 4, 5, 89
Limitation Act (c. 58) . 3, 4, 5, 10, 19, 21, 22, 31, 41, 68, 89, 97, 114, 115, 119
Pt. I 3, 61
Pt. II 3
Pt. III 3
ss. 2–10 64
s. 2 .... 44, 59, 60, 114
s. 3 59
(1) 59, 60, 61
(2) 3, 60, 61
s. 4 .... 59, 60
(1) 59, 60
(2) 59–60
(5) 59
(a) 59

1980   Limitation Act—*cont.*

s. 4A	44, 56, 57
s. 5	31, 32, 114
s. 6	38
(2)(*a*)	38
(*b*)	38
(3)	38
s. 7	114
s. 8	31, 114
(1)	33
(2)	33
s. 9	33, 114
s. 10	17
(3)	17
(4)	17
s. 11	14, 62, 66, 67, 76, 77, 78, 79
(1)	66
(4)	44, 64
(*a*)	66
(*b*)	66, 67
(5)	118
(6)	118
(7)	118
s. 11A	3, 62, 76
(3)	62
(4)	62
s. 12	14, 76, 79, 117
(8)	117
s. 13	117
s. 14	53, 54, 56, 62, 84
(1)	67–68, 69
(*a*)	67
(*b*)	67, 69
(*c*)	67
(*d*)	67–68
(2)	71
(3)	68, 72, 74
(*a*)	67
(*b*)	68, 73
s. 14A	4, 9, 42, 43, 52, 58, 62
(1)	53
(4)	52
(5)	53
(6)	53
(7)	54
(8)	53
(10)	55
s. 14B	4, 9, 52
s. 15	88, 114
(1)	86
(2)	86
(*a*)	86
(*b*)	86
(7)	87
s. 16	86, 114
s. 17	3, 86, 97
s. 18	97
s. 19	33, 97
s. 20	33
(1)	86
(2)	114
(4)	114

1980   Limitation Act—*cont.*

s. 21	114
(1)	118
(*a*)	115
(*b*)	116
(2)	116, 118
(3)	115
(4)	116
s. 22	114, 115, 118
s. 24	114
s. 26(*b*)	22
s. 28	83, 117
(1)	19
s. 29	38
(2)	96
(5)(*a*)	38, 39
s. 30(1)	38
(2)(*a*)	38
(*b*)	38
s. 32	21, 23, 24, 25, 26, 27, 28, 29, 30, 61, 74
(1)	21, 26, 27, 28
(*a*)	21, 22, 61
(*b*)	22, 23, 61
(*c*)	24, 25
(2)	22
(3)	29
(4)	29
(4A)	63
s. 32A	57
(*a*)	57
s. 33	9, 11, 14, 16, 19, 20, 57, 58, 71, 72, 73, 75, 76, 77, 78, 79, 84, 85, 117
(1)(*a*)	75, 76
(*b*)	75
(3)	75, 80, 117
(*a*)	80
(*b*)	81
(*c*)	82
(*d*)	83
(*f*)	84
(4)	117
(5)	117
s. 34	1
(1)	3, 7
(2)	10
s. 35	13, 14, 15
(1)(*a*)	16
(*b*)	16, 18
(2)	16
(*a*)	14
(*b*)	16
(3)	16
(5)	14
(*a*)	14
(7)	14
(8)	14
s. 36	114
s. 38	20, 96
(1)	3, 64, 86, 115
(2)	20, 83

1980	Limitation Act—*cont.*	
	s. 38(3)	83
	s. 39	5
	Sched. 1	3, 88, 97
	Pt. I	88
	Pt. II	87
	para. 1	88, 95
	para. 5(1)	97
	(2)	97
	para. 8(4)	93
	para. 11(1)	87
	(2)(*a*)	87
	(*b*)	87
	Sched. 2	3, 4, 5
	Sched. 3	3
	Sched. 4	3
1981	Supreme Court Act (c. 54)—	
	s. 31	108
	(6)	108, 109
	(*a*)	108
	(*b*)	108
1982	Administration of Justice Act (c. 53)—	
	s. 4	117
1983	International Transport Conventions Act (c. 14)	42
	Mental Health Act (c. 20)	83
1984	Foreign Limitation Periods Act (c. 16)	5, 7, 29
	s. 1(1)(*a*)	6
	(2)	7
	(3)	6
	(4)	6
	s. 2(1)	6
	(2)	6, 7
	s. 3	7
	s. 4(2)	6
	s. 5	7
1985	Companies Act (c. 6)—	
	s. 14	32
	(2)	32
	s. 651	8, 72
	Administration of Justice Act (c. 61)	4
	s. 57(2)	56
	(4)	57
1986	Latent Damage Act (c. 37)	4, 8, 9, 22, 30, 37, 42, 43, 46, 52–56, 58, 59
1987	Consumer Protection Act (c. 43)	3, 4, 9, 62
	s. 4	62
	s. 6(6)	62
	Sched. 1	62
1988	Criminal Justice Act (c. 33)—	
	Sched. 7	
	para. 2(*a*)	74
	(*b*)	74
	para. 3	74
	Copyright, Designs and Patents Act (c. 48)—	
	s. 303	59
	Sched. 8	59
1989	Law of Property (Miscellaneous Provisions) Act (c. 34)—	
	s. 1(1)(*b*)	31
	(2)	31
	(3)	31
	Companies Act (c. 40)—	
	s. 141	8, 72
1990	Contracts (Applicable Law) Act (c. 36)	7, 110
	Sched. 1	7
	Courts and Legal Services Act (c. 41)—	
	s. 102	18

TABLE OF E.C. AND INTERNATIONAL TREATIES AND CONVENTIONS

EUROPEAN COMMUNITY TREATIES AND CONVENTIONS

1951 Paris. European Coal and Steel Community (E.C.S.C.) Treaty (April 18, 1951) 261 U.N.T.S. 140; U.K.T.S. 16 (1979), Cmnd. 7461—
    Art. 33(3) 109
1957 Rome. Treaty establishing the European Atomic Energy Community (Euratom) (March 27, 1957) 298 U.N.T.S. 167, U.K.T.S. 15 (1979), Cmnd. 7480—
    Art. 146(3) 109
    Rome. Treaty establishing the European Economic Community (E.E.C.) (March 25, 1957) 298 U.N.T.S. 11; U.K.T.S. 15 (1979), Cmnd. 7480—
    Art. 173(3) 109
    Art. 175(2) 109
    Art. 215 110
1980 Rome. Convention on the law applicable to contractual obligations (June 19, 1980) (O.J. 1980 L266/1) 7
    Art. 10(1)(d) 7

RULES OF PROCEDURE OF THE EUROPEAN COURT OF JUSTICE

    Rules of Procedure of the European Court of Justice (1991) O.J. L176/7; [1991] 3 C.M.L.R. 745 .... 109, 110
    Art. 80(1) 113
        (a) 112
        (2) 113
    Art. 81(1) 112
    Annex II 110
    Court of Justice Protocol 109
    Art. 42(2) 111
    Art. 43 110

INTERNATIONAL TREATIES AND CONVENTIONS

1955 Warsaw. Treaty on friendship co-operation and mutual assistance (Warsaw Pact) (May 14, 1955) 219 U.N.T.S. 3 .... 42, 64
    Art. 29(1) 42
1956 Geneva. Convention relative au contrat de transport international de marchandises par route (C.M.R.) (May 19, 1956) 399 U.N.T.S. 189; U.K.T.S. 90 (1967) Cmnd. 3455 42
    Art. 32 42
1968 The Hague–Visby Rules (the Brussels Protocol) 41
    Art. III(6) 42
1970 Berne. International conventions concerning the carriage (A) of goods by rail (C.I.M.) and (B) passengers and luggage by rail (C.I.V.) with additional protocol (February 7, 1970) U.K.T.S. 40, 41 (1975), Cmnd. 5897, 5898—
    Part (A) Art. 58 42
    Part (B) Art. 55 42
    Paris. Convention on the means of prohibiting and preventing the illicit import, export and transfer of ownership of cultural property (November 14, 1970) 823 U.N.T.S. 231 30
1974 Athens. Convention relating to the carriage of passengers and their luggage by sea (December 13, 1974) Cmnd. 6326 .. 42
    Art. 16 42
1980 Berne. Convention relative aux transports internationau ferroviaires (C.O.T.I.F.) (May 9, 1980) Cmnd. 8535 42
    Appendix A 42
    Appendix B 42

1 NATURE AND PURPOSE OF LIMITATION PERIODS

A limitation period is the time laid down by statute[1] within which legal and arbitral[2] proceedings must be commenced in a particular action; if proceedings are started outside the stipulated time, the plaintiff may be met with a plea from the defendant that the action is time-barred and should consequently be struck out.

Purpose of limitation periods

The imposition of strict time limits within which actions must be started serves to encourage plaintiffs to commence proceedings within a reasonable time so as to ensure, as far as possible, that actions are tried at a time when the recollection of witnesses is still clear.[3] In addition, such time limits permit those against whom claims might be brought to calculate the time for which they should keep records of accidents or proof of payment of debts.[4]

Differing lengths of limitation periods

The length of a limitation period in any given case should, therefore, be sufficient to permit the plaintiff to take cognisance of the damage which he has suffered, to consult appropriate experts, whether legal or otherwise, to make investigations into the cause of his damage and finally to issue a writ against the defendant. At the same time, however, the interests of the defendant should be taken into account: the primary purpose of the limitation period is to protect a defendant from the injustice of having to face a stale claim, *i.e.* a claim with which he never expected to have to deal.[5] The defendant should not be left for an unreasonable length of time in a state of uncertainty as to whether or not proceedings will be brought against him, since this may make it difficult for him to conduct his business efficiently. Moreover, if the action is eventually brought a number of years after the occurrence of disputed events, he may be prejudiced by the passage of time since some witnesses may be untraceable or dead, and the memory of others may have faded.

The setting of limitation periods of differing lengths represents recognition of the fact that the various competing factors referred to in the last paragraph operate differently

---

[1] The concept of limitation was not known to the common law. The earliest statute of limitations dates from 1623 and was in force until repealed by the Limitation Act 1939.

[2] Limitation Act 1980, s.34.

[3] *R.B. Policies at Lloyd's* v. *Butler* [1950] 1 K.B. 76.

[4] *A'Court* v. *Cross* (1825) 3 Bing. 329. See the Report of the Committee on Limitation of Actions in Cases of Personal Injury, Cmnd. 1829 (1962), para. 17 and the Law Reform Committee, Final Report on Limitation of Actions, Cmnd. 6293 (1977), para. 1.7. See also *Yew Bon Tew* v. *Kenderaan Bas Mara* [1983] 1 A.C. 553 at p. 563, P.C.

[5] See *Donovan* v. *Gwentoys Ltd.* [1990] 1 All E.R. 1018 at p. 1024.

according to the nature of the action at issue[6]: in a claim for damages for personal injury, the recollection of witnesses may be paramount, consequently a comparatively short limitation period of three years is imposed (but with a generous interpretation of the date when time starts to run, together with the possibility of exclusion of the time limit in appropriate cases),[7] whereas in an action for the recovery of land a limitation period of 12 years is appropriate given the traditional importance attached to the ownership of land.[8]

Judicial attitudes towards limitation periods

The statute of limitation has been described as "an Act of peace",[9] a beneficial statute which is to be construed liberally and not strictly.[10] Judicial attitudes towards defendants seeking to rely on the expiry of the limitation period vary greatly; it has been said that "long dormant claims have often more of cruelty than of justice in them"[11] and, alternatively, that a plea of limitation is "an unattractive plea at the best of times."[12] Although the plaintiff is clearly entitled to the full benefit of the limitation period laid down by statute, there have been criticisms in recent years of the unreasonable delays in the conduct of litigation within the limitation period itself: it has been stated that:

> "it is highly questionable whether plaintiffs should be allowed the benefit of the full periods of limitation, with virtual impunity, where the facts are known and there is no obstacle to the speedy institution and prosecution of claims."[13]

Limitation period not usually prescriptive

In relation to the majority of actions, a limitation period is not prescriptive: it bars the remedy rather than extinguishing the right itself.[14] Thus, if the plaintiff is able to find an alternative method (*e.g.* a lien) of asserting his right against the defendant,[15] he is entitled to do so.[16] Moreover, as the right is not extinguished, the defendant, in order to take advantage of the expiry of any limitation period, must plead it specifically in his defence[17]; the court will not intervene to declare an action time-barred.[18]

---

[6] Whilst it has been suggested that a common limitation period should apply in respect of all claims, these have been rejected, partly on the basis of differing requirements for different causes of action. Moreover, even if limitation periods were harmonised internally, it would not be possible to avoid the differing periods which exist in the international conventions to which the United Kingdom is a party: see the Law Reform Committee Final Report on Limitation of Actions, Cmnd. 6293 (1977) where it is stated at para. 1.10 that "the ideal of a single uniform period applicable to every cause of action is plainly unattainable."

[7] See further Chap. 7.

[8] See further Law Reform Committee Report, Cmnd. 6293 (1977), para. 1.10.

[9] *A'Court* v. *Cross* (1825) 3 Bing. 329 at p. 333, *per* Best C.J.

[10] *Murray* v. *East India Co.* (1821) 5 B. & Ald. 204 at 215.

[11] *A'Court* v. *Cross*, see above, n. 9.

[12] *Midland Bank Trust Co. Ltd.* v. *Hett Stubbs & Kemp* [1979] Ch. 384, *per* Oliver J.

[13] *Westminster City Council* v. *Clifford Culpin & Partners (a firm)* (1987) 137 New L.J. 736 at p. 738, C.A. *per* Kerr L.J.

[14] See *Ronex Properties Ltd.* v. *John Laing Construction Ltd.* [1982] 3 All E.R. 961 at p. 965.

[15] On the question of the burden of establishing whether or not the action is time-barred, see Chap. 2.

[16] *Allen* v. *Waters* [1935] 1 K.B. 200, C.A.

[17] R.S.C., Ord. 18, r. 8.

[18] *Thursby* v. *Warren* (1628) Cro. Car. 159; *Stile* v. *Finch* (1634) Cro. Car. 384.

Exceptions   Prescriptive limitations which extinguish the right of the owner are laid down in relation to conversion (section 3(2) of the Limitation Act 1980) and title to land (section 17 of the 1980 Act). A prescriptive period is also to be found in the 10 year longstop introduced by the Consumer Protection Act 1987 (section 11A of the 1980 Act).

Distinction illusory   However, in most cases, the distinction between a mere limitation period and the more draconian period of prescription is illusory—after the expiry of the limitation period, the plaintiff will be left with no means of enforcing his right and therefore the right itself will have effectively disappeared.

Statute must provide for limitation   Limitations, other than those in equity, result from statute only and, in order to rely on a limitation period, the defendant must point to the relevant statute: if there is no statutory provision laying down a time limit for that particular action, the action cannot be held to be time-barred, notwithstanding delay[19] unless the remedy requested is discretionary, in which case the court may apply the equitable doctrine of laches.[20]

The legislation

The Limitation Act 1980

Actions governed by Limitation Act   The Limitation Act 1980, which came into force on May 1, 1981, gives the time limits for the bringing of the various types of action specified in the Act. Under section 38(1), "action" is stated to include any proceedings in a court of law, including an ecclesiastical court. The term will be interpreted to include an application by a local authority to issue a distress warrant in respect of arrears of rent, community charge and uniform business rates.[21] The 1980 Act applies to arbitrations in the same way as it applies to actions in the High Court.[22] Time limits in relation to proceedings before tribunals are governed by the legislation applicable to the tribunal in question.[23]

Layout of statute   The Act is divided into three parts, followed by four schedules. Part I lays down the ordinary time limits for different classes of action, Part II deals with extension or exclusion of the ordinary time limits and Part III with miscellaneous matters such as interpretation and transitional matters. Schedule 1 contains a number of provisions with respect to actions for the recovery of land, Schedule 2, transitional provisions, Schedule 3, consequential amendments and Schedule 4, repealed enactments.

---

[19] *Bray* v. *Stuart A. West & Co.* (1989) 139 New L.J. 753. See also *Collin* v. *Duke of Westminster* [1985] Q.B. 581 at p. 600, where it was stated by Oliver L.J. that "the limitation of actions is entirely statutory and an action will be barred only if there is some period of limitation applicable to it under the statute."
[20] See further Chap. 11.
[21] *China* v. *Harrow Urban District Council* [1953] 2 All E.R. 1296.
[22] Limitation Act 1980, s.34(1).
[23] See, for example, s.67(2) of the Employment (Protection) Consolidation Act 1978. A discussion of the time limits in social security law is outside the scope of this work: see further Partington, *Claim in Time* (2nd ed., 1989, L.A.G.).

Statutes incorporated in the 1980 Act

The 1980 Act was passed in order to consolidate a number of statutes previously in force[24] and has itself now been amended by the Administration of Justice Act 1985,[25] the Latent Damage Act 1986[26] and the Consumer Protection Act 1987.[27] Previous legislation had been subjected to, at times, strong criticism by the judiciary, both by reason of its harshness[28] and its complex and, occasionally, obscure drafting.[29] Although it is a consolidating statute, the 1980 Act has not maintained the wording of its predecessors and has sought to introduce clarity into those provisions which were previously criticised.[30]

The Prescription Act 1832

Easements and right to light

Mention should also be made of the Prescription Act 1832 which provides a supplementary means of establishing, by virtue of the running of time, an easement (including a right to light) over the property of another person.[31]

Retrospective effect of limitations legislation

Transitional provisions

With the coming into force of the 1980 Act, and also of previous amending legislation, questions have arisen as to which provisions should be applied where the plaintiff's action appears to straddle two statutes. Schedule 2 of the Act deals with transitional provisions and provides that nothing in the Act shall enable an action to be brought which was barred by either the 1939 Act or by the Limitation Amendment Act 1980. Special provisions apply in relation to contribution[32] and acknowledgement.[33]

---

[24] Limitation Acts 1939 and 1975 and Limitation Amendment Act 1980.

[25] This Act introduces new time limits in relation to defamation: see pp. 56–58.

[26] See pp. 52–56.

[27] See pp. 61–62.

[28] *Cartledge* v. *Jopling* [1963] 1 All E.R. 341, where all the Law Lords expressed hope that the law relating to the running of time in personal injuries cases would be changed, Lord Reid commenting (at p. 344) that "the fact that the present law requires us to dismiss this appeal shows that some amendment of the law is urgently necessary" (the date of accrual of the cause of action in personal injuries cases was subsequently changed by the Limitation Act 1963). More recently, in *Pirelli General Cable Works Ltd.* v. *Oscar Faber & Partners* [1983] 2 A.C. 1, Lord Scarman commented (at p. 19) "it must be . . . unjustifiable in principle that a cause of action should be held to accrue before it is possible to discover any injury (or damage). A law which produces such a result is . . . harsh and absurd." The harshness of the decision in this case led to the passing of the Latent Damage Act 1986, now inserted into the Limitation Act 1980, ss.14A and 14B.

[29] In *Central Asbestos* v. *Dodd* [1973] A.C. 518, H.L., Lord Reid stated (at p. 529) that the 1963 statute (amending the date of accrual of the cause of action in personal injuries cases) had "a strong claim to the distinction of being the worst drafted Act on the statute book"; in *Eddis* v. *Chichester Constable* [1969] 2 Ch. 345, C.A., Winn L.J., when considering the effect of fraudulent concealment of a cause of action under the 1939 legislation, commented (at p. 362) "I am all the more ready to refrain from any [attempt to expound the meaning of the proviso at issue] because I do not understand the scope of its meaning."

[30] See the debate on the statute as it passed through the House of Commons, particularly H.C. Vol. 991, cols. 856–857.

[31] See below, Chap. 9.

[32] See below, p. 17. See also *Lampitt* v. *Poole Borough Council, Taylor (Third Party)* [1991] 2 Q.B. 545; [1990] 3 W.L.R. 179.

[33] See below, pp. 38–39.

It has been said that where a statute is substantive, in that it deals with rights of action, there is a presumption that an existing right of action will not be taken away (unless the contrary is expressed in the statute), but that where the statute deals with procedure only, there will be a presumption that it applies to all actions, whether passed before or after the passing of the statute (again, unless the contrary is expressed in the statute).[34] Although the length of a limitation period is generally viewed as a procedural matter, this will be so only as long as the limitation period in question has not yet expired.[35] Upon expiry, substantive rights accrue to the defendant: he can, from this date, assume that he is no longer at risk from a stale claim and may then part with his papers and generally order his affairs on the basis that his potential liability has gone.[36] The limitations legislation will, therefore, not act retrospectively so as to deprive a defendant of the protection of the limitation period which had previously expired, but may so act so as to extend an as yet unexpired period of limitation.[37]

Limitation period procedural only where time has not expired

Although the 1980 Act was a consolidating statute, some of the provisions of the 1939 Act are no longer included.[38] The 1939 Act will apply to all actions in which the period of limitation expired prior to August 1, 1980 (the date on which the Limitation Amendment Act 1980 came into force), the 1980 Act to those expiring after that date.[39]

Other legislation

The provisions of the 1980 Act will not be applicable in any action or arbitration for which a period of limitation is prescribed by any other statute.[40] Such statutes include the various carriage statutes implementing international conventions,[41] the Sex Discrimination Act 1975 and the Race Relations Act 1976, the Equal Pay Act 1970, the Employment Protection (Consolidation) Act 1978, the Defective Premises Act 1972 and the Matrimonial Causes Act 1973. Details of the limitation periods applicable in actions brought under these statutes and others may be found in the table on pages 121–126.

Limitation periods and conflict of laws

The Foreign Limitation Periods Act 1984[42] changed the common law rules relating to limitations in private international law. Whereas at common law a foreign rule of *prescription* (or

---

[34] *The Ydun* [1899] P. 236 at p. 245, C.A.
[35] *Maxwell* v. *Murphy* (1957) 96 C.L.R. 261 at p. 277, High Court of Australia.
[36] *Yew Bon Tew* v. *Kenderaan Bas Mara* [1983] 1 A.C. 553, at p. 563, P.C.
[37] See *Arnold* v. *C.E.G.B.* [1988] A.C. 228, H.L.; *Maxwell* v. *Murphy* (1957) 96 C.L.R. 261, High Court of Australia.
[38] These were repealed by the Limitation Amendment Act 1980 prior to the coming into force of the Limitation Act 1980.
[39] Sched. 2 to the Limitation Act 1980; for examples, see the first instance decision in *Colchester Borough Council* v. *Smith* [1991] 2 All E.R. 29 at p. 50 and *B.P. Properties* v. *Buckler* [1987] 2 EGLR 168, C.A.
[40] Limitation Act 1980, s.39.
[41] See further the table of limitation periods at pp. 121–126.
[42] For accounts of the Act, see Stone, "Time limitation in the English conflict of laws" [1985] L.M.C.L.Q. 497 and Carter, "The Foreign Limitation Periods Act 1984" (1985) 101 L.Q.R. 68.

extinction) was always given effect by the English courts, a foreign rule of *limitation* was treated as a procedural issue and was thus governed by the *lex fori*, with the result that the relevant English limitation period would be applied. The English courts[43] could thus deny the plaintiff a remedy even though that remedy was not yet barred by the *lex causae* or could permit an action to proceed against a defendant where time had expired under the *lex causae*.[44] Now, where the court has to take into account the law of another country when determining any matter, by section 1(1)(a) of the 1984 Act, "the law of that other country relating to limitation shall apply in respect of that matter for the purposes of the action or proceeding." A foreign limitation period is thus now to be regarded as a substantive matter rather than a procedural one. It is irrelevant that under the proper law, the limitation period would be regarded as procedural.[45]

Foreign limitation periods now substantive

The relevant law to be applied includes both substantive and procedural law, but the doctrine of *renvoi* is excluded: section 4(2). However, English procedural rules continue to determine the question of when proceedings have been commenced for the purpose of stopping the running of time: section 1(3). The English court is required to exercise any discretion conferred by the law of another country, in so far as is practicable, in the manner in which it would be exercised by the courts of that other country: section 1(4).

Date of commencement governed by English law

If the application of a foreign limitation period would conflict with public policy, it may be excluded: section 2(1). In such a case it would seem that the court should apply the English rules of limitation, rather than reverting to the position adopted before the Act.[46] An example of a public policy issue (although there are other potential grounds of conflict) which may lead a court to disapply the foreign limitation period is in section 2(2) where "undue hardship to a person who is, or might be made, a party to the action or proceedings." The meaning of "undue hardship" was considered by the Court of Appeal in *Jones* v. *Trollope Colls Cementation Overseas Ltd*.[47] where it was held that the meaning of "undue" is excessive, implying greater hardship than the circumstances warrant. The court is not required to conduct a balancing operation as between the plaintiff on the one hand and the defendant on the other in order to see who would be the more prejudiced by the application of the alternative rules.[48]

Public policy

Undue hardship

---

[43] This was contrary to the approach adopted by most other European countries where rules of limitation have always been treated as substantive issues: see, in relation to France, "Les conflits dans l'espace et dans le temps en matière de prescription", Hage-Chahine, Dalloz 1977.

[44] *Huber* v. *Steiner* (1835) 2 Bing. N.C. 202.

[45] *Bank of America National Trust and Savings Association* v. *Epidavros Gulf Shipping Co. S.A.* [1990] 2 Lloyd's Rep. 329.

[46] *The Komninos S.* [1991] 1 Lloyd's Rep. 370.

[47] *The Times*, January 26, 1990, C.A.

[48] *Jones* v. *Trollope Colls* was a personal injury case, the tort having been committed in Pakistan where the relevant limitation period was just 12 months. In deciding that the plaintiff would suffer undue hardship if the Pakistani limitation period were applied, the Court of Appeal took into account the fact that, for the bulk of the limitation period, the plaintiff was incapacitated in hospital as a result of the accident and that the defendants (or their insurers) had led her to believe that her claim for her injuries would be

A decision by a foreign court that a particular action is time-barred is henceforth to be treated as a judgment on the merits: section 3.

Section 1(2) applies to cases "in the determination of which both the law of England and Wales and the law of some other country fall to be taken into account." Accordingly, in those

Double actionability

cases where English law requires double actionability for an action to succeed, as in tort,[49] the plaintiff may now be confronted with a limitation defence where either the English or the foreign limitation period has expired.[50]

Arbitrations

The Act applies to arbitrations in the same way as to actions in the High Court.[51] Since limitations legislation is essentially procedural in nature, the Foreign Limitation Periods Act will be applicable in those arbitration actions where the substantive law to be applied is foreign, but which are governed by English procedural law.

The Act came into force on October 1, 1985 and applies to all actions and proceedings commenced after that date. The fact that the plaintiff's cause of action accrued prior to this date will not be relevant, unless the case can properly be decided on the "undue hardship" ground under section 2(2).[52]

New rules for conflicts in contract

The Contracts (Applicable Law) Act 1990,[53] in addition to providing a series of rules which determine the way in which the applicable law of a particular contract should be determined, states[54] that the applicable law will govern the prescription and limitation of actions. The rules for determining the applicable law of the contract are very similar to the common law procedure for finding the proper law of the contract.[55] The 1990 Act therefore has the same effect as the Foreign Limitation Periods Act in that, where the substantive law governing proceedings in contract is other than English, that law should govern limitations issues. It should be noted that, although the 1990 Act implements an EEC Convention, it will apply to any litigation involving a choice between the laws of different countries, even though neither of those countries is a Member State of the EEC.

---

met. The fact that she was based throughout in a foreign country, while of some weight, was less important than the first two factors.

[49] *Phillips* v. *Eyre* (1870) L.R. 6 Q.B. 1; *Chaplin* v. *Boys* [1971] A.C. 356.

[50] *Metall und Rohstoff AG* v. *Donaldson Lufkin & Jenrette Inc.* [1989] 3 All E.R. 14 at p. 26.

[51] Foreign Limitation Periods Act 1984, s.5; Limitation Act 1980, s.34(1) provides "this Act and any other limitation enactment shall apply to arbitrations as they apply to actions in the High Court."

[52] See *Jones* v. *Trollope Colls*, above, n. 47.

[53] This statute implements the EEC Convention on the Law Applicable to Contractual Obligations 1980 (the Rome Convention). The aim of the Convention was the unification of the rules of contractual private international law within the Community.

[54] Article 10(1)(d) of the Rome Convention, which is contained in Sched. 1 to the Contracts (Applicable Law) Act 1990.

[55] See, *inter alia*, Dicey and Morris, *The Conflict of Laws* (11th ed., 1987) pp. 1251–1253; Cheshire and North, *Private International Law* (11th ed., 1987), pp. 504–506.

2 GENERAL ISSUES RELATING TO LIMITATION PERIODS

Accrual of the cause of action

Time runs from date of accrual

Subject to some exceptions[1] the limitation period runs from the date of the accrual of the cause of action. This will be the date on which there is in existence "every fact which it would be necessary for the plaintiff to prove, if traversed, in order to support his right to the judgment of the court."[2]

Defendant capable of being sued

The cause of action will not accrue until there is in existence a defendant capable of being sued[3]: this does not mean to say that such a person should be capable of being identified, since time will continue to run, other than in personal injury actions, even where the identity of the defendant is unknown.[4]

Where the defendant is a company which has been dissolved subsequent to the accrual of the cause of action, the plaintiff may apply to the court, within two years of the date of dissolution, for an order declaring the dissolution to have been void.[5] Such an order will be made on such terms as the court thinks fit: this may include an order that all or part of the time for which the company was not on the register should be ignored for Limitation Act purposes.[6]

The cause of action will accrue on the date on which the plaintiff is first in a position to succeed in an action against the defendant, notwithstanding that he may be unaware of this fact and may have suffered no damage.[7] The accrual of the cause of action is not necessarily coterminous with the date on which the plaintiff first had the right to bring an action: in *Coburn* v. *Colledge*[8] it was held that a solicitor's cause of action for payment

---

[1] See below, p. 19, (Disability); pp. 52–56 (Latent Damage Act 1986) and pp. 67–74 (Knowledge).
[2] *Read* v. *Brown* (1888) 22 Q.B.D. 128 at p. 131; *Coburn* v. *Colledge* [1897] 1 Q.B. 702 at p. 706; cited with approval in *Sevcon Ltd.* v. *Lucas CAV Ltd.* [1986] 1 W.L.R. 462 at p. 464.
[3] In the case of an ambassador, diplomat or other person enjoying immunity from suit within the jurisdiction, time will begin to run in respect of any tort committed or debt incurred within the jurisdiction only once that immunity has been lifted: *Musurus Bey* v. *Gadban* [1894] 2 Q.B. 352, C.A. See also *Re Russo-Asiatic Bank* [1934] Ch. 720.
[4] *R.B. Policies at Lloyd's* v. *Butler* [1950] 1 K.B. 76.
[5] Companies Act 1985, s.651 as amended by Companies Act 1989, s.141.
[6] See *Re Workvale Ltd. (No. 2)* [1992] 2 All E.R. 627.
[7] *Pirelli General Cable Works Ltd.* v. *Oscar Faber & Partners* [1983] 2 A.C. 1; *Cartledge* v. *Jopling* [1963] 1 All E.R. 341; *Archer* v. *Catton & Co. Ltd.* [1954] 1 W.L.R. 775. However, as a result of the injustice of the strict application of the rule as to accrual of cause of action in these cases, special rules now apply in respect of personal injury and damage caused by negligence: see below, Chaps. 6 and 5.
[8] [1897] 1 Q.B. 702, C.A.

for work done arose as soon as the work was finished, even though there was a statutory provision to the effect that he could not commence an action for recovery of his fees until the expiration of one month after he had delivered to the party to be charged a bill for the fees. It was held that this statutory provision did not affect the cause of action, only the remedy for enforcing it.

Date of accrual

A cause of action for breach of contract will accrue upon breach, regardless of whether the plaintiff has suffered damage or is even aware of the breach,[9] unless the defendant has acted fraudulently or has deliberately concealed his breach from the plaintiff.[10] In respect of some torts (for example, trespass and libel) the cause of action will accrue upon the commission of the tort since damage is not a necessary ingredient of the tort, but for others (for example, negligence) the cause of action will accrue only once some damage has been suffered by the plaintiff. The question to be asked in any dispute as to the date on which the cause of action accrued, is whether an action brought on the date contended for by the defendant would have been thrown out as disclosing no cause of action. The injustice which such an approach can cause has to some extent been alleviated by the discretionary provisions of section 33 of the 1980 Act (which permits the exclusion of the time limit in personal injury actions)[11] and the passing of the Latent Damage Act 1986, now incorporated into the 1980 Act in sections 14A and 14B.[12] However, it is still true to say that in some situations a plaintiff may find that time has expired before he became aware that his cause of action had accrued. For example, where the plaintiff's cause of action is in contract and where there is no alternative cause of action in tort[13] or where the plaintiff is caught by either the 15 year longstop under the Latent Damage Act 1986 or the 10 year longstop under the Consumer Protection Act 1987.

Retrospective effect of decisions

In some instances a decision taken under ministerial or statutory authority may be held to have retrospective effect. The result may be to cause a cause of action to have accrued at a date some years prior to the date of the decision itself. For example, in *Sevcon Ltd.* v. *Lucas CAV Ltd.*[14] it was held by the House of Lords that the plaintiffs' right to pursue an action in respect of infringement of their patent was time-barred even though the letters patent had been granted less than two years prior to the issue of the writ. This was because the patent had been applied for in 1967 and, when granted in 1982, was dated and "made patent as of" June 7, 1968. In order to determine such cases, it will be necessary to ask whether an early action would have been dismissed as disclosing no cause of action, or whether proceedings might have been stayed pending a decision on the

---

[9] *Lynn* v. *Bamber* [1930] 2 K.B. 72.
[10] See below, Chap. 3.
[11] See below, Chap. 7.
[12] See below, Chap. 5.
[13] *Islander Trucking Ltd.* v. *Hogg Robinson & Gardner Mountain (Marine) Ltd.* [1990] 1 All E.R. 826; *Iron Trade Mutual Insurance Co. Ltd.* v. *J. K. Buckenham Ltd.* [1990] 1 All E.R. 808 approved by the Court of Appeal in *Société Commerciale de Réassurance* v. *ERAS (International) Ltd.* [1992] 2 All E.R. 82, C.A.
[14] [1986] 1 W.L.R. 462.

issue.[15] Where the ministerial decision on which the plaintiff bases his action created no new right or liability on the date of decision, but merely confirmed the existence of a right or liability, this will not have the effect of causing a new cause of action to accrue.[16]

Arbitral awards   Previously, an arbitration clause in the *Scott* v. *Avery*[17] form (making the arbitral decision a condition precedent to the existence of any liability) would have the effect of postponing the accrual of the cause of action until the date of the arbitral decision. Section 34(2) of the Limitation Act 1980 now provides that, notwithstanding the insertion of such a clause in the agreement between the parties, the cause of action shall be deemed to have accrued at the time when it would have accrued but for the agreement.[18]

Issue of writ   The running of time will be suspended by the issue of a writ.[19] It is also possible to effect such a suspension by virtue of an agreement between the parties; however, very clear wording will be required to establish such an agreement.[20] The mere fact that the parties have been in negotiations for a settlement will not serve to suspend the running of time.[21]

The calculation of time

Date of accrual not included   When calculating the precise length of the limitation period, the courts will ignore the day on which the cause of action arose[22]: the relevant provisions of the Limitation Act 1980 state that an action shall not be brought after the expiration of the specified number of years *from the date* on which the cause of action accrued. Thus in a personal injury action where the accident giving rise to the claim occurred on February 11, 1992, the limitation period will start to run at midnight on February 11 with the result that the writ must be issued on or before the close of court on February 11, 1995.

Closure of court office on last day   Where the court office is closed on the last day of the limitation period, time is extended to the first day on which the office re-opens.[23] However, this will be so only where the act of the plaintiff which will stop the running of time requires some co-operation or action by the court or tribunal. This is clearly the case in relation to the issue of a writ, but is not so where the claimant is required merely to "present" his complaint to a

---

[15] *Central Electricity Board* v. *Halifax Corporation* [1963] A.C. 785, H.L.

[16] *Ibid.*

[17] (1865) 5 H.L.Cas. 811.

[18] See also *Agromet Motoimport Ltd.* v. *Maulden Engineering Co. (Beds.) Ltd.* [1985] 2 All E.R. 436.

[19] It should be noted that in most other European countries, the running of time will be suspended only by the service of the writ. A clause in the Courts and Legal Services Bill which would have introduced such an amendment into English law failed to reach the statute book.

[20] *Adams Holden & Pearson* v. *Trent Regional Health Authority* (1989) 47 B.L.R. 34.

[21] *Jones* v. *Jones* [1970] 2 Q.B. 576; [1970] 3 All E.R. 47.

[22] *Marren* v. *Dawson Bentley & Co. Ltd.* [1961] 2 Q.B. 135; affirmed in *Trow* v. *Ind Coope (West Midlands) Ltd.* [1967] 2 Q.B. 899.

[23] *Pritam Kaur* v. *S. Russell & Sons Ltd.* [1973] Q.B. 336; *Hartley* v. *Birmingham City D.C.* [1992] 2 All E.R. 213, C.A.

tribunal in which case the running of time will be stopped by the mere placing of the complaint in the letter box of the tribunal.[24]

Expiry of limitation period prior to issue of writ

Limited power to strike out It is only in a "very clear case" that an action which is alleged to be statute-barred may be struck out under R.S.C., Order 18, rule 19(*b*) on the ground that it is frivolous, vexatious and an abuse of the process of the court[25] or where it is manifest that the plea of limitation must succeed.[26]

Determination of limitation issue: final or interlocutory?

R.S.C., Order 59, rule 1A lays down rules for determining whether a judgment or order is to be treated as final or interlocutory. Paragraph (3) of R.S.C., Order 59, rule 1A provides that a judgment or order shall be treated as final if the entire cause or matter would (subject only to any possible appeal) have been finally determined whichever way the court below had decided the issues before it. Notwithstanding this, paragraph (6)(*ff*) states that an order determining limitation issues is to be treated as interlocutory unless it is part of a final order or judgment within the meaning of paragraph (3). Determination of such issues as the date of accrual of the cause of action or the question of whether or not there has been deliberate concealment will therefore be treated as interlocutory, unless they are part of the final judgment. A direction pursuant to section 33 of the 1980 Act that the three year limitation period in respect of personal injuries actions should not apply will, however, be treated as final, with the result that leave to appeal against this direction will not be necessary.[27]

Onus of proving validity or expiry of writ

Burden on plaintiff Where the defendant has pleaded that the action is time-barred, the burden is on the plaintiff to prove that the relevant limitation period has not expired.[28]

---

[24] *Swainston* v. *Hetton Victory Club Ltd.* [1983] 1 All E.R. 1179, a case which concerned the presentation of a complaint under section 67(2) of the Employment Protection (Consolidation) Act 1978.
[25] *Ronex Properties Ltd.* v. *John Laing Construction Ltd.* [1981] 1 Q.B. 398 C.A. at p. 405, *per* Donaldson L.J.; see also *National Graphical Association* v. *Peter Thimbleby* [1984] 25 B.L.R. 94.
[26] *Leicester Wholesale Fruit Market Ltd.* v. *Grundy (No. 1)* [1990] 1 W.L.R. 107.
[27] *Dale* v. *British Coal Corporation (No. 1), The Times,* June 25, 1992, C.A.
[28] *London Congregational Union Inc.* v. *Harriss & Harriss* (1986) 35 B.L.R. 58, C.A.

Calculation of the period of validity of the writ

Date of issue included

A writ *may not be served more than four calendar months after* the date stated on its face. This wording indicates that the calculation of the period of validity of a writ will be different from that applicable to the limitation period itself, which runs *from* the date of the accrual of the cause of action. In the case of a writ, the date of issue must be taken into account, so that a writ issued on February 24 must be served on or before June 23.[29]

Extension of the writ

Four months validity

While the issue of a writ will suspend the running of time for the period of its validity, it must be served on the defendant within four months of issue (six months if it is to be served out of the jurisdiction).[30]

Extensions

Upon application to the court, the writ may be extended for a further period of four months; more than one application for such an extension may be made. Where the plaintiff can show that, despite making reasonable efforts, it may be impossible to serve the writ within the four-month period, the court has a discretion, after due consideration of all the circumstances of the case, to permit an extension of up to 12 months.

Three categories of case may be envisaged in which the plaintiff may seek an extension:

    (a) where the writ is still valid and the limitation period has not yet expired;

    (b) where the writ is still valid but the limitation period has expired;

    (c) where the writ is no longer valid and the limitation period has expired.[31]

The approach of the courts when exercising their discretion as to whether or not to extend will differ according to which category the application falls into.[32] In practice, the majority of applications fall within category (c) where, owing to the double expiry of both the limitation period and the validity of the writ, the discretion is sparingly exercised.

Only good cause need be shown

The plaintiff is not obliged to show exceptional circumstances justifying the extension of the writ, merely that there is "good cause" or "good reason" for doing so.[33] It has

---

[29] *Trow* v. *Ind Coope (West Midlands) Ltd.* [1967] 2 Q.B. 899, C.A.

[30] R.S.C. (Amendment No. 4) 1989 (S.I. 1989 No. 2427). Writs issued prior to June 4, 1990, continue to be governed by the former rules, *i.e.* an initial validity of 12 months.

[31] See the speech of Lord Brandon in *Kleinwort Benson Ltd.* v. *Barbrak Ltd., The Myrto (No. 3)* [1987] 2 All E.R. 289.

[32] In *Portico Housing Association Ltd.* v. *Brian Moorehead and Partners* (1985) 1 Const.L.J. 226; *The Times*, February 5, 1984, the Court of Appeal stated that an extension would be more readily granted if the application was made before the expiry of the period of validity of the writ and prior to the end of the limitation period.

[33] *Kleinwort Benson Ltd.* v. *Barbrak Ltd., The Myrto (No. 3)* [1987] 2 All E.R. 289; *Battersby* v. *Anglo-American Oil Co. Ltd.* [1945] K.B. 23, C.A.

been said that the best reason is either that the defendant has been avoiding service or that his address is unknown.[34] However, other effective reasons may also exist, and the matter may not be defined: whether or not there is good reason will depend on all the circumstances of the case and must be left to be decided by the judge.[35] If such good cause or good reason can be shown,[36] the court will proceed[37] to determine the relative hardship and injustice between the parties in the event that the extension is granted or refused.[38]

Amendment of the writ and of pleadings

Once the writ has been issued, the plaintiff may wish to amend it, either before or after service. Either the plaintiff or the defendant may wish to amend subsequent pleadings. Prior to service, the writ may be amended once without leave, any subsequent amendments requiring the leave of the court.

Wide discretion to permit amendments However, the court has a wide discretion under R.S.C., Order 20 to permit amendments and permission will generally be given wherever it is necessary in order to do justice between the parties by permitting the real issues in the case to be raised by the pleadings.[39]

Where the relevant limitation period has expired, amendments may be made in the following situations where the court considers it just to do so[40]: to correct the name of a party, to alter the capacity in which a party sues and to add a new cause of action, provided that this new cause of action arises out of substantially the same facts as relied on by the party seeking to amend in the present action.[41]

Correction of the name of a party may be permitted where the **Genuine mistake** court is satisfied that the mistake in name was a genuine one,[42] even if it resulted from the plaintiff's own carelessness or that of his advisers.[43] The amendment will not be permitted where the effect of the original name was misleading or causes reasonable doubt as to the identity of the party suing or being sued. The correction may even extend to the substitution of a new party, subject to R.S.C., Order 15, rule 6, which provides that no

[34] *Battersby* v. *Anglo-American Oil Co. Ltd.* [1945] K.B. 23 at pp. 32–33, *per* Lord Goddard C.J.
[35] *Kleinwort Benson Ltd.* v. *Barbrak Ltd., The Myrto (No. 3)* [1987] 2 All E.R. 289 at p. 300, *per* Lord Brandon.
[36] The mere fact that negotiations are being conducted by the parties for a settlement will not in itself be a good reason for extending the validity of the writ, even if there has been an implied agreement between the parties deferring service of the writ: *The Mouna* [1991] 2 Lloyd's Rep. 221, C.A.
[37] This balancing operation will not be undertaken unless the plaintiff has initially established good cause or good reason for the extension: *Waddon* v. *Whitecroft-Scovill* [1988] 1 W.L.R. 309, H.L.
[38] See particularly *Jones* v. *Jones* [1970] 2 Q.B. 576.
[39] *G.L. Baker Ltd.* v. *Medway Building and Supplies Ltd.* [1958] 1 W.L.R. 1216, where the amendment sought was rendered necessary by reason of the obscure drafting of the plaintiffs' statement of claim.
[40] R.S.C., Ord. 20, r. 5(2); s.35 of the Limitation Act 1980.
[41] R.S.C. Ord. 20, r. 5(3), (4) and (5).
[42] *Katzenstein Adler Industries* v. *Borchard Lines Ltd., The Gladys* [1988] 2 Lloyd's Rep. 274; (1988) 138 New L.J. 94.
[43] *Mitchell* v. *Harris Engineering Co. Ltd.* [1967] 2 Q.B. 703.

person shall be added or substituted as a party after the expiry of any relevant period of limitation, unless:

> (a) the relevant period was current at the date when proceedings were commenced and it is necessary for the determination of the action that the new party should be added or substituted; or
>
> (b) the relevant period arises under section 11 or 12 of the 1980 Act (action for personal injuries or death) and the court directs under section 33 that those provisions should not apply to the action by or against the new party.

In such a situation, it is necessary for an application to be made under section 33 to disapply the limitation period before or at the same time as the application for leave to amend the writ is made.[44]

Alteration of the capacity of a party may be made if the new capacity is one which the party had at the date of the commencement of proceedings or has since acquired.[45] A widow suing in her personal capacity in respect of the death of her husband is entitled to amend the writ upon obtaining letters of administration, so as to claim as administratrix of the estate even though the title of an administrator dates only from the grant.[46] In the case of a claim for breach of contract, the plaintiff is entitled to amend his statement of claim so as to sue as an equitable assignee of the contract, rather than as a principal, since this will not alter the nature of the action.[47]

Addition of a new cause of action will be allowed only where the new cause of action arises out of substantially the same facts as a cause of action in respect of which relief has already been claimed in the action by the party seeking the amendment.[48] Although section 35(5) states that the amendment may be made where the new cause of action arises out of the same or substantially the same facts as are "at issue" in the original action, the words "at issue" should not be narrowly construed. The amendment will not be permitted simply because the new facts which it is sought to introduce are not disputed: the words "at issue" should be interpreted as meaning "material to".[49] The question of whether or not a proposed amendment would introduce a new claim for the purpose of section 35 of the 1980 Act is a mixed question of fact and law, and, a matter of degree.[50]

An amendment will be refused if it would represent a significant change in the nature of the proceedings, involving consideration of factual material which did not arise on the original claim.[51] The mere fact that the plaintiff's statement of

Substantially the same facts

---

[44] *Howe* v. *David Brown Tractors (Retail) Ltd.* [1991] 4 All E.R. 30, C.A.

[45] R.S.C., Ord. 20, r. 5(4); s.35(7) and (8) of the Limitation Act 1980.

[46] See *Beswick* v. *Beswick* [1968] A.C. 58; [1967] 3 W.L.R. 932.

[47] *Robinson* v. *Unicos Property Corpn. Ltd.* [1962] 1 W.L.R. 520, C.A.

[48] R.S.C., Ord. 20, r. 5(5); s.35(2)(*a*), (5)(*a*) and (8) of the Limitation Act 1980.

[49] *Fannon* v. *Backhouse, The Times,* August 22, 1987; (1988) B.L.M. February, p. 8, C.A.

[50] *Steamship Mutual Underwriting Association Ltd.* v. *Trollope & Colls (City) Ltd.* (1986) 33 Build.L.R. 77, C.A.

[51] *Hydrocarbons Great Britain Ltd.* v. *Cammell Laird Shipbuilders Ltd.* (1991) 25 Con.L.R. 131. See also *Balfour Beatty Construction Ltd.* v. *Parsons Brown & Newton Ltd., The Financial Times,* November 7, 1990, C.A.

claim in an action against an architect alleges, for example, faults in a building, will not necessarily permit him to amend the statement of claim so as to include further damage: even where all the separate items of damage arise out of breaches of the same duty by the same defendant, it is not possible to say that they

One or more causes of action? will all give rise to a single cause of action.[52] Such a rigid approach could cause injustice to the plaintiff, who is obliged to bring forward his entire case in respect of one and the same cause of action at the same time,[53] and may consequently find that damage occurring at a later date will be time-barred on the basis that the cause of action accrued at the date of the first damage.[54]

Following the decision of the House of Lords in *Murphy* v. *Brentwood District Council*[55] that there exists no duty of care in negligence to avoid economic loss consequent upon a negligent act, plaintiffs may need to consider whether or not pending

Amendments to claim for negligent misstatement claims, originally framed as actions in respect of a negligent act, can be amended so as to be classed as being for negligent misstatement.[56]

Such an amendment will be permitted only where the original pleadings disclosed all the facts necessary to support such a claim.[57]

Where a plaintiff, having previously abandoned or elected not to proceed with a claim, subsequently seeks to revive that claim, the court has discretion to allow the claim to be revived. However, that discretion will be exercised in favour of the plaintiff only where he can give a good explanation for the dropping of the claim and the desire to revive it.[58]

When exercising its discretion in this matter, the court must have regard to the fact that, if leave to amend is granted, the defendant will be deprived of an accrued defence.

In circumstances other than those listed above, an amendment after the expiry of the limitation period will be permitted only where the party seeking it can point to the

Amendment not retrospective existence of exceptional circumstances. If leave to amend is granted, it will not be retrospective to the date when the action as a whole was begun: it will take effect from the date of amendment.[59]

[52] *Steamship Mutual* v. *Trollope & Colls*, above; n. 50. However, see also *Horbury* v. *Craig, Hall & Rutley* (1991) C.I.L.L. 692, noted in (1991) B.L.M. Dec., p. 8, where it was held that the various heads of damage, occurring at different times, gave rise to a single cause of action dating from the date of the manifestation of the first head of damage. If there has been a single breach by the defendant giving rise to several heads of damage, this will constitute a single cause of action.

[53] *Conquer* v. *Boot* [1928] 2 K.B. 336.

[54] *Steamship Mutual* v. *Trollope & Colls*, above, n. 50.

[55] [1990] 2 All E.R. 908.

[56] Thus permitting recovery on the basis of the principles established in *Hedley Byrne & Co.* v. *Heller & Partners* [1963] 2 All E.R. 575.

[57] *Hydrocarbons Great Britain Ltd.* v. *Cammell Laird Shipbuilders Ltd.* (1991) 25 Con LR 131; (1992) B.L.M. 5. See the six factors listed by Neill J. in *McNaughton* v. *Hicks Anderson* [1991] 1 All E.R. 134 at pp. 144–145.

[58] *Leicester Wholesale Fruit Market Ltd.* v. *Grundy (No. 2)* (1990) 53 B.L.R. 1 at p. 14.

[59] *Banks* v. *CBS Songs Ltd.*, The Times, January 30, 1992, C.A. It should be noted that *Ketteman* v. *Hansel Properties* [1987] A.C. 189, H.L. where it was stated that the joinder of a new party would have retrospective effect, was decided under the equivalent provision in the 1939 legislation, the wording of which differs from section 35 of the 1980 Act.

Addition of a new party

No addition of new party unless within time or section 33 applies

R.S.C., Order 15, rule 6(5) applies where it is sought to add or substitute a party after the expiry of any relevant period of limitation. This will not be possible unless either:

> "(a) the relevant period was current at the date when proceedings were commenced and it is necessary for the determination of the action that the new party should be substituted; or
>
> (b) the relevant period arises under the provisions of section 11 or 12 of the Limitation Act 1980 and the court directs that those provisions should not apply to the action by or against the new party."

Where the court allows a new party to be joined either as plaintiff or defendant to the existing proceedings, section 35(1)(b) and 35(2)(b) provides that the claim is deemed to have been made at the date of commencement of the original action. However, section 35(3) provides that, subject to the operation of section 33 (exclusion of the time limit in personal injury actions: see Chapter 7), no person should be added as a party to an existing action after the expiry of the relevant limitation period.[60]

Applicability of section 33 must be determined prior to addition

It is clear from the wording of rule 6(5)(b) that a party may be added in a personal injury claim where the three year limitation period has expired, provided that the court directs that section 33 (which gives the court discretion to exclude the three year period) is applicable. The question of exclusion of the three year limit must consequently be decided prior to the addition of the new party.[61] If, however, the party sought to be added has previously been properly joined in the proceedings, Order 15 will not be applicable and a new claim against that party may proceed, even though it is prima facie time-barred: it will then be for the party facing the new claim to take the point that the claim is barred leaving the other party to seek an exclusion of the limitation period under section 33.[62]

Third party proceedings

Deemed to be a separate action

Third party proceedings, *i.e.* a claim brought in the course of the action against a new party, other than a claim to add a new defendant to an existing claim, will be treated as a separate action and will be deemed to have been commenced on the date when these proceedings were commenced (and not the date of the original action): section 35(1)(a) and (2). The provision therefore relates to the situation where a party is to be joined as a second (or more) defendant, rather than where he is being added by the plaintiff as a defendant in the original claim.

---

[60] See generally *Ketteman* v. *Hansel Properties Ltd.* (1984) 27 B.L.R. 1 at pp. 16–19, C.A.; *Chelmsford District Council* v. *Evers* (1983) 25 B.L.R. 99 at pp. 104–106.

[61] *Howe* v. *David Brown Tractors (Retail) Ltd.* [1991] 4 All E.R. 30, C.A.

[62] *Kennett* v. *Brown* [1988] 2 All E.R. 600, C.A.

Contribution

Where the plaintiff's loss has been caused by more than one person, he may choose whether to sue just one or all or some of those responsible. The distribution of the burden of financial responsibility amongst those persons will be effected through the process of contribution. The Civil Liability (Contribution) Act 1978 details the way in which such contribution will be effected.

Two-year limitation period Section 10 of the Limitation Act 1980 provides for a two-year limitation period in an action brought by a person entitled to a right to recover contribution. Time will begin to run in such an action from the date of judgment (in civil proceedings) or the date of award (in an arbitration). In the case of an award of damages which is varied on appeal, the relevant date remains the date of judgment at first instance.[63] Where a settlement is reached between the plaintiff and one or more of the parties liable, the right of contribution will run from the earliest date on which the amount to be paid is agreed between them.[64]

Counter-claims/set-off

The defendant may assert in his defence, that the plaintiff's claim should fail, either in whole or in part, by reason of some connected right which he possesses against the plaintiff. A

Distinction between defence and cross-claim distinction must then be drawn between a matter which is in the nature of a defence and one which is in the nature of a cross-claim. When a defendant is sued, he can raise any matter which is properly in the nature of a defence, without fear of being met by a period of limitation. No defence, properly so-called, is subject to a time-bar.[65] However, the defendant cannot raise a matter which is properly the subject of a cross-claim, except within the period of limitation allowed for such a claim.[66] A cross-claim will be subject to the time-bar whether it is made in a separate action or by way of set-off or counterclaim in the original proceedings brought against him by the plaintiff.

The distinction between a defence and a cross-claim may, therefore, be vital. Where the defendant's assertion goes directly in diminution or extinction of the plaintiff's claim, this will be a

Defence cannot be time-barred matter of defence and cannot be time-barred. This will be so where there is an assertion by the defendant that work performed by the plaintiff for which he is claiming payment is defective by reason of some breach by the plaintiff, and consequently the contractual price is not owing.[67] Similarly, where the defendant sets up what is known as an "equitable set-off" (or, in the words of Lord Denning M.R., an "equitable

---

[63] Limitation Act 1980, s.10(3).
[64] *Ibid.* s.10(4).
[65] *Henriksens Rederi A/S* v. *T.H.Z. Rolimpex, The Brede* [1973] 3 All E.R. 589 at p. 593, C.A.; approved *Aries Tanker Corporation* v. *Total Transport Ltd.* [1977] 1 All E.R. 398, H.L.
[66] *Ibid.*
[67] *Mondel* v. *Steel* (1841) 8 M. & W. 858; *Modern Engineering* v. *Gilbert Ash* [1974] A.C. 689; *Acsim (Southern) Ltd.* v. *Danish Contracting and Development Co. Ltd.* (1989) 47 B.L.R. 55, (1990) B.L.M., July, p. 1. See also section 53(1) of the Sale of Goods Act 1979.

defence"[68]), an assertion, not that the value of the goods or services has been diminished by reason of the plaintiff's breach, but that other consequential damage has been caused (for example, by late delivery) there will be no time-bar.[69] If the amendment of the defence relates to the question of which remedies he will pursue following the plaintiff's breach, this will not be seen as introducing a new cause of action.[70] Where the defendant's assertion relates to a matter which either arises out of the plaintiff's claim or is sufficiently closely connected to it, the plaintiff will not be permitted to avail himself of the defence of limitation.[71]

New claim deemed commenced on date of original action

Where the defendant's claim against the plaintiff is not sufficiently closely related to the original action, it will be subject to the provisions of the Limitation Act 1980. Section 35(1)(b) provides that a new claim made in the course of the action will be deemed to have been commenced on the same date as the original action. Consequently, if the defendant's claim was time-barred at the date when the plaintiff started proceedings, he will be unable to assert it. If, however, his claim was not then time-barred, he will be free to plead it, notwithstanding that the requisite limitation period may have elapsed between the date of start of proceedings and the date when the cross-claim was first raised.

Dismissal for want of prosecution

Delays by plaintiff prior to expiry of limitation period

If, following issue and service of the writ, the plaintiff delays unduly in prosecuting his action, the defendant may apply to the court to have the action dismissed for want of prosecution.[72] In general, the defendant's application will be dismissed if it is made at a time when the limitation period in respect of the plaintiff's action has not yet expired: *Birkett* v. *James*.[73] This is logical, since, if the application were refused, the plaintiff could simply issue another writ, which would be to the detriment of the defendant, since it would further delay the trial of the action and allow the plaintiff the benefit of new time limits for the service of the second writ. However, in exceptional circumstances[74] the court may be justified in dismissing the first action even though the limitation period has not yet expired and the plaintiff may start a fresh action.

---

[68] *Henriksens Rederi A/S* v. *Rolimpex, The Bede* [1973] 3 All E.R. 589, C.A.

[69] However, different rules apply in the case of freight; see *ibid.*

[70] *Tilcon Ltd.* v. *Land and Real Estate Investments Ltd.* [1987] 1 W.L.R. 46; [1987] 1 All E.R. 615.

[71] See *British Anzani (Felixstowe) Ltd.* v. *International Marine Management (U.K.) Ltd.* [1980] Q.B. 637; [1979] 2 All E.R. 1063.

[72] A similar power now exists in relation to arbitration proceedings: Courts and Legal Services Act 1990, s.102 which inserts a new s.13A into the Arbitration Act 1950.

[73] [1978] A.C. 297, H.L. The principles laid down in this case have been criticised as being "far too lenient to deal with excessive delays . . . the regime of *Birkett* v. *James* should be replaced by a system of rules which are much stricter, more effective and simple to apply." *Per* Kerr L.J. in *Westminster City Council* v. *Clifford Culpin & Partners* (1987) 137 New L.J. 736 at pp. 737–738, C.A.

[74] See the speeches of Lord Diplock and Lord Edmund-Davies in *Birkett* v. *James* [1978] A.C. 297, H.L.

Not applicable in section 33 cases

In personal injury actions where the initial three year limitation period has expired, but the plaintiff argues that he would be entitled to an exclusion of the time limit under section 33, the principles established in *Birkett* v. *James*[75] will not apply.[76]

Power to dismiss not to be exercised lightly

Even where the limitation period has expired, the power to dismiss an action for want of prosecution should not be exercised lightly.[77] The defendant should be able to point to intentional and contumelious default on the part of the plaintiff. Such default might be disobedience to a peremptory order, or else where inordinate and inexcusable delay on the part of the plaintiff has given rise to a substantial risk that a fair trial would not be possible or where there would be serious prejudice to the defendant.[78] A claim will similarly be dismissed as an abuse of the process of court where the writ has been issued with no reasonable evidence or ground on which to serve the statement of claim (a "protective writ").[79]

An application to strike out will be dismissed even where the limitation period has expired, if the defendant has led the plaintiff to believe that the application would not be made.[80]

The principles applicable to striking out for want of prosecution in an action commenced by writ apply equally to proceedings begun by originating summons.[81]

Delay prior to expiry irrelevant

Although the court is entitled to consider the entire period of delay when deciding whether or not to strike out for want of prosecution,[82] it will be necessary for the defendant to establish prejudice which has resulted specifically from the delay which has arisen following issue of the writ.[83] Delay prior to the expiry of the limitation period is impliedly tolerated by the Limitation Act and cannot, therefore, serve as a ground for dismissing the action.[84] If a causal link cannot be found between the post-writ delay of the plaintiff and the prejudice to the defendant then, notwithstanding that that delay might be classed as "inordinate and inexcusable", the action will not be struck out.[85]

Disability

Running of time suspended

Where the plaintiff is under a disability at the time when the cause of action accrues, the running of time will be suspended until such time as he is no longer under that disability.[86] The plaintiff will then have the benefit of the full limitation period from the date of cessation of the disability.

---

[75] See the speeches of Lord Diplock and Lord Edmund-Davis in *Birkett* v. *James* [1978] A.C. 297, H.L.
[76] *Walkley* v. *Precision Forgings Ltd.* [1979] 1 W.L.R. 606. See further Chap. 7.
[77] *Department of Transport* v. *Chris Smaller (Transport) Ltd.* [1989] 1 All E.R. 897.
[78] See also *Allen* v. *Sir Alfred McAlpine & Sons Ltd.* [1968] 2 Q.B. 229.
[79] *Steamship Mutual* v. *Trollope & Colls*, see above, n. 77.
[80] *Simpson* v. *Smith, The Times*, January 19, 1989, C.A.
[81] *Halls* v. *O'Dell* (1991) 35 S.J. (L.B.) 204, C.A.
[82] *William C. Parker* v. *F.J. Ham & Son Ltd.* [1972] 1 W.L.R. 1583.
[83] *Department of Transport* v. *Chris Smaller (Transport) Ltd.* [1989] 2 W.L.R. 578, H.L. See also *Halls* v. *O'Dell, The Times*, November 5, 1991, C.A.
[84] See *Birkett* v. *James*, see above, n. 73; *Rath* v. *C. S. Lawrence & Partners* (1990) 26 Con LR 16.
[85] *Halls* v. *O'Dell*, see above, n. 81.
[86] Limitation Act 1980, s.28(1).

A person is under a disability if he is a minor[87] or of
unsound mind.[88] Section 38(2) provides that a person is of
unsound mind if he is a person who, by reason of mental
disorder within the meaning of the Mental Health Act 1959, is
incapable of managing and administering his property and
affairs.[89] If the disability arises after the accrual of the cause of
action, the running of time will not be suspended. However, in
personal injury actions, the subsequent disability may constitute
a ground for the court to exercise its discretion under section 33
to permit exclusion of the time limit.[90]

---

[87] The suspension will apply whether the minor is in the custody of a parent or
not.
[88] Limitation Act 1980, s.38. A minor is a person under the age of 18: Family
Law Reform Act 1969, s.1.
[89] See *Kirby* v. *Leather* [1965] 2 Q.B. 367; *Dawson* v. *Spain Gower*, October 18,
1988; unrep., Glidewell L.J. sitting as a single judge of the Court of Appeal.
[90] See further Chap. 7.

3 FRAUD, CONCEALMENT AND MISTAKE

Postponement

Section 32(1) of the Limitation Act 1980 provides for the postponement of the commencement of the limitation period in three situations:

   (a) where the action is based upon the fraud of the defendant;

   (b) where any fact relevant to the plaintiff's right of action has been concealed from him by the defendant;

   (c) where the action is for relief from the consequences of a mistake.

The limitation period will start to run only when the plaintiff has discovered the fraud, concealment or mistake or when he could with reasonable diligence have discovered it. The subsection specifically states that references to the defendant include references to the defendant's agent and to any person through whom the defendant claims and his agent.

   In order for section 32 to apply, the fraud, concealment or mistake must have occurred before time started to run in the action in question: section 32(1) states "the period of limitation

No interruption of running of time

shall not begin to run. . ."[1]; this is in line with the traditional principle that, once time begins to run, it runs continuously.[2]

Extinction of title and the fraud provisions

Even though title may have been extinguished by the running of time following the tortious act, (*i.e.* the provisions of the Limitation Act are prescriptive rather than merely limiting, see Chap. 1), title may be revived by the operation of section 32.[3]

Fraud

Where the plaintiff seeks to rely on the application of section 32(1)(*a*) as postponing the running of time, it is necessary to

Action based on fraud

show that "the action is based upon the fraud of the defendant," *i.e.* that fraud must be proved in order for the plaintiff to succeed in the main action. In *Beaman* v. *A.R.T.S. Ltd.*[4] the plaintiff claimed damages for conversion outside the six-year

---

[1] See Megarry V.-C. in *Tito* v. *Waddell (No. 2)* [1977] Ch. 106 at p. 245: "If time has already begun to run, I do not think that a supervening fraudulent concealment will start time running again."; seemingly accepted in *Kaliszewska* v. *John Clague & Partners* (1984) 5 Con LR 62: see below, p. 23.

[2] *Prideaux* v. *Webber* (1661) 1 Lev. 31.

[3] *Eddis* v. *Chichester Constable* [1969] 2 Ch. 345 at p. 361.

[4] [1949] 1 K.B. 550, C.A.

limitation period, arguing that the actions of the defendants had been fraudulent and that, therefore, section 32(1)(a) applied. It was held by the Court of Appeal that, in order to rely on this subsection, fraud should be an essential ingredient of the cause of action, which is not the case in an action at common law for conversion.[5]

Where part of the subject-matter of the claim, irrespective of the limitation point, consists in an allegation of fraud, section 32(1)(a) may apply.[6]

Deliberate concealment

The running of time will be postponed where the defendant or his agent has deliberately concealed any fact relevant to the plaintiff's cause of action. The concept of "deliberate concealment" is further defined in section 32(2) which provides that "deliberate commission of a breach of duty in circumstances in which it is unlikely to be discovered for some time amounts to deliberate concealment of the facts involved in that breach of duty."[7] Under the precursor to section 32(1)(b), section 26(b) of the Limitation Act 1939, the running of time would be postponed where "the right of action is concealed by the fraud" of the defendant. This provision was extremely widely interpreted,[8] and it would seem that the wording inserted into the 1980 legislation was intended to reflect this generous interpretation.[9] In order to rely on this provision it is now necessary for the plaintiff to show only that the cause of action has been "deliberately" concealed from him by the defendant or his agent. It would seem that those cases decided under the former provision, "fraudulent concealment", will continue to apply in respect of "deliberate concealment".

Conscious decision to conceal It will in all cases be necessary to distinguish deliberate concealment of facts relating to the cause of action, and merely negligent concealment: in the latter situation, time will run normally.[10] The subsection will apply where the defendant has taken a conscious decision to conceal some fact from the plaintiff, rather than merely overlooking it.[11] If, at the time of

---

[5] For limitation periods in relation to conversion, see pp. 58–61.
[6] G.L. Baker Ltd. v. Medway Building & Supplies Ltd. [1958] 1 W.L.R. 1216.
[7] This subsection constitutes statutory endorsement of the decision in Bulli Coal Mining Co. v. Osborne [1899] A.C. 351, P.C. where it was held that the commission of a tort (in this case trespass) in a surreptitious manner would prevent the running of time. It was not necessary that the wrongdoer should have taken steps to prevent detection if he has acted in such a way as to avoid being found out for a long time.
[8] In order to avail himself of the fraudulent concealment provision, it was not necessary for the plaintiff to show that fraud in the normally accepted sense of the term had been committed: " 'fraud' in this context does not necessarily involve any moral turpitude", per Lord Denning M.R. in Applegate v. Moss [1971] 1 Q.B. 406 at p. 413; see also Beaman v. A.R.T.S. Ltd. [1949] 1 K.B. 550, C.A., Shaw v. Shaw [1954] 2 Q.B. 429 and Kitchen v. Royal Air Forces Association [1958] 2 All E.R. 241, C.A.
[9] See the Law Reform Committee, Report on Limitation of Actions, Cmnd. 6923, para. 2.22.
[10] However, the provisions of the Latent Damage Act 1986, as inserted into the Limitation Act 1980, may be applicable where the cause of action is based on negligence. See Chap. 5.
[11] In Kitchen v. R.A.F.A. [1958] 2 All E.R. 241, C.A. it was held that the running of time should be postponed where the defendant solicitors had consciously concealed from the plaintiff the source of an ex gratia payment; the

the act or omission, the defendant was quite unaware that he was committing a wrong or a breach of contract the subsection will not apply.[12] However, once it has been established that the defendant knowingly (or recklessly[13]) committed the wrong without informing the plaintiff, it is not necessary to go further and show that he took active steps to conceal the wrongdoing if the effect of the failure to inform is the same as active concealment.[14]

Plaintiff's knowledge

In determining whether or not there has been concealment, the court will consider the knowledge which the plaintiff could reasonably be expected to possess.[15] For example, where a builder of a bungalow had substituted bricks of an inferior quality to those specified in his contract with the plaintiff purchasers, it was held that although the bricks had not been covered or concealed, the right of action had been concealed. This was because the builder knew that the plaintiffs were relying upon him "to perform his contract and treat them in a decent, honest way. He also knew that there was nobody supervising the work on their behalf and that they were dependent upon him for the honest performance of the contract."[16] Where the defect would or should be immediately apparent to someone in the position of the plaintiff, the running of time will not be postponed.

Duty to trace witnesses

Where the plaintiff seeks to rely on section 32(1)(b) he will be making a serious allegation against the defendant and accordingly he will be expected to have made every endeavour to trace any witness[17] who can give evidence on the manner in which the concealment may have been effected.[18] In some cases, however, the seriousness of the defects discovered, for example in a building, may lead the court to infer that there was deliberate concealment.[19]

Application of estoppel

As stated above,[20] section 32 will apply only to postpone the commencement of the running of time: where time has already started to run, a subsequent act of concealment will not come within the provision. However, it may in some cases be possible for the plaintiff to rely on the doctrine of estoppel in order to avoid the harsh consequences of the operation of the limitation period. In *Kaliszewska* v. *John Clague & Partners*[21] the defendant

---

effect of this was to conceal from the plaintiff the existence of a cause of action against the maker of the payment and, ultimately, against the solicitors for having thrown away any case which she may have possessed under the Fatal Accidents Act.

[12] *King* v. *Victor Parsons & Co.* [1973] 1 All E.R. 206 at p. 209, *per* Lord Denning M.R.

[13] *Ibid.*

[14] *Ibid.*

[15] See also below, p. 25 (Discoverable with reasonable diligence).

[16] *Clark* v. *Woor* [1965] 1 W.L.R. 650, at p. 655, *per* Lawton J.

[17] On the question of the extent to which the plaintiff's claim will be affected by any lack of reasonable diligence on the part of his agents, see below, p. 27.

[18] See the commentary immediately preceding the report of *William Hill Organisation Ltd.* v. *Bernard Sunley & Sons Ltd.* (1982) 22 B.L.R. 1, C.A.

[19] *Gray* v. *T.P. Bennett & Son* (1987) 43 B.L.R. 63 where it was apparent that work had not been merely negligently performed, but that there had been destructive action in relation to parts of a supporting wall, the results of which had been covered with cladding, making it impossible for the plaintiff to discover the damage within the limitation period.

[20] See above, p. 21.

[21] [1984] C.I.L.L. 131; (1984) 5 Con LR 62.

architect had been engaged to design a building for the plaintiff. The building was completed in 1970; when cracks began to appear in 1974, the defendant returned and assured the plaintiff that these were trivial, as a result of which they were filled in and no further investigation was undertaken. However, in 1978, following further cracking and subsidence, the plaintiff took independent advice which revealed that the foundations were inadequate. Proceedings were commenced in 1982; the defendant argued that the action was time-barred on the ground that the cause of action had accrued in 1974 at the latest. The plaintiff did not seek to rely on section 32, presumably because the principle in *Tito* v. *Waddell*[22] was tacitly accepted, but asserted instead that the defendant was estopped from relying on the limitation period by virtue of his conduct in 1974. The conditions required for the operation of estoppel were satisfied since the plaintiff, following the representation of the defendant, had acted to his detriment by relying on the representation and failing to bring an action within the remainder of the limitation period. It was held that, while the cause of action had prima facie accrued in 1970, when the building was completed, the effect of the estoppel would be to grant a further six-year limitation period running from the date when the truth was discovered in 1978.

Mistake

Section 32(1)(c) postpones the running of time where "the action is for relief from the consequences of a mistake." It has been held that the provision applies only where the mistake is an essential ingredient of the cause of action.[23] It is not, however, necessary for the plaintiff to show that he himself committed the mistake on which he relies.[24] It will not be enough for the plaintiff to assert that the action was not commenced in time by virtue of a mistake, even where the effect of that mistake is to conceal the existence of the right of action from the plaintiff. Thus an action by an employee to recover alleged under-payments of salary should properly be regarded as a simple claim to recover money due under a contract. Although there may have been a mistake in that the employee failed to realise at the time of payment that the balance was due, and by that mistake the right of action was concealed, this will not be sufficient to activate section 32(1)(c).[25] The courts will similarly reject an argument that section 32(1)(c) should apply where the defendant has negligently or inadvertently failed to perform an undertaking made to the plaintiff, for example solicitors who fail to register an option as a lands charge.[26] It has been stated that[27]:

[22] [1977] Ch. 106.
[23] *Phillips-Higgins* v. *Harper* [1954] 1 Q.B. 411, [1954] 1 All E.R. 116, *per* Pearson J. at p. 418 and p. 119 respectively; *Singer* v. *Harrison Clark*, April 15, 1987; unrep., Jeffs Q.C. sitting as Deputy Judge of the Chancery Division.
[24] *Ministry of Health* v. *Simpson* [1951] A.C. 251 at p. 276, H.L., affirming the decision of the Court of Appeal in the same case, *sub nom: Re Diplock's Estate* [1948] 2 All E.R. 318 at p. 344.
[25] *Phillips-Higgins* v. *Harper* [1954] 1 Q.B. 411.
[26] *Singer* v. *Harrison Clark*, see above n. 23.
[27] *Ibid.*

"on the face of it, almost every professional negligence action involves a mistake of some kind, if the word mistake is given its widest possible meaning, and if the argument succeeded it would result in most negligence cases being no longer subject to being barred. It would also have the astonishing result that an action would not be time-barred if it arose from a mere mistake but would be time-barred if it was the result of deliberate misconduct."

Examples of mistakes within section 32(1)(c)

In order to postpone the running of time under the subsection, it is necessary to show something more than a mistake which has had the effect of concealing the right of action. In *Phillips-Higgins* v. *Harper*[28] Pearson J. cited examples of "familiar mistakes":

(a) where money is paid in consequence of a mistake—the mistake is made, in consequence of the mistake the money is paid so there can be an action to recover that money back[29];

(b) where a contract has been entered into in consequence of a mistake, there can be an action to obtain the rescission, or in some cases, the rectification of the contract;

(c) where there has been an account settled in consequence of mistakes—if the mistakes are sufficiently serious, there can be a re-opening of the account.

It would seem that the subsection will apply irrespective of whether the mistake in question was shared by both parties or affected only one.[30]

Discoverable with reasonable diligence

What is reasonable diligence?

Section 32 will serve to postpone the running of time only in those cases where the fraud, mistake or concealment has not been discovered by the plaintiff or could not with "reasonable diligence" have been discovered by him. Time will then start to run from the date of discoverability.[31] What, then, is "reasonable diligence" in the context of section 32? A number of building cases have considered the question of the diligence to be expected of an architect or engineer employed by a building owner to supervise the performance of a construction contract.[32] The architect or engineer will not be expected or required to be on site for the duration of the contract, but will be expected or required to pay regular visits to inspect the work as it progresses. It has been held that, in the case of defective work which has been deliberately concealed from the architect or

---

[28] [1954] 1 All E.R. 116 at p. 119.

[29] The provision will apply either to an action to recover money paid under a mistake of fact or to an analogous claim in equity in respect of money paid under a mistake of fact or law: *Ministry of Health* v. *Simpson* [1951] A.C. 251 at p. 270.

[30] *Baker* v. *Courage & Co.* [1910] 1 K.B. 56, now seemingly overruled by the wording of s.32 itself; see *Phillips-Higgins* v. *Harper* [1954] 1 All E.R. 116 at p. 118; however, see also *Peco Arts Inc.* v. *Hazlitt Gallery Ltd.* [1983] 3 All E.R. 193 at p. 196 where Webster J. left open this question.

[31] *Leicester Wholesale Fruit Market Ltd.* v. *Grundy (No. 2)* (1990) 53 B.L.R. 1 at p. 16.

[32] See below, p. 28.

engineer at a time when it is known that he will not be present on site, those defects were not discoverable with "reasonable diligence".[33] However, it might also be argued that, where the architect is aware that a major piece of work might be undertaken at a time when he is not on site, he is under an obligation to request the contractor to refrain from covering that work until it has been inspected.[34]

The meaning to be given to the term "reasonable diligence" in this context was considered in some detail by Webster J. in *Peco Arts Inc.* v. *Hazlitt Gallery Ltd.*[35] The plaintiff had bought a picture, believing it to be an Ingres original. Some 11 years later, upon being apprised by an expert that it was merely a reproduction, she sought to bring an action. It was argued by the defendants that a plaintiff could not show that he or she had exercised due diligence if there was available a means of discovering the mistake which the plaintiff did not use and it was contended that the plaintiff could, soon after acquiring the drawing, have had it independently authenticated, at which point she would have discovered that it was a reproduction. This argument was rejected by Webster J. who concluded that[36]:

> "reasonable diligence means not the doing of everything possible, not necessarily the doing of anything at all, but. . .the doing of that which an ordinarily prudent buyer and possessor of a valuable work of art would do having regard to all the circumstances, including the circumstances of the purchase."

Since, to the knowledge of both the plaintiff and the defendant in this case, major works of art are almost invariably authenticated prior to sale at the expense of the seller, a prudent purchaser in the position of the plaintiff would not normally obtain independent authentication in the circumstances of a sale of this kind.

In order to avail himself of section 32, the plaintiff is required merely to show that he has acted reasonably in the circumstances and is not required to be constantly looking for evidence of fraud, concealment or mistake. If the action is brought against the plaintiff's own professional adviser (*e.g.* accountant, solicitor or surveyor) it will not be open to the adviser to argue that the plaintiff could have discovered the existence of the concealment or mistake by obtaining a second opinion or by checking up on the work done.

Act of the defendant's agent

All references to the defendant in section 32(1) include "references to the defendant's agent and to any person through whom the defendant claims and his agent." The Court of Appeal

---

[33] *Gray* v. *T.P. Bennett* (1987) 43 B.L.R. 63.
[34] See *Florida Hotels Pty. Ltd.* v. *Mayo* (1965) 113 C.L.R. 588, which did not involve a limitation point, but where the Australian High Court held that the architect had been negligent in not ordering the contractors to keep open for inspection a major piece of reinforced concrete.
[35] [1983] 3 All E.R. 193.
[36] *Ibid.* at p. 199.

Wide definition of agent
has held[37] that the concept of "agent" in the context of section 32 is wider than the ordinarily accepted meaning of the term and that it should not be confined to a person who represents the principal in relations with third parties. For the purposes of section 32 a builder may be considered to be the agent of the developer, so that, even where the developer is unaware that defective building work has been concealed from the purchaser with whom the developer has a contract, the developer must take responsibility for the conduct of the builder.[38]

This wide interpretation of the term "agent" has also been applied in the context of payments, to a company, of money which had been fraudulently obtained by a director of that company.[39] The company had received the money from its director in good faith, but, as it was not established that value had been given for the payments, an action for retention lay at the instance of the company which had been defrauded. As the plaintiff company did not discover the fact of the payments for a number of years, a limitation point arose and, as the defendant company had clearly not been guilty of fraudulent (or deliberate) concealment of the cause of action, it became necessary to consider whether there had been concealment by the defendant's agent or any person through whom the defendant claimed.[40] Danckwerts J. considered that section 32 was indeed applicable on the ground that the defendants, although equally innocent victims of the director's fraudulent conduct, were claiming, in regard to the subject-matter of the claim, through the director: they had got the money from the director and were not holders for value, therefore their claim to the money must be *through* the director.

Relevance of acts of plaintiff's agent
An alleged lack of diligence on the part of the plaintiff's agent in discovering the fraud, concealment or mistake has been argued in a number of cases as providing justification for the normal running of time. Section 32 mentions expressly only the acts of the agent of the defendant and, as the dicta on the point are conflicting, it is not possible to state the position with certainty. In *Peco Arts Inc.* v. *Hazlitt Gallery Ltd.*[41] the plaintiff had purchased a picture represented to be an original Ingres. Some time later, within the limitation period, she took the picture to Sotheby's to be valued. Sotheby's failed to discover that the picture was in fact a reproduction—this fact being discovered only upon a subsequent valuation some years later. Webster J. was asked to consider whether this failure of Sotheby's should be attributed to the plaintiff so as to prevent the limitation period from being postponed. He stated that[42] "as a matter of construction arising out of the express words contained in the last sentence of section 32(1) the acts or omissions of an agent of a plaintiff are not to be attributed to the plaintiff for the purposes of this section."

---

[37] *Archer* v. *Moss, Applegate* v. *Moss* [1971] 1 All E.R. 747 at p. 752, *per* Edmund Davies L.J.

[38] *Ibid.* at p. 751, *per* Lord Denning M.R.; see also *Eddis* v. *Chichester Constable* [1969] 2 Ch. 345, [1969] 2 All E.R. 912, C.A.

[39] *G.L. Baker Ltd.* v. *Medway Building Supplies Ltd.* [1958] 1 W.L.R. 1216. It should be noted that, although the case was also heard on appeal, s. 32 was discussed only at first instance.

[40] Limitation Act 1980, s.32(1).

[41] [1983] 3 All E.R. 193.

[42] *Ibid.* at p. 202.

Construction cases

However, a number of construction cases have taken a different line of approach, without referring specifically to the wording of the last sentence of section 32(1). The plaintiff in a dispute involving a faulty piece of building work will in many cases have been represented throughout the performance of the contract by one or more agents: the architect, engineer and/or clerk of works. Where it is alleged that there has been deliberate concealment of the faulty work with the result that the defects could not reasonably have been discovered by the plaintiff prior to the expiry of the limitation period, the defendant may seek to argue that the failure of the plaintiff's agents, present on site for long periods of time during the construction work, to discover the defect before it was concealed will serve automatically to prevent the application of section 32. The general approach in such cases has, however, been to consider what the architect or other agent of the plaintiff could have discovered by exercise of reasonable diligence. It will not be sufficient, in order to prevent the application of section 32, for the defendant to show that the plaintiff had architects and engineers on site who could have spotted the defects. There is no distinction between a small house with hidden defects and the situation of a large developer represented on site by his own agents.[43] However, the courts are not prepared to ignore the presence of such agents: they must be called by the plaintiff as witnesses wherever available.[44] The failure to call such witnesses in a case where the plaintiff is alleging deliberate concealment will be regarded as "unattractive"[45] and[46]:

> "where a building owner employs his own expert supervisors. . .and claims that defective work was concealed, it is incumbent upon him to lead evidence to establish the fact that the work was carried out in such a manner that, in exercising reasonable skill, the supervisors could not have been expected to have observed the defects. The burden of proof falls on the plaintiffs."

The court will require the plaintiff to discharge the burden of proof that his own supervisors could not have been expected to have observed the defects. If the plaintiff does not call his supervisors or if it is found that, by exercising reasonable diligence, they could and should have discovered the concealed defects, section 32 will not avail the plaintiff. If, however, it is found that the deliberate concealment was directed at the plaintiff's supervisors (for example, specifically performed at times when the supervisor was scheduled to be absent from the site and immediately covered up) the building owner will be entitled to rely on section 32 to prevent the running of time.[47]

Conflicting approaches

It is submitted that, notwithstanding the considerable dicta to the contrary, the approach of Webster J. in *Peco Arts* v. *Hazlitt*[48] is to be preferred. Section 32 does not state that references to the plaintiff should be taken to include his agents,

---

[43] *London Borough of Lewisham* v. *Leslie & Co. Ltd.* (1978) 12 B.L.R. 22, C.A.
[44] *William Hill Organisation Ltd.* v. *Bernard Sunley & Sons Ltd.* (1982) 22 B.L.R. 1, C.A.
[45] *Ibid.* at p. 17, *per* Cumming-Bruce L.J.
[46] *Ibid.* at p. 22, *per* Cumming-Bruce L.J.
[47] *Gray* v. *T.P. Bennett & Son* (1987) 43 B.L.R. 63, Sir William Stabb Q.C.
[48] [1983] 3 All E.R. 193.

whereas this is the case in respect of the defendant. Although it might be argued that the architect, engineer or clerk of works is employed partly in order to identify any instances of shoddy work and concealment and that consequently the appropriate action should lie against him personally for failing to detect the defects, such an action will in many cases be time-barred. Section 32 will not be available here since the agent will most probably have been merely negligent and will not have deliberately concealed any cause of action from the building owner. It would seem more logical that section 32 should serve to permit an action to be brought against the actual perpetrator of the deliberate concealment in such circumstances.

Third parties and postponement of limitations

Innocent purchasers

Section 32(3) provides protection for the innocent purchasers of property which was originally acquired as a result of fraud, concealment or mistake. Once the limitation period has expired, section 32 will not serve to postpone the running of time in an action to recover either the property or its value or to enforce any charge affecting the property, where, following the fraud, concealment or mistake, the property has been purchased for valuable consideration by an innocent third party. A definition of the "innocent third party" is given in section 32(4) as someone who was not a party to the fraud or concealment and had no reason to suspect that this had taken place, or, in the case of mistake, as someone who did not know or have reason to believe at the time of purchase that the mistake had been made.

The subsection (or rather its predecessor, section 26 of the 1939 Act) was unsuccessfully invoked in *Eddis* v. *Chichester Constable*[49] where an action in conversion was brought against an art consortium which had acquired a valuable painting which had been sold contrary to the terms of a family settlement. The family trust argued that the circumstances of the disposal of the painting amounted to fraudulent concealment and that, consequently, the running of time against them should be postponed. It was held that the running of time should indeed be postponed since (on the assumed facts) the art consortium should have known, and the person through whom they claimed did in fact know, that the sale of the picture was a breach of trust; the art consortium could not be said to be innocent purchasers within the meaning of the section.[50]

The problem of the inherent conflict between the certainty requirements of the implementation of limitation periods and the legitimate rights of dispossessed works of art and items of cultural heritage has been recognised in a number of countries throughout the world.[51] Such problems will indeed frequently arise in an international, rather than a purely domestic, context, and reference should be made to the rules of private

International dimensions

[49] [1969] 2 Ch. 345.
[50] See also *Vane* v. *Vane* (1873) 8 Ch. App. 383.
[51] See particularly S. A. Williams, *The International and National Protection of Movable Cultural Property: a Comparative Study*, New York 1978, pp. 178–191.

international law[52] and to appropriate international conventions on the subject[53] in order to determine the length of the applicable limitation period and the circumstances in which it may be overridden in cases of theft and subsequent acquisition by innocent third parties. The United States decision in *Autocephalus Greek-Orthodox Church of Cyprus* v. *Goldberg*[54] provides an interesting discussion of the way in which national courts will seek to apply the limitation periods in such a way as to strike a balance between the competing interests of free trade in cultural heritage and the right of an owner to recover stolen property even after the lapse of a number of years. The question is also addressed in the 1970 UNESCO Convention on the means of prohibiting and preventing the illicit import, export and transfer of ownership of cultural property and a draft UNIDROIT convention on stolen or illegally exported cultural objects.[55]

Relevance of the Latent Damage Act 1986

Where the plaintiff has suffered loss as a result of the negligence of the defendant and that loss is not discoverable with reasonable diligence within the limitation period, the provisions of the Latent Damage Act 1986 may apply.[56] In such cases it will not be necessary to show that there has been deliberate concealment or mistake, merely that it was not reasonable to expect the plaintiff to have discovered the damage in time. Section 32 of the Limitation Act 1980 will continue to be relevant in those situations where the claim is not founded in negligence[57] or where the 15-year longstop laid down by the Latent Damage Act 1986 has expired.

---

[52] See Cheshire and North, *Private International Law* (11th ed., 1987); Foreign Limitation Periods Act 1984.

[53] See the 1970 UNESCO "Convention on the means of prohibiting and preventing the illicit import, export and transfer of ownership of cultural property", and the UNIDROIT "Preliminary Draft Convention on stolen or illegally exported cultural objects".

[54] 171 F.Supp. 1374 (5 D.Ind. 1989) (District Court) and transcript No. 89–2809 of the United States Court of Appeals for the Seventh Circuit, the subject of a casenote by Quentin Byrne-Sutton in (1992) *International Journal of Cultural Property*, 151.

[55] See Byrne-Sutton, *ibid.*

[56] See Chap. 5.

[57] See *Iron Trade Mutual Insurance Co. Ltd.* v. *J. K. Buckenham Ltd.* [1990] 1 All E.R. 808; *Islander Trucking Ltd.* v. *Hogg Robinson and Gardner Mountain (Marine) Ltd.* [1990] 1 All E.R. 826; *Société Commerciale de Réassurance* v. *ERAS (International) Ltd.* [1992] 2 All E.R. 82, C.A.

4 PERIODS OF LIMITATION IN CONTRACT

Differing limitation periods

The limitation period in contract differs according to whether the litigation concerns a simple contract or a specialty: in the former case the limitation period will be six years from the date on which the cause of action accrued, and in the latter, 12 (unless a shorter period is otherwise prescribed by the Limitation Act 1980).[1] The parties are free to stipulate a shorter or longer limitation period in their contract, but, in the case of consumer contracts and contracts on one party's written standard terms of business, the provisions of the Unfair Contract Terms Act 1977 may apply so as to render a shorter limitation period inapplicable on the basis that it was unreasonable.[2]

Specialties

The Act does not define either a simple contract or a specialty, but it has been stated that "[t]he most obvious and most common case of an action upon a specialty is an action based on a contract under seal."[3] Since, under section 1(1)(*b*) Law of Property (Miscellaneous Provisions) Act 1989 a seal is no longer necessary for the valid execution of a deed by an individual, it may now be necessary to consider whether the contractual document at issue constituted a deed, in which case the limitation period will be 12 years. Section 1(3) of the 1989 Act requires that the deed be signed by the individual in the presence of a witness who attests the signature or alternatively at his direction and in the presence of two witnesses who each attest the signature. Under section 1(2) of that Act it must be made clear that a particular document is intended to be a deed.

A distinction must be drawn between, on the one hand, those contracts which are either made under seal or in the form of a deed and, on the other, those which are merely evidenced by a contract under seal or a deed. The 12-year limitation period will apply only in respect of the former.

It has recently been confirmed by the Court of Appeal that the term "specialty" should not be confined merely to contracts

Statutes as specialties

under seal or deeds[4]: it may also apply to statutes with the effect that, where the plaintiff's cause of action is derived from statute

---

[1] Limitation Act 1980, ss.5 and 8 respectively. A shorter limitation period is prescribed in respect of actions for breach of contract claiming damages for personal injury: see further Chap. 6.

[2] Unfair Contract Terms Act 1977, s.13(1)(*a*) provides that the Act shall apply to terms which make the liability or its enforcement subject to restrictive or onerous conditions.

[3] *Collin* v. *Duke of Westminster* [1985] Q.B. 581 at p. 601, C.A., *per* Oliver L.J.; see also *R.* v. *Williams* [1942] A.C. 541 at p. 555. For a general discussion of the requirements relating to specialties, see *Chitty on Contracts* (26th ed., 1989) at paras. 20–33.

[4] *Collin* v. *Duke of Westminster* [1985] Q.B. 581 where the Court of Appeal stated that the Limitation Acts of 1939 and 1980 have not caused the meaning of the term "specialty" to be reduced, thereby rejecting the *obiter* view expressed in *Leivers* v. *Barber, Walker & Co.* [1943] 1 K.B. 385 (*per* Goddard

and from statute alone, the applicable limitation period is that of a specialty.[5]

In *Collin* v. *Duke of Westminster*[6] the applicant claimed that he was entitled under the Leasehold Reform Act 1967 to acquire the freehold of his house. The right to apply for the freehold under the 1967 Act is a statutory procedure which produces incidents akin to, but not precisely the same as, those produced by a simple contract; as such section 5 of the Limitation Act 1980 was inapplicable. However, the Court of Appeal rejected the argument that such a finding implied that no period of limitation would be applicable, holding that where the plaintiff's claim is under a statute in that he must rely on the terms of the statute in order to succeed, the action should be regarded as an action upon a specialty. A distinction should be drawn between those cases where all that the statute does is to make binding a contract which otherwise would not be binding[7] and those where the action rests on the statute and only on the statute.[8] In the former, the limitation period will be six years and in the latter, 12.

The distinction between simple contracts and specialties has been the subject of careful consideration in a number of

Company law cases

company law cases where liquidators have sought clarification of the period of limitation where capital or dividends are to be returned to members of the company. The issue relates to the nature of the contract between the member and the company. Section 14 of the Companies Act 1985 provides "Subject to the provisions of this Act, the memorandum and articles, when registered, bind the company and its members to the same extent as if they respectively had been signed and sealed by each member. . ."

In *Re Compania de Electricidad de la Provincia de Buenos Aires Ltd.*[9] the court rejected the previously held view that a claim by shareholders in respect of the declaration of a dividend was a claim on a specialty,[10] on the ground that it was wrong to regard the wording of section 14 (and its predecessors in previous companies legislation) as creating a contract under seal. Although section 14 states that the contract between the company and its members should be deemed to have been executed by the members under seal, it makes no equivalent assumption as far as the company itself is concerned. This interpretation is reinforced by the express provision in section 14(2) which states that money payable by a member to the company under the memorandum or articles is in the nature of a specialty debt. Where a company owes money to a member, whether in the form of a dividend or as capital to be returned, the relevant limitation period is consequently six years; where a

---

L.J. at p. 398) and upholding the older cases of *Cork and Brandon Rly. Co.* v. *Goode* (1853) 13 C.B. 826 and *Aylott* v. *West Ham Corporation* [1927] 1 Ch. 30.
[5] See below, p. 33.
[6] [1985] Q.B. 581.
[7] See *Aylott* v. *West Ham Corporation* [1927] 1 Ch. 30, C.A.; *Gutsell* v. *Reeve* [1936] 1 K.B. 272.
[8] See *Collin* v. *Duke of Westminster* [1985] Q.B. 581; *Pratt* v. *Cook, Son & Co. (St. Paul's) Ltd.* [1940] A.C. 437.
[9] [1980] Ch. 146, Slade J.
[10] See *Re Artisans' Land and Mortgage Corpn.* [1904] 1 Ch. 796.

member owes money to the company under the memorandum or articles, the action is time-barred only after 12 years.

Exceptions to the 12-year rule

In certain circumstances, although the plaintiff's action is based upon a specialty or a statute, the 12-year limitation period will not be applicable and a shorter six-year period may be substituted: section 8(2) provides that the 12-year limitation period laid down for specialties shall not apply in respect of any action for which a shorter period of limitation is prescribed by any other provision of the Act.

Money due under a statute
    Section 9 imposes a six-year time limit in respect of actions to recover a sum of money due under a statute. While it is true that a statute, being sealed, is a form of specialty, section 9 provides an exception to the general rule laid down in section 8(1). However, the wording of the section should be read restrictively: it applies only in respect of "any sum recoverable by virtue of any enactment." Differing views have been expressed on the subject of whether or not an action to recover compensation which is payable only by virtue of a statute should be considered to fall within section 9. The preferable view is that such actions should be considered to be actions to recover a sum recoverable by virtue of an enactment and therefore the shorter limitation period will apply.[11]

Non-pecuniary rights
    An action which seeks to assert a non-pecuniary right which exists only by virtue of a statute will be considered to be an action on a specialty and the 12-year limitation period will apply.[12]

Rent and mortgage interest
    Section 19 provides that the period of limitation to recover arrears of rent is six years from the date on which the arrears became due. Similarly, by section 20, there is a six-year limitation in respect of actions to recover arrears of interest on a mortgage. These provisions apply irrespective of whether or not the lease or mortgage is a deed.

Accrual of the cause of action

Cause of action accrues on breach
The cause of action in contract accrues upon breach, irrespective of whether damage has been suffered by the plaintiff at that time.[13] It will therefore be necessary to establish the date on which the breach occurred; if this is outside the limitation period it will be necessary to determine whether the breach can be classified as a continuing one[14] and/or whether a separate

[11] See *Pegler* v. *Railway Executive* [1948] A.C. 332, H.L. and *Brueton* v. *Woodward* [1941] 1 K.B. 680 at p. 686. The contrary view was expressed in *Leivers* v. *Barber, Walker & Co. Ltd.* [1943] 1 K.B. 385, C.A.
[12] *Collin* v. *Duke of Westminster* [1985] Q.B. 581, where the claimant was seeking to acquire the freehold of his house in accordance with the Leasehold Reform Act 1967.
[13] *Lynn* v. *Bamber* [1930] 2 K.B. 72; see also *Forster* v. *Outred & Co.* [1982] 1 W.L.R. 86, [1982] 2 All E.R. 753, C.A. and *Bell* v. *Peter Browne & Co.* [1990] 3 All E.R. 124 discussed in Chap. 5, "Tort" at pp. 49–50.
[14] See *Midland Bank Trust Co. Ltd.* v. *Hett, Stubbs & Kemp* [1979] 1 Ch. 384.

cause of action is available in tort (where the cause of action generally accrues upon damage being suffered by the plaintiff).[15]

Date of breach

Question of fact

In many situations the date of the breach of contract will be apparent from the circumstances of the case; however, if this is not so, the determination of the date of breach will be a question of fact, to be determined by the judge after consideration of all the surrounding circumstances.[16] Thus, where a charterparty provided that the charterer should nominate a safe port, and the port chosen, while safe at the date of nomination, subsequently became unsafe, the date of breach was held to be the date of damage.[17]

Sale of goods

In a contract for the sale of goods where there is an implied condition that the goods shall be fit for their purpose,[18] it has been held that that condition exists not only at the time of sale, but also for a reasonable time thereafter.[19] It may be argued, therefore, that where a product becomes defective after a reasonable period of use (which will differ according to the particular product) the breach of the implied condition may be held to have occurred at the time when the defect arose, rather than at the time of sale or delivery. However, where there exists a latent defect in the product which manifests itself some time after the date of delivery, the date of breach will be the date of delivery.[20]

Anticipatory breach

Time begins to run against the plaintiff from the moment when he would have been able to obtain judgment against the defendant in respect of the breach which has occurred. Where the defendant has indicated in advance of the time for performance that he will not perform his obligations under the contract, *i.e.* where he has committed an anticipatory breach,[21] the promisee has a choice as to whether to accept this anticipatory repudiation immediately, or to treat the contract as continuing in existence. If he chooses the former option, he may sue at once to recover damages for his loss, and time will start to run immediately. If, however, he chooses to continue, there will be no immediate cause of action for damages and time will start to run only when the date for performance is passed.[22]

Continuing breaches

Although the general rule is that the cause of action accrues upon the date of the breach of contract, it may be possible to

[15] See below, p. 35 and further, Chap. 5.
[16] *Transoceanic Petroleum Carriers* v. *Cook Industries Inc., The Mary Lou* [1981] 2 Lloyd's Rep. 272; *The Hermine* [1978] 2 Lloyd's Rep. 37.
[17] *Ibid.*
[18] Sale of Goods Act 1979, s.14(3).
[19] See *Lambert* v. *Lewis* [1982] A.C. 225.
[20] See *Transoceanic Petroleum Carriers* v. *Cook Industries Inc., The Mary Lou* [1981] 2 Lloyd's Rep. 272.
[21] See *Hochster* v. *de la Tour* (1853) 2 E. & B. 678 on the question of the right to sue in respect of an anticipatory breach.
[22] See comments of Mustill L.J. in *Bell* v. *Peter Browne & Co.* [1990] 3 All E.R. 124 at p. 135.

extend the time within which an action may be brought by establishing that, after the original breach, the relationship between the parties subsisted such that there may be found to exist a continuing duty under the contract to rectify the original breach. This was the explanation preferred by the Court of Appeal[23] for the decision of Oliver J. in *Midland Bank Trust Co. Ltd.* v. *Hett, Stubbs & Kemp.*[24]

Construction of the contract

It will in all cases be a question of construction of the contract to determine whether the defaulting party's obligation is indeed a continuing contractual obligation. An example of such an obligation would be the repairing clause in a tenancy agreement where the obligation of the tenant or the landlord to repair is broken afresh every day the property is out of repair.[25]

Building cases

The existence of a continuing contractual duty has been affirmed in a number of building cases, where architects and engineers have been held to be under such a duty to consider their design during the course of the erection of a building which they have designed.[26] Thus where an architect or engineer has produced a faulty design for a building, while the cause of action will initially accrue upon completion of the design, he will be "under a continuing duty to check that his design will work in practice and to correct any errors which may emerge"[27] and that duty will continue until the building is completed. Where the relationship between the parties continues after the completion of the building, as for example where the defendant is both builder/designer and landlord and the plaintiff is a tenant injured as a result of a design now acknowledged to be unsafe, the court may hold that there exists a continuing duty to keep abreast of developments and, where practicable, to alter the structure of the building so as to avoid physical injury.[28]

No continuing duty after completion

The Court of Appeal has recently rejected, albeit cautiously, the argument that the duty of the architect or engineer should generally continue after the completion of the building, but such a development may materialise in the future.[29] It was held at first instance[30] in the litigation arising out of the explosion at the Abbeystead water pumping station, that the first defendants, the civil engineers, were to some slight degree negligent in not keeping abreast with and considering, in relation to design, developing knowledge about methane between the time of completion and the time of the explosion and passing such information and knowledge to the third defendants: the water authority which had commissioned the works. On appeal, Bingham L.J., while of the opinion that the

---

[23] *Bell* v. *Peter Browne & Co.* [1990] 3 All E.R. 124.

[24] [1979] 1 Ch. 384.

[25] *Spoor* v. *Green* (1874) L.R. 9 Exch. 99 at p. 111, *per* Bramwell B.

[26] *Brickfield Properties Ltd.* v. *Newton* [1971] 1 W.L.R. 862, C.A.; *London Borough of Merton* v. *Lowe* (1981) 18 B.L.R. 130, C.A.; *Chelmsford District Council* v. *Evers* (1983) 25 B.L.R. 99, Judge Newey Q.C.

[27] *Brickfield Properties Ltd.* v. *Newton* [1971] 1 W.L.R. 862 at p. 873, *per* Sachs L.J.

[28] *Rimmer* v. *Liverpool City Council* [1985] Q.B. 1.

[29] See *Eckersley* v. *Binnie and Partners* (1988) 18 Con L R 1, C.A., commented on in (1988) B.L.M., April, p. 7.

[30] *Eckersley* v. *Binnie and Partners* March 13, 1987; unrep., Rose J.; see commentary in (1987) B.L.M., July, pp. 10–14.

imposition of such duties would be "novel and burdensome", did not rule out altogether the possible future development of such a duty, stating that "if any such duty at all is to be imposed, the nature, scope and limits of such a duty require to be very carefully and cautiously defined. The development of the law on this point, if it ever occurs, will be gradual and analogical."[31]

Continuing relationship necessary

In general, where a breach of contract consists in a failure to perform an act, the mere fact that the breach could be rectified and the damage to the plaintiff altogether averted by performance of the act within the limitation period, will not convert the breach into a continuing one. The cause of action will accrue at the date of breach, and the subsequent passing of opportunities to rectify the breach will not themselves constitute further breaches.[32] In order to establish a continuing duty of care it will be necessary to show, not only that a contractual relationship between the parties has continued up to a point within the limitation period, but also that the defendant should have continued in some way to retain responsibility for the relevant transaction or advice.

Availability of a concurrent action in tort[33]

No imposition of wider duty in tort

Where the plaintiff's cause of action consists of the breach of a contractual duty of care, it is now established that the action may be framed in either contract or tort.[34] The plaintiff may not, by virtue of framing his action in tort rather than contract, avoid any exclusion clauses contained in the contract[35] or seek to impose a wider liability than would have been possible under the terms of the contract.[36] The plaintiff may, however, by framing his action in tort rather than contract, take advantage of the more favourable operation of the limitation period which may occur in tort, where time runs from the date of damage rather than the date of the breach of duty.[37]

Where the breach in respect of which the plaintiff is claiming consists of the giving of negligent advice or the making of a negligent statement, while it may be possible to claim damages in respect of economic loss incurred following reliance

---

[31] (1988) 18 Con LR 1 at pp. 146–147.
[32] *Bell* v. *Peter Browne & Co.* [1990] 3 All E.R. 124.
[33] See also Chap. 5.
[34] *Midland Bank Trust Co. Ltd.* v. *Hett, Stubbs and Kemp* [1979] Ch. 384; *Esso Petroleum Co. Ltd.* v. *Mardon* [1976] Q.B. 801; *Pirelli General Cable Works Ltd.* v. *Oscar Faber & Partners* [1983] 2 A.C. 1; *Bell* v. *Peter Browne & Co.* [1990] 3 All E.R. 124. Older cases asserting the contrary (*e.g. Bagot* v. *Stevens Scanlan & Co. Ltd.* [1966] 1 Q.B. 197) must now be taken to have been overruled. However, a recent decision of the Court of Appeal has emphasised that "[t]he different treatment for limitation purposes of claims in contract and tort is . . . unsatisfactory . . . if a contract is in existence this is the natural vehicle for recourse.": *Société Commerciale de Réassurance* v. *ERAS International Ltd.* [1992] 2 All E.R. 82 at p. 85, C.A. *per* Mustill L.J.
[35] *William Hill Organisation* v. *Bernard Sunley & Sons Ltd.* (1982) 22 B.L.R. 1, C.A.
[36] *Tai Hing Cotton Mill Ltd.* v. *Liu Chong Hing Bank Ltd.* [1985] 2 All E.R. 947; *Greater Nottingham Co-operative Society Ltd.* v. *Cementation Piling and Foundations Ltd.* [1988] 3 W.L.R. 396, C.A.
[37] *Bell* v. *Peter Browne & Co.* [1990] 3 All E.R. 124.

Date of damage is date of reliance

on the statement,[38] the date of damage, for the purpose of calculating the date of accrual of the cause of action, will generally be held to be the date of reliance on the statement, rather than the date on which the damage manifested itself. Recourse to tortious limitation periods will be of little help to the plaintiff. Moreover, where the plaintiff's action is framed as a breach of a contractual duty of care, the provisions of the Latent Damage Act 1986 will not assist where the damage has manifested itself outside the limitation period.[39]

Action for money had and received

Where money has been paid, or other services rendered, in consequence of a mistake of fact, recovery may be possible on the basis of the principles of the law of restitution or unjust enrichment.[40] Similarly, in those situations where, after a period of negotiation, the parties have failed to agree on the terms to a contract, but one party has acted in reliance upon a contract coming into existence and has conferred property or a valuable benefit on the other, a restitutionary remedy may be available.[41] In such cases, the appropriate period of limitation is six years, as for a simple contract,[42] with the cause of action accruing at the time when the money is paid or the service rendered. In the case

Contracts which fail to materialise

of, for example, a building contract which has failed to materialise, the plaintiff may be left in a very insecure position as the date of the rendering of the building service will be considerably earlier than the date on which a breach of the building contract (had there been one) would have been held to have occurred (*i.e.* the date of practical or substantial completion). It has been argued,[43] however, that use of the contractual limitation period in actions based on unjust enrichment is inappropriate, and that a more flexible approach, akin to the equitable doctrine of laches,[44] should be adopted.

Contracts of loan

Accrual when payment due or on demand

In the case of a contract of loan, the cause of action will normally accrue on the date when payment is due, or, if the debt is repayable on demand, on the date of demand.[45]

---

[38] On the basis of the principles established in *Hedley Byrne & Co. Ltd.* v. *Heller & Partners Ltd.* [1962] 1 Q.B. 396 and *Caparo Industries plc* v. *Dickman* [1990] 1 All E.R. 568; economic loss is widely construed (see Chap. 5) and will not generally be recoverable where the claim asserts merely a negligent act: *D. & F. Estates* v. *Church Commissioners for England* [1988] 2 All E.R. 992; *Murphy* v. *Brentwood District Council* [1990] 2 All E.R. 908.

[39] *Iron Trade Mutual Insurance Co. Ltd.* v. *J.K. Buckenham Ltd.* [1990] 1 All E.R. 808; see also the commentary on this case in (1990) B.L.M., May, pp. 1–4).

[40] See generally Goff and Jones, *Law of Restitution* (3rd ed., 1986).

[41] See *William Lacey (Hounslow) Ltd.* v. *Davis* [1957] 1 W.L.R. 932; *British Steel Corp.* v. *Cleveland Bridge & Engineering Co. Ltd.* [1984] 1 All E.R. 504, Goff J.

[42] *Re Diplock* [1948] Ch. 465 at p. 514, C.A., affirmed in *Ministry of Health* v. *Simpson* [1951] A.C. 251; *Chesworth* v. *Farrar* [1967] 1 Q.B. 407.

[43] McLean "Limitation of Actions in Restitution" [1989] C.L.J. 472.

[44] See Chap. 11.

[45] *Lloyds Bank Ltd.* v. *Margolis* [1954] 1 W.L.R. 644.

If no date for repayment, demand is necessary

Prior to the enactment of the current legislation, where any contract of loan which did not specify a date for repayment (as is frequently the case in respect of loans between family or friends), time began to run against the creditor from the date of making the loan. Section 6 now provides that where a loan is made which contains no specific date for repayment (section 6(2)(a)) and does not effectively make the obligation to repay conditional on demand or the occurrence of some other event (section 6(2)(b)) time will begin to run only when the creditor (or if there is more than one creditor, any one of them) makes a demand in writing for repayment (section 6(3)).

In the case of the relationship between banker and customer, a demand will always be a prerequisite for repayment, whether the person seeking repayment is the customer[46] or the bank (or building society).[47]

Acknowledgment and part payment of debt

Accrual at date of acknowledgment of liquidated pecuniary claim

Section 29(5)(a) of the Limitation Act 1980 provides that, where there has been any acknowledgment or part payment by the person liable of a debt or other liquidated pecuniary claim, the cause of action will be treated as having accrued on and not before the date of the acknowledgment. The Act contains no definition of the term "acknowledgment"; this will be a question of fact to be determined according to the circumstances of each case.[48] It is not necessary that the document relied upon as constituting an acknowledgment should expressly specify the sum owed, but that sum should be ascertainable by reference to extrinsic evidence.[49] A statement that a sum *might* be due on an *ex gratia* basis does not constitute an acknowledgment.[50] A refusal to pay may be construed as an acknowledgment that the money is owing,[51] but a denial of liability, whether it be a simple denial that the debt was incurred or an assertion that liability to pay does not exist by virtue of a right of set-off, will not be interpreted as an acknowledgment.[52]

Acknowledgment in writing

In order to start the running of time afresh, the acknowledgment must be in writing and be signed by the person who is liable: section 30(1), or his agent: section 30(2)(a).[53] It must be made to the person to whom the debt is owed or his authorised agent: section 30(2)(b). Initialling of a document acknowledging a debt will bring the acknowledgment within the terms of section 29.[54]

---

[46] *Joachimson* v. *Swiss Bank Corp.* [1921] 3 K.B. 110; *Arab Bank* v. *Barclays Bank* [1954] A.C. 495.

[47] See generally *Atkinson* v. *Bradford Third Equitable Benefit Building Society* (1890) 25 Q.B.D. 377; *Lloyds Bank* v. *Margolis* [1954] 1 W.L.R. 644 at p. 649, *per* Upjohn J.; *Limpgrange* v. *Bank of Commerce and Credit International S.A.* [1986] F.L.R. 36; *National Bank of Commerce* v. *National Westminster Bank* [1990] 2 Lloyd's Rep. 514.

[48] *Jones* v. *Bellgrove Properties* [1949] 2 K.B. 700.

[49] *Ibid.*

[50] *Kamouh* v. *Associated Electrical Industries International* [1979] 2 W.L.R. 795, Parker J.

[51] *Good* v. *Parry* [1963] 2 Q.B. 418.

[52] *Surrendra Overseas* v. *Government of Sri Lanka* [1977] 1 W.L.R. 565.

[53] On the question of who is authorised to act as an agent in making such acknowledgments, see *Wright* v. *Pepin* [1954] 2 All E.R. 52.

[54] *Lord St. John* v. *Boughton* (1838) 9 Sim. 219.

Acknowledgment of any form of unliquidated claim (*i.e.* a claim for damages) will not serve to restart the running of time.

Acknowledgment of quantum meruit claim

Where the action relates to a *quantum meruit* claim for the value of works rendered under a contract which failed to materialise or which failed to stipulate the price to be paid, it has been held that such a claim is a liquidated pecuniary claim within the meaning of section 29(5)(*a*).[55]

Assignment of debt

Assignee takes subject to limitation period

Where the benefit of a contract has been assigned, the assignee will take "subject to equities", *i.e.* he cannot recover more from the promisor than the assignor might himself have recovered. Thus, if the promisor could have pleaded the defence of limitation against the assignor, he will be entitled so to plead against the assignee. Similarly, where there has been subrogation of rights under a contract of loan.[56] However, where there has been a novation of an existing contract, time may start to run afresh.[57]

Contracts of guarantee

Two forms of contract of guarantee

It has been stated[58] that there are at least two possible forms of contract of guarantee:

    (a) where the guarantor promises only that, if the principal debtor fails to pay any instalment, he will pay it; and

    (b) where the guarantor undertakes that the principal debtor will carry out the contract.

It would seem that the date of accrual of the cause of action for breach of his obligations by a guarantor will differ according to the type of guarantee envisaged. In the first case, the date of accrual would be the date when the guarantor fails to pay the instalment when called upon to do so, for that is the date of his breach. In the second case, the date of accrual is the date of the principal's breach, not the date when the guarantor is called upon to pay.[59] An example of the second type of guarantee is one where the guarantor states that he "personally guarantees the performance" of a third party of its obligations under a contract between the third party and the beneficiary of the guarantee.

Contracts of indemnity

The question of when a cause of action accrues in relation to a contract of indemnity has been considered in a number of cases. The indemnity may be express or implied.[60] At common law, time ran against a person seeking to enforce an indemnity (the beneficiary) from the time when he was called upon to discharge

---

[55] *Amantilla Ltd.* v. *Telefusion plc* (1987) 9 Con LR 139; see also McLean "Limitation of Actions in Restitution" [1989] C.L.J. 472, at pp. 477–479.

[56] *Central Insurance Co.* v. *Seacalf Shipping Corp.* [1985] 2 Lloyd's Rep. 25.

[57] *Chatsworth Investments Ltd.* v. *Cussins (Contractors) Ltd.* [1969] 1 W.L.R. 1.

[58] *Moschi* v. *Lep Air Services Ltd.* [1972] 2 All E.R. 393 at p. 398, *per* Viscount Dilhorne.

[59] *Moschi* v. *Lep Air Services Ltd., ibid.;* see also *Hyundai Heavy Industries Co. Ltd.* v. *Papadopoulos* [1980] 2 All E.R. 29.

[60] See *Telfair Shipping Corporation* v. *Inersea S.A.* [1985] 1 W.L.R. 553 at p. 566.

Common law rule relaxed

his own liability, rather than from the time when the event giving rise to his liability occurred.[61] This rule has, however, now been relaxed by equity so that the beneficiary is not forced to face possible ruin by discharging the liability before being entitled to maintain an action against the debtor, but may take proceedings under the contract of indemnity once the extent of his liability has been ascertained.[62]

Equity cannot override "pay to be paid" clauses

However, where the contract of indemnity contains an express "pay to be paid" clause (as in the standard provisions of marine protection and indemnity associations or clubs), equity cannot intervene so as to override this express provision.[63]

It has been suggested[64] that there is no general rule relating to the date of the accrual of the cause of action in contracts of indemnity, but that in all cases the document itself must be construed in order to determine the legal consequences which flow from it. However, in *County and District Properties Ltd.* v. *C. Jenner & Son Ltd.*[65] Swanwick J. reaffirmed the former rule, stating[66]: "an indemnity against a breach, or an act, or an omission, can only be an indemnity against the harmful consequences that may flow from it, and I take the law to be that the indemnity does not give rise to a cause of action until those consequences are ascertained." This view was recently upheld by the House of Lords in *Bradley* v. *Eagle Star Insurance Co. Ltd.*[67]

Two general categories of indemnity can be envisaged: those which seek to indemnify in respect of any liability which may arise on the part of the beneficiary and those which indemnify in respect of any losses incurred by the beneficiary. The cases indicate that the court will be slow to find the existence of the former category, where time will be held to run from the moment of the wrongful act of the indemnor which gives rise to liability on the part of the beneficiary. Ultimately,

Construction of the contract

however, it will turn upon the construction of the contract at issue.

Joinder of third parties

However, the fact that a cause of action on an indemnity has not yet accrued against the indemnor will not prevent the indemnor from being joined as a third party in the proceedings under which the liability of the beneficiary is to be established.[68]

Statutory indemnities

In the case of a statutory indemnity it will again be necessary to look to the wording of the statute in order to determine the date upon which the cause of action accrued.[69] Accordingly, where a statute[70] provided that compensation shall

---

[61] *Collinge* v. *Heywood* (1839) 9 A. & E. 633.
[62] See *Re Richardson, ex p. Governors of St. Thomas's Hospital* [1911] 2 K.B. 705 at pp. 709–710, *per* Lord Cozens-Hardy M.R.
[63] *Firma C-Trade* v. *Newcastle Indemnity Association* [1990] 2 All E.R. 705, H.L.
[64] *Bosma* v. *Larsen* [1966] 1 Lloyd's Rep. 22, McNair J.
[65] [1976] 2 Lloyd's Rep. 728.
[66] *Ibid.* at p. 736. See also *Telfair Shipping Corp.* v. *Inersea S.A.* [1985] 1 W.L.R. 553 at p. 567; and *R. & H. Green & Silley Weir Ltd.* v. *British Railways Board* [1985] 1 W.L.R. 570 at p. 574, *per* Dillon J.
[67] [1989] A.C. 957. See also *Post Office* v. *Norwich Union Fire Insurance Society Ltd.* [1967] 2 Q.B. 363.
[68] *County and District Properties* v. *C. Jenner & Son Ltd.* [1976] 2 Lloyd's Rep. 728.
[69] *Yorkshire Electricity Board* v. *British Telecommunications plc* [1986] 1 W.L.R. 1029, H.L.
[70] Public Utilities Street Works Act 1950, s.26.

be paid "equal to the expense reasonably incurred by the [plaintiffs] of making good damage" caused by the defendants, it was held by the House of Lords that the cause of action accrued only when the plaintiffs had incurred the expenditure necessary in order to make good the damage caused by the defendants. Such an interpretation may, of course, extend the limitation period some considerable time beyond that which would apply in a negligence action.[71]

Insurance contracts

Simple contract An action on a policy of insurance is an action on a simple contract. As such, the limitation period will expire six years from the date on which the cause of action accrued. As a contract of insurance is a form of indemnity contract, it will be necessary to look at the precise terms in order to determine the date on which the cause of action accrues. In general, however, this will be the date on which the loss in respect of which the claim is being made occurred. With marine insurance the very lengthy process of average adjustment (without which payment will not be made) may occasionally result in limitation problems, although it would seem that the point is rarely pleaded by the insurance companies involved. However, where the average adjustment award is made at such a time that the plaintiff is unable to formulate his claim against the insurers within six years of the loss, the action will be held to be time-barred if the insurers choose to plead the point since the cause of action will be held to have accrued at the time of the loss.[72]

Limitation periods in contracts of carriage

Special limitation periods apply In the case of international carriage contracts, the limitation periods specified in the Limitation Act 1980 will not apply in respect of actions brought against the carrier of the goods for death, personal injury or loss of or damage to the goods; reference should be made to the relevant international Convention together with its implementing legislation. In the case of claims brought by the carrier against the consignor, in respect, for example, of claims for payment of freight, the normal contractual limitation periods will apply.

Carriage by sea   Carriage of goods by sea will be governed by the Hague-Visby Rules, as implemented by the Carriage of Goods by Sea Act 1971, under which the limitation period for claims in respect of damage to cargo or breach of the carriage contract is one year (with notice of any such claim being notified to the carrier

---

[71] In *Yorkshire Electricity Board* v. *British Telecommunications plc* [1986] 1 W.L.R. 1029, H.L. the damage to the plaintiffs' underground cables occurred in 1971, but was made good by them only in 1976. In accordance with *Pirelli General Cable Works Ltd.* v. *Oscar Faber & Partners* [1983] 2 A.C. 1, it was held that the cause of action in negligence was barred at the time the writ was issued in 1978. However, the action under the Public Utilities Street Works Act 1950 was held to run from the date when the cables were repaired.

[72] *Chandris* v. *Argo Insurance Co.* [1963] 2 Lloyd's Rep. 65.

immediately upon arrival of the goods or within three days if the damage was not immediately apparent).[73] The carrier is entitled to plead the one-year limitation period to defeat a claim for set-off by the cargo owner in any action brought to recover freight after a period of more than one year has elapsed.[74] A two-year limitation period is laid down by the Athens Convention of 1974 relating to the Carriage of Passengers and their Luggage by Sea (as amended by the 1976 Protocol thereto) where damages are claimed by or on behalf of a passenger in respect of death, personal injury, or loss of or damage to luggage.[75]

Carriage by air

The limitation period will be two years in the case of claims arising out of the international carriage of goods and passengers by air (see Warsaw Convention as amended at The Hague and the Carriage by Air Act 1961), with notice in writing required within 14 days of arrival for cargo and seven days for luggage.[76]

Carriage by road

A general one-year limitation period is provided for in the case of goods carried by road (C.M.R. as implemented by the Carriage of Goods by Road Act 1965), but this is extended to three years where the damage has been caused by wilful misconduct.[77]

Carriage by rail

A one-year limitation period is again laid down in respect of damage to goods carried by rail (C.O.T.I.F. as implemented by the International Transport Conventions Act 1983), with an extension to two years if cash on delivery was charged or if there has been fraud or wilful misconduct.[78] In the case of death or personal injury to passengers, the Convention lays down a limitation period of three years from the date of the accident (where the action is brought by the passenger himself) or, where the plaintiff is someone other than the passenger, three years from the date of death, with a maximum limit of five years from the date of the accident.[79]

Contracts and the Latent Damage Act 1986

Act does not apply to claims framed in contract

It has been held that section 14A of the Limitation Act 1980, as inserted by the Latent Damage Act 1986, does not apply to claims framed in contract where the breach alleged is a breach of an implied duty of care: a claim of "contractual negligence".[80] Section 14A applies to "any action for damages for negligence"

---

[73] Article III(6) of the Hague-Visby Rules.

[74] *The Aries Tanker* [1977] 1 Lloyd's Rep. 334; see also *Bank of Boston Connecticut (formerly Colonial Bank)* v. *European Grain and Shipping, The Dominique* [1989] A.C. 1056; [1989] 2 W.L.R. 440.

[75] Article 16 of the Athens Convention.

[76] Article 29(1) of the Warsaw Convention as amended at The Hague; by s.5(1) of the Carriage by Air Act 1961, this limitation period also applies in actions against servants and agents of the carrier.

[77] Article 32 of the Convention Relative au Contrat de Transport International de Marchandises par Route (C.M.R.).

[78] Article 58 of the C.I.M. uniform rules to be found in Appendix B of the Convention Relative aux Transports Internationaux Ferroviaires (C.O.T.I.F.).

[79] Article 55 of the C.I.V. uniform rules to be found in Appendix A of C.O.T.I.F.

[80] *Iron Trade Mutual Insurance Co. Ltd.* v. *J.K. Buckenham Ltd.* [1990] 1 All E.R. 808; *Société Commerciale de Réassurance* v. *ERAS (International) Ltd.* [1992] 2 All E.R. 82, C.A.

and in the view of Rokison Q.C. (sitting as a deputy Judge of the High Court), since the 1980 Act specifically distinguishes actions in contract and actions in negligence, it was not possible to read section 14A as applying to any claim framed in contract, even where the breach of contract complained of consisted in a failure to exercise reasonable care and skill.[81] Where the plaintiff is able to establish the breach of a concurrent duty of care in tort, the 1986 Act may be applicable.[82]

---

[81] See further Chap. 5.
[82] *Berg* v. *Glentworth Bulb Co. Ltd.* July 25, 1988, C.A., unrep.; *Bell* v. *Peter Browne & Co.* [1990] 3 All E.R. 124.

5 TORT

Differing limitation periods

The usual limitation period in respect of actions brought in tort is six years from the date of the accrual of the cause of action: section 2 of the Limitation Act 1980. However, actions seeking to recover damages for personal injury are subject to a shorter time limit of three years,[1] as are actions in defamation.[2]

Accrual of the cause of action

As in other areas, the cause of action will accrue on the date when the plaintiff is first in a position to succeed in an action against the defendant, the date when all the facts necessary to support an action in tort have occurred.[3] For those torts which are actionable *per se* or without proof of special damage, *e.g.* trespass to the person, false imprisonment, libel and some forms of slander, time will run from the date of the commission of the tort; whereas for those in respect of which damage is a necessary part of the cause of action, *e.g.* negligence, nuisance and most forms of slander, time will begin to run from the date when damage is suffered. A definition of the concept of "damage" is therefore an important starting point in the discussion of limitation periods in negligence.[4]

Negligence

Date of actionable damage

The cause of action in negligence accrues, not at the date of the negligent act or omission, but at the date when actionable damage is sustained by the plaintiff.[5] When determining the date on which damage to property was sustained, account must be taken of any cause of action which had already accrued to the plaintiff's predecessors in title: so where damage occurs to property it is irrelevant that the plaintiff has owned the property for only two years if the damage can be shown to have occurred more than six years previously.[6] Clearly, no owner in the chain

---

[1] Limitation Act 1980, s.11(4): see further Chaps. 6 and 7.
[2] *Ibid.* s.4A: see below, p. 56.
[3] *Coburn* v. *Colledge* [1897] 1 Q.B. 702, C.A.; for a more detailed discussion of this issue see Chap. 2, pp. 8–10.
[4] On the difficulties of attempting such a definition, see Stapleton (1988) 104 L.Q.R. 213 and 389.
[5] In relation to personal injury see *Cartledge* v. *E. Jopling & Sons Ltd.* [1963] A.C. 758 at p. 777; *Archer* v. *Catton & Co. Ltd.* [1954] 1 W.L.R. 775; Chap. 6; in relation to damage to property see *Pirelli General Cable Works Ltd.* v. *Oscar Faber & Partners* [1983] 2 A.C.1 discussed below, pp. 45–49; and in relation to damage suffered as a result of reliance upon a negligent misstatement see *Forster* v. *Outred* [1982] 2 All E.R. 753; *UBAF Ltd.* v. *European American Banking Corp.* [1984] 2 All E.R. 226, discussed below, pp. 49–52.
[6] *Pirelli General Cable Works Ltd.* v. *Oscar Faber & Partners* [1983] 2 A.C. 1, overruling *Sparham-Souter* v. *Town and Country Developments (Essex) Ltd.* [1976] 1 Q.B. 858.

can have a better claim than his predecessor in title; if time started to run afresh each time a property changed ownership, defendants would be left in a permanent state of uncertainty, unable to avail themselves of the protection which limitation periods were designed to afford to them.

Onus on plaintiff

Where the defendant asserts that the action is barred by the Act, the plaintiff bears the burden of establishing on a balance of probabilities that the damage giving rise to the action occurred within the limitation period.[7]

Accrual of the cause of action in relation to damage to property

Cause of action accrues upon date of damage, not discoverability

After some doubt during the course of the 1970s, the House of Lords held in 1983 that, in relation to negligently-caused damage to property, the cause of action will accrue and time begin to run against the plaintiff on the date when the property itself first suffers damage.[8] This will be so even where the plaintiff could not reasonably have been expected to have discovered the damage within the limitation period, and where he was not the owner of the property at the time when the damage occurred. Thus in *Pirelli*, which was an action against an engineer in respect of the negligent design of a chimney built in 1969, cracks first appeared in the chimney no later than 1970, but were not discoverable until 1972 and not, in fact, discovered until 1977. The writ was issued in 1978, and the defendants pleaded that the action was time-barred. The House of Lords held that the cause of action accrued, not upon discoverability of the cracks, but on the date when significant cracks first appeared, even though they could not reasonably have been discovered until some two years later.[9] The unfairness of this result was lamented by their Lordships,[10] but no other conclusion was possible without overruling *Cartledge* v. *Jopling*,[11] which their Lordships were not prepared to do: "the reform needed is not the substitution of a new principle or rule of law for an existing one but a detailed set of provisions to replace existing statute law. The true way forward is not by departure from precedent but by amending legislation."[12] Parliament responded to the injustice of the decision in *Pirelli* by

---

[7] *London Congregational Union Inc.* v. *Harriss & Harriss* (1986) 35 B.L.R. 58; see further Chap. 2.

[8] *Pirelli General Cable Works Ltd.* v. *Oscar Faber & Partners* [1983] 2 A.C. 1.

[9] The infamous "doomed from the start" principle was first mooted by Lord Fraser in *Pirelli*, *ibid.* at p. 16 when he stated that there may be exceptional cases in which "the defect is so gross that the building is doomed from the start, and where the owner's cause of action will accrue as soon as it is built." This would have provided defendants with an extremely favourable starting point for the accrual of any action against them precisely in those cases where, arguably, negligence was greatest. The principle was applied in a small number of early cases (*Tozer Kemsley & Millbourn (Holdings) Ltd.* v. *J. Jarvis & Sons Ltd.* (1983) 1 Const. L.J. 79; *Chelmsford District Council* v. *T.J. Evers Ltd.* (1983) 1 Const.L.J. 65), but has generally been rejected in more recent years (*Ketteman* v. *Hansel Properties Ltd.* [1989] 1 All E.R. 38 at pp. 50–51, H.L.; *London Congregational Union Inc.* v. *Harriss & Harriss* (1986) 35 B.L.R. 58 at pp. 77–80, C.A.).

[10] The decision was also widely criticised: see, *inter alia*, Burrows (1983) 46 M.L.R. 509, Baxter (1983) 133 New L.J. 414 and 437.

[11] [1969] A.C. 758; see Chap. 6 "Personal injury actions".

[12] [1983] 2 A.C. 1 at p. 19, *per* Lord Scarman.

enacting the Latent Damage Act 1986[13] which, while not altering the date on which a cause of action accrues, provides an alternative limitation period of three years from the date when the damage could reasonably have been discovered.[14]

Defects in property are economic loss

However, more recent authority has established that, where a property owner suffers loss in the form of defects occurring in the structure of the property as a result of negligent design or construction, such loss should properly be classified as economic rather than physical[15] and will usually be irrecoverable in negligence. The recovery of economic loss in negligence will now generally be confined to those situations where there exists a sufficient relationship of proximity, such as to impose a duty of care on one party to prevent damage to those persons whom he might reasonably foresee as being likely to suffer damage as a result of relying on the former's negligently made statement.[16]

Emergence of a previously latent defect

Where the plaintiff's loss consists merely of the manifestation of a latent defect, and is classified as economic rather than physical, no cause of action will arise against the person responsible in the absence of a sufficiently proximate relationship, as outlined above. The question then arises as to whether the early discovery of a defect in a structure at a time when it has caused no physical damage in the form of personal injury or damage to other property, will preclude a later accrual of a cause of action if the defect should subsequently cause such physical damage. In *Murphy* it was emphasised that the basis for recovery of damages in respect of physical damage caused by a defective structure lay in the latency of the defect: Lord Oliver stated[17]: "once the danger ceases to be latent there never could be any liability" and according to Lord Bridge "if the defect becomes apparent before any injury or damage has been caused, the loss sustained by the building owner is purely economic." Once the defect has manifested itself, the plaintiff is not entitled to wait, on the basis that compensation will not be available for mere repairs, until physical damage has occurred. He will have the invidious choice of either repairing at his own expense or abandoning the property. There will be no later accrual of a cause of action if he chooses simply to ignore the defect.

Result when a defect manifests itself

It is important to determine the precise nature of the early discovery which will preclude the plaintiff from bringing a subsequent action in respect of physical damage. Is it discovery of the defect alone, or is it discovery of the defect, together with realisation of the implications for possible future physical damage? That is to say, is it the defect which should remain

---

[13] Following the recommendations of the Law Reform Committee, Twenty Fourth Report on Latent Damage, Cmnd. 9390.

[14] See below, pp. 52–56.

[15] *D. & F. Estates Ltd.* v. *Church Commissioners for England* [1988] 2 All E.R. 992; *Murphy* v. *Brentwood District Council* [1990] 2 All E.R. 908, overruling *Anns* v. *Merton London Borough Council* [1978] A.C. 728.

[16] *Hedley Byrne & Co. Ltd.* v. *Heller & Partners Ltd.* [1962] 1 Q.B. 396; *Caparo Industries plc* v. *Dickman* [1990] 1 All E.R. 568. This is now the explanation given by the House of Lords in *Murphy* v. *Brentwood District Council* [1990] 2 All E.R. 908 for the decisions in *Junior Books Ltd.* v. *Veitchi Co. Ltd.* [1983] 1 A.C. 520 and *Pirelli General Cable Works Ltd.* v. *Oscar Faber & Partners* [1983] 2 A.C.1 . See also below, pp. 49–52, (Accrual of the cause of action following negligent execution of documents).

[17] [1990] 2 All E.R. 908 at p. 936.

latent, or is it the danger which should remain so? If it is the danger which should remain latent, should the behaviour of the plaintiff be assessed objectively or subjectively? In other words, will the plaintiff's ability to recover depend on what he actually foresaw as the likely result of leaving the defect unrepaired, or what he should, as a reasonable person, have foreseen?

Accrual of cause of action where there is economic loss followed by physical damage

It has recently been held that early discovery of a defect in a chattel which led to physical damage to other property some time after the initial discovery did not preclude a cause of action from accruing at the date of physical damage. In *Nitrigin Eireann Teoranta* v. *Inco Alloys Ltd.*[18] the plaintiffs discovered in 1983 that tubing supplied by the defendants was cracked. The plaintiffs repaired the tubing and continued to use it. The loss up to that point was clearly economic and consequently irrecoverable. In 1984 the tubing exploded, causing damage to the structure of the plant around it. The writ alleging negligent manufacture was issued in 1990 (less than six years after the explosion, but more than six years after the discovery of the defect) and the defendants claimed that the action was time-barred. It was held that, as there was no cause of action in respect of the economic loss which occurred in 1983, the cause of action must be considered to have accrued in 1984 at the date of the explosion. Such a finding must, however, be subject to a reasonableness requirement: it cannot be open to the plaintiff to carry on using a manifestly defective product without ascertaining the risk that physical damage might ensue. In the view of May J., a plaintiff who had continued to use a defective product in such circumstances would have his damages reduced or extinguished by reason of contributory negligence, but the accrual of a cause of action in negligence would not be affected.[19]

Accrual of cause of action for economic loss

Although *Pirelli* was not expressly overruled in *Murphy* or *D. & F. Estates*, it is clear that the statement of their Lordships in relation to the date of accrual of the cause of action against the defendant engineers must now be re-read in the light of these later decisions. The loss suffered in *Pirelli* (severe cracking in a chimney designed by the defendant engineers) must now be regarded as economic rather than physical: the plaintiffs, as a result of the negligence of the defendants, acquired a chimney which was either valueless or worth significantly less than was paid for it and required substantial expenditure in order to remedy the defects.

Was Pirelli a Hedley Byrne situation?

The interpretation given by Lord Keith in *Murphy* of the decision in *Pirelli* was that the latter was, in fact, a *Hedley Byrne* type of situation with a duty of care being imposed on the engineers by reason of a negligent statement made by them in tendering the design for the chimney.[20] Such a contention is, however, contrary to an express dictum of Lord Fraser in *Pirelli*, although it should be noted that no consideration of the

---

[18] [1992] 1 All E.R. 854.

[19] *Ibid.* at p. 862.

[20] "In a case such as *Pirelli*, where the tortious liability arose out of a contractual relationship with professional people, the duty extended to take reasonable care not to cause economic loss to the client by the advice given. The plaintiffs built the chimney as they did in reliance on that advice. The case would accordingly fall within the principles of *Hedley Byrne*." [1990] 2 All E.R. 908 at p. 919.

issue was given as it was not necessary for the purpose of deciding the case. The defendants in *Pirelli* (in seeking to establish that the cause of action arose at the earliest possible date) argued that any fault in advising on the design of the chimney should be regarded as analogous to that of a solicitor who gives negligent advice on law; Lord Fraser stated that it was not necessary to consider whether the fault of the engineers was analogous to that of a solicitor who gives negligent advice on the law, but "as at present advised, I do not think it is."

When did the cause of action accrue?

However, even if the action is reclassified as one for negligent misstatement, the problems raised by *Murphy* do not stop there: it becomes necessary to establish the date on which the cause of action accrued.[21] This might be the date when the cracks appeared, the date when the plaintiffs acquired the chimney or the date when the plaintiffs (in reliance on the defendants' design) caused the chimney to be built.

Date of cracking?

The latest possible date on which the cause of action could accrue, following the rule that time begins to run from the date when actionable damage is first suffered, would be the date when cracks appeared, as was held to be the case in *Pirelli* itself. However, while this would clearly be true in a case in which physical damage formed the basis of the action, it is unlikely to be so where the action is seeking damages in respect of economic loss. Although the cracking represents a form of economic loss, it may be held to be merely a physical manifestation of economic loss which had occurred at an earlier date. Economic loss will include not only the cost of repairs to the defective structure or chattel, but will also take into account the diminution in value which arises when a defective product is acquired. The running of time will not be postponed to the date of occurrence of physical damage, since the actionable damage must now be defined as economic rather than physical.

Date of reliance on plans?

Actionable damage, as in *Pirelli*, must now be taken to occur at the time when the plaintiff suffered a financial detriment.[22] This date would be, in *Pirelli*, the date when the plaintiffs relied on the defendants' negligent design specifications and instructed the contractors to commence construction work, as it was then inevitable that, unless there was a substantial revision of the design specifications, the plaintiffs would eventually acquire a defective chimney.

The date of reliance has frequently been used as the starting point for the running of time in cases alleging negligence by a solicitor in the execution of documents,[23] and it was argued by the defendants in *Pirelli* that the position of engineers was analogous to that of solicitors with the result that the accrual of the cause of action should be the same but this argument was rejected by Lord Fraser, albeit without full consideration of the issues. It can also be argued that it would not be appropriate to use the date of reliance on the misstatement as the starting date in cases of negligence by engineers or architects, since the plaintiff does not at this time possess property which has been

---

[21] The date of accrual of the cause of action in relation to negligent misstatements or negligent execution of documents is discussed below.
[22] See discussion of cases involving negligent execution by solicitors of legal documents, below, pp. 49–52.
[23] See below, pp. 49–52.

subject to some diminution in value or other incumbrance. In cases involving solicitors, the alleged fault of the solicitor invariably involved some form of negligent action or inaction in relation to property or rights already possessed by the plaintiff.[24] In cases such as *Pirelli*, it is arguable that a starting date based on reliance would be inappropriate since the effect of reliance was not to damage, incumber or alter in any way an existing piece of the plaintiff's property. The economic loss would affect the chimney and, on the date of reliance, this was not yet in existence.

Date of acquisition
We are therefore left with the date on which the plaintiffs acquired the chimney as the starting date for the running of time. It was at this time that the plaintiffs had in their possession something which was defective and was ultimately going to require substantial repairs and it was at this point that economic loss was first suffered. While it is true that Lord Fraser in *Pirelli* rejected this as the starting date, it should be remembered that the case was at that time considered to be one of physical rather than economic loss and consequently the issue was not fully explored.

Accrual of the cause of action following negligent execution of documents

Concurrent action in contract and tort
Where a solicitor, in breach of the duty of care imposed on him by contract, fails to register a charge or option or other interest in land on behalf of his client, an action may lie in either contract or tort.[25] However, the scope of the tortious duty imposed cannot exceed the terms of the contract between the parties: the presumption is that where two parties have entered into a contractual relationship, the contract will define exhaustively the rights and duties existing between them.[26] The main advantage of the concurrent action lies, therefore, not in the widening of the duties owed by the defendant, but in the possibility of a more favourable interpretation of the date of the accrual of the cause of action in tort. In contract, the cause of action accrues upon breach, as this is the time when the plaintiff's cause of action is complete, regardless of whether or not damage has in fact been suffered.[27] In negligence the cause of action accrues only upon the occurrence of some damage to the plaintiff. It is therefore necessary to consider what is meant by "damage" in this context.

In line with physical damage cases, it is now clear that damage may be held to have occurred even though the plaintiff was unaware of it and, indeed, could not possibly have

[24] See, *inter alia*, *Forster* v. *Outred*; *Bell* v. *Peter Browne & Co.*; *Moore* v. *Ferrier*, all discussed below.
[25] *Bell* v. *Peter Browne & Co.* [1990] 3 All E.R. 124; *D.W. Moore & Co. Ltd.* v. *Ferrier* [1988] 1 All E.R. 400; *Midland Bank Trust Co. Ltd.* v. *Hett Stubbs & Kemp* [1979] Ch. 384. However, see the *dicta* of Mustill L.J. in *Société Commerciale de Réassurance* v. *ERAS (International) Ltd.* [1992] 2 All E.R. 82, C.A., above Chap. 4, n. 36.
[26] *Tai Hing Cotton Mill Ltd.* v. *Liu Chong Hing Bank Ltd.* [1986] A.C. 80, P.C.; *Greater Nottingham Co-operative Society Ltd.* v. *Cementation Piling and Foundations Ltd.* [1988] 3 W.L.R. 396, C.A.
[27] See Chap. 4 at pp. 33–36.

What is damage?

discovered its existence. What, then, is damage? In order to bring an action in negligence, damage must be "actual" rather than presumed, as in trespass or libel. "Actual" damage does not, however, necessarily imply damage which is immediately precisely quantifiable, but may include loss which may arise on a contingency over which the plaintiff has no control.[28] In relation to a failure to register a charge or an option to purchase land, it was formerly thought that the damage occurred and consequently the cause of action accrued only upon the occurrence of a quantifiable, tangible loss, such as the sale of the property in breach of the terms of the charge or the option agreement.[29] However, more recent authority has established that this is false: the cause of action accrues at the time when the plaintiff was first in a position to maintain an action against the defendant. If a solicitor is negligent in the performance of an operation entrusted to him, an action may be brought immediately by the client; the court will not strike out an action in negligence merely because the precise extent of the loss remains a contingency. By reason of the negligent execution or failure to execute the charge, some interest of the client's has been substantially reduced, or even rendered non-existent. Some examples will serve to illustrate this proposition:

In *Foster* v. *Outred*[30] the plaintiff's solicitors negligently failed to advise her as to the extent of a mortgage executed by her in 1973 in order to guarantee business debts of her son. It was held by the Court of Appeal that actual damage occurred and her cause of action was complete at the date when she acted in reliance on the negligent advice, rather than the date on which the finance company foreclosed on the mortgage. This was because the effect of entering into the mortgage deed was to encumber her interest in her freehold estate with a legal charge, thus reducing the equity of redemption of the property. The fact that the *quantum* of damages would be difficult to assess and that the damage suffered by foreclosure was significantly greater than the reduction in value of the property did not prevent the cause of action from accruing at the earlier date.

Encumbrance of interest in land

Similarly, in *Bell* v. *Browne*[31] the Court of Appeal held that the cause of action in respect of a negligent failure by a solicitor to register a client's interest in the former matrimonial home following a divorce, accrued upon the date when the breach of duty occurred, rather than the date upon which the client's former spouse sold the property and disposed of the profits.[32]

Loss of interest in matrimonial home

Negligent drafting of contract

Where a contract has been negligently drafted, with the result that its terms do not protect the plaintiff's interest in the way in which was intended, the cause of action accrues upon the date of execution of the contract, rather than the date when the defect was discovered. In *D. W. Moore & Co. Ltd.* v. *Ferrier*[33]

---

[28] *Forster* v. *Outred & Co.* [1982] 2 All E.R. 753, C.A.; *Bell* v. *Peter Browne & Co.* [1990] 3 All E.R. 124.

[29] See the decision of Oliver J. in *Midland Bank Trust Co. Ltd.* v. *Hett, Stubbs & Kemp* [1979] Ch. 384, now explained on alternative grounds, discussed below.

[30] See above n. 28.

[31] See above n. 28.

[32] See also *Melton* v. *Walker & Stanger* (1981) 125 S.J. 861; *Baker* v. *Ollard & Bentley* (1982) 126 S.J. 593, C.A. and *Aikman* v. *Hallett & Co.*, March 20, 1987; unrep., where the principles laid down in *Forster* v. *Outred* were applied.

[33] [1988] 1 All E.R. 400.

the plaintiff company approached a firm of solicitors with a view of drawing up a restrictive covenant which would prevent one of the directors from setting up in competition if he should leave the company. The clause stated that the restrictive covenant was to operate if the said director "ceased to be a member of the company". Some time later, the director relinquished his directorship, but remained as a shareholder; it was discovered that the restrictive covenant was ineffective since he was still a member of the company. It was held by the Court of Appeal that, while there is no presumption that, in the case of giving negligent advice, damage is presumed to occur at the time when the advice is acted upon, on the facts of the case damage occurred at the time of the execution of the restrictive covenant, since it was immediately less valuable than it would have been had it been correctly drafted.

Non-disclosure of material facts in insurance policy

Limitation problems have also arisen following the avoidance of insurance policies where the broker has negligently failed to disclose material facts. The courts have followed the approach of the Court of Appeal outlined above in relation to the negligent execution of documents by solicitors, holding that the damage occurred at the date of the execution of the voidable insurance policy, rather than at the date when the policy was avoided by the insurer.[34] The plaintiff, by virtue of entering into a voidable contract of insurance, suffered damage immediately and could have sustained an action against the broker.

No general rule as to accrual

However, the fact that the plaintiff has entered into a disadvantageous transaction as a result of relying on a negligent misstatement will not necessarily mean that a cause of action accrued upon the making of the statement: it will always be necessary to determine the point at which the plaintiff first suffered actual damage, *i.e.* the point at which he first had a sustainable claim against the maker of the statement.[35] In all the above cases the plaintiff suffered loss from the moment of the execution of the document, either because his property immediately became subject to a charge or because he obtained a voidable rather than a valid contract of insurance. In *UBAF Ltd.* v. *European American Banking Corp.*[36] the Court of Appeal, after consideration of a number of the above solicitors' negligence cases, came to the conclusion that the cause of action in such a situation will not necessarily accrue upon reliance on the negligent misstatement.

The plaintiff in the *UBAF* case, an English banking corporation, had relied on statements made by the defendant, a New York banking corporation, when deciding whether to participate in two loans which the defendant was intending to make to two Panamanian corporations. The Panamanian corporations defaulted on the loans with U.S.$880,000 owing to the plaintiff. The main representations as to the financial standing of the Panamanian corporations were made in a letter dated September 12, 1974, and, in reliance on that letter and

---

[34] *Iron Trade Mutual Insurance Co. Ltd.* v. *J.K. Buckenham Ltd.* [1990] 1 All E.R. 808; *Islander Trucking Ltd.* v. *Hogg Robinson & Gardener Mountain (Marine) Ltd.* [1990] 1 All E.R. 826.

[35] See the judgment of Neill L.J. in *D. W. Moore & Co. Ltd.* v. *Ferrier* [1988] 1 All E.R. 400 at pp. 409–410.

[36] [1984] 2 All E.R. 226.

other representations, the plaintiff lent U.S.$500,000 to each company. In October 1981 the plaintiff sought leave to issue and serve out of the jurisdiction a writ claiming damages against the New York corporation in respect of the alleged negligent misrepresentation. Ackner L.J. emphasised that "the mere fact that the innocent but negligent misrepresentations caused the plaintiff to enter into a contract which it otherwise would not have entered into does not inevitably mean that it had suffered damage by merely entering into the contract."[37] In *Forster* v. *Outred*[38] and *Baker* v. *Ollard & Bentley*[39] the negligent advice of the solicitors led in each case to the plaintiff entering into a transaction under which he immediately suffered a loss, albeit one which was not apparent and not immediately quantifiable. However, in the present case, Ackner L.J. was prepared to accept that evidence would need to be led in order to determine whether, at the date when the plaintiff advanced the money, the value of the chose in action which it then acquired was in fact less than the sum which the plaintiff lent. The mere fact that the defendant had misrepresented the true state of the Panamanian corporations' financial standing did not *necessarily* mean that loss was suffered upon reliance on the statements. A major contributing factor in the difficulties suffered by the Panamanian corporations was the collapse of the shipping market in 1975–76, and it was possible, though perhaps not probable, that without this additional factor the loans would have been repaid without any damage being suffered by the plaintiff.

The Latent Damage Act 1986

Accrual still on date of damage

The Latent Damage Act 1986 was enacted in response to criticism of the harshness of the rule laid down in *Pirelli* (that a cause of action in negligence accrues upon damage being suffered, irrespective of whether the plaintiff could reasonably have discovered that damage within the limitation period). The Act proceeds, not by altering the date of accrual of the cause of action or the length of the normal limitation period, but by adding an alternative three year limitation period which will run from the date of reasonable discoverability of the damage. The relevant provisions of the 1986 Act have been inserted into the Limitation Act 1980 as sections 14A and 14B. Section 14A is described in the 1980 Act as a "special time limit for negligence actions where facts relevant to cause of action are not known at date of accrual." In such cases there are now two alternative

Six year period and alternative three year period

limitation periods: the first is the normal six year period from the date on which the cause of action accrued (accrual remaining the same as it was in *Pirelli*), and the second is three years from the date of "knowledge" of the cause of action, where that period expires later than the normal six year period.[40]

Fifteen year longstop

In order to achieve a balance as between the interests of plaintiffs and defendants, the Act introduces a "longstop" limitation of 15 years: no action for damages for negligence

[37] [1984] 2 All E.R. 226 at pp. 234–235.
[38] [1982] 2 All E.R. 753, C.A.
[39] (1982) 126 S.J. 593, C.A.
[40] Limitation Act 1980, s.14A(4).

(other than for personal injury) may now be brought after the expiration of 15 years from the date on which the act or omission alleged to constitute negligence occurred. This longstop will apply regardless of whether the plaintiff's cause of action has yet accrued. Thus, in some situations the plaintiff will find that his position has been rendered considerably worse by the implementation of the Latent Damage Act, since his cause of action may be time-barred before any physical damage is suffered.

Action must not be barred at date of entry into force of Act

The Act will apply only where the plaintiff's cause of action was not already time-barred on the date of its entry into force: September 18, 1986. The plaintiff will, therefore, be required to establish that his cause of action arose on or after September 18, 1980.

By section 14A(1) the latent damage provisions may apply to "any action for damages for negligence" (other than an action seeking damages for personal injury). The Act does not define what is meant by an "action for damages for negligence" but it has recently been confirmed that the term will be interpreted narrowly and that an action framed in contract claiming damages in respect of a breach of a contractual duty to exercise care and skill will not fall within the scope of the provisions.[41] Similarly, the Act is unlikely to apply in those situations where a duty of care is imposed by statute. In order to avail himself of the alternative three year limitation period, the plaintiff must establish that his cause of action arises in the tort of negligence. The mere fact that the parties are in a contractual relationship will not necessarily preclude the establishment of a duty of care in tort and possible reliance on the latent damage provisions.[42]

Narrow interpretation of "negligence"

Act's scope not confined to building cases

Although the impetus for the legislation was the specific problem of latent damage in buildings, early decisions which sought to confine the scope of the Act to such situations have not been confirmed.[43] The Act may be used in all cases where the action is in negligence, the claim is for damages in respect of loss, whether economic or physical and is started within three years of the date of reasonable discoverability.

"Knowledge"

By section 14A(5) the starting date for the period of limitation is "the earliest date on which the plaintiff or any person in whom the cause of action was vested before him first had both the knowledge required for bringing such an action for damages in respect of the relevant damage and a right to bring such an action." "Knowledge" is further defined in section 14A (6) and (8) as knowledge of the material facts about the damage in respect of which damages are claimed and that the damage was attributable in whole or in part to the act or omission which is alleged to constitute negligence and the identity of the defendant. This definition of knowledge is similar to that contained in section 14 in relation to personal injury and it is likely that it will be interpreted in a similar manner.[44]

---

[41] *Iron Trade Mutual Insurance Co. Ltd.* v. *J.K. Buckenham Ltd.* [1990] 1 All E.R. 808; *Société Commerciale de Réassurance* v. *ERAS (International) Ltd.* [1992] 2 All E.R. 82.

[42] *Bell* v. *Peter Browne & Co.* [1990] 3 All E.R. 124.

[43] See particularly the discussion of the Court of Appeal in *Berg* v. *Glentworth Bulb Company Ltd.* July 25, 1988, C.A.; unrep.

[44] See further pp. 67–74.

"Material facts"

When seeking to ascertain the date on which the plaintiff first had the requisite degree of knowledge, it will be necessary to determine what are the "material facts", knowledge of which will start the running of time. Section 14A(7) provides that these are "such facts about the damage as would lead a reasonable person who had suffered such damage to consider it sufficiently serious to justify his instituting proceedings for damages against a defendant who did not dispute liability and was able to satisfy a judgment." Again, this provision is couched in identical wording to section 14 relating to the running of time in actions seeking damages in respect of personal injury. However, in a recent case it was held that a reasonable person may endure suffering of a more extensive nature in relation to personal injury than when financial expenditure is concerned.[45]

Surveyors and the Latent Damage Act

In *Horbury* v. *Craig Hall & Rutley* the plaintiff, the widow of a Baptist minister who had died suddenly leaving her with two small children, accepted the financial assistance of the London Baptist Association (LBA) in relation to the purchase of a house after she was obliged to leave the manse which the family had occupied rent-free. The LBA also provided the services of their solicitors and surveyors (the defendants). Contracts were exchanged on the property in November 1980 (the date of reliance on the survey), and the writ alleging negligence in the performance of the survey was issued in February 1988. The plaintiff was entitled to plead the provisions of the Latent Damage Act as her cause of action was not time-barred at the date of coming into force of the Act (September 18, 1986).

When would the reasonable person consider the damage sufficiently serious?

The first question which fell to be considered by the court was the date on which a reasonable person who had suffered such damage would consider it sufficiently serious to justify his instituting proceedings against a defendant who did not dispute liability and was able to satisfy a judgment. In April 1984 it had been brought to the attention of the plaintiff that the chimney breasts in the house were unsupported and consequently constituted a danger to herself and her children, clearly a fact which the defendants had overlooked in their survey of the premises. She was obliged to spend £132 in order to rectify the defects. It was held that, taking into account 1984 money values, a reasonable person in the plaintiff's circumstances would have considered the claim sufficiently serious to institute proceedings against a defendant who did not dispute liability, especially given the fact that she and her two children had been in danger of serious injury for two years. Although section 14A(7) appears to provide for an objective test (at what date would the reasonable person consider the damage sufficiently serious to

Objective or subjective test?

institute proceedings?) the judge applied a partially subjective test to the detriment of the plaintiff. This took into account the plaintiff's personal circumstances in relation to her lack of

[45] "Although personal injuries, when not severe, can be more important than 'mere' money, it is regarded as reasonable in this country at present to endure a moderate amount of pain without bringing an action unless financial loss results (that may change). On the other hand, when one is forced to pay out money which one has earned partly for the benefit of one's dependants, it is reasonable to be more ready to bring an action." *Horbury* v. *Craig Hall & Rutley* (1991) C.I.L.L. 692, *per* Judge Peter Bowsher Q.C.

resources and that she was a mother of young children, but it ignored the relationship which she had with the LBA, which had provided the services of the surveyors, and her own mentality which, whether for religious or other reasons, meant that she did not wish to institute proceedings to claim that amount. It was only when the full extent of the loss (some £56,500) became apparent in late 1985 that the plaintiff sought to bring her action against the surveyors.

The action was held to be time-barred under the provisions of the 1986 Act since the discovery of the damage in respect of which a reasonable person would have instituted proceedings occurred more than three years prior to the issue of the writ. On this reasoning, wealthy plaintiffs who can afford to lose several hundred pounds without undue worry may be protected as it would not be reasonable for them to start proceedings, while less affluent plaintiffs who are reluctant to have recourse to legal action may find that their action is time-barred. Either the section should be interpreted by the courts in a fully subjective manner (including the fact that for a plaintiff with some resources and thereby just preventing qualification for legal aid, an action against a defendant who does dispute liability may be almost impossible) so as to recognise that certain individuals may quite reasonably not commence proceedings in respect of minor damage, or in a fully objective manner, so that damage of a certain level would be recognised as actionable for all.

The plaintiff in *Horbury* sought to avoid the consequences of the finding that she had the necessary knowledge in 1984 following the discovery of the defective chimney breasts by arguing that she was not claiming in respect of the £132, but only in respect of the £56,500 which represented the loss incurred in rectifying extensive problems of dry rot. She further claimed that, as this damage could not reasonably have been discovered more than three years prior to the issue of the writ, she should be permitted to proceed with her action. The judge

Distinction between "damage" and "damages"

emphasised that it is essential to distinguish between "damage" and "damages". The plaintiff's case was not assisted by the fact that the damages in respect of which she was claiming were to compensate in respect of the dry rot which was discovered fewer than three years prior to the issue of the writ. The Act could not apply where the plaintiff had knowledge of the damage outside the three year period: damage in this context being the purchase of a property which would require substantial repair and maintenance work. In this respect the plaintiff had a single cause of action, despite the fact that the damage manifested itself in various different forms. She was consequently held to have had the knowledge of the relevant damage outside the limitation period laid down by the Act.

Date of reasonable discoverability

Section 14A(10) further provides that a person's knowledge must be taken to include knowledge which he might reasonably have been expected to acquire from facts observable or ascertainable by him, together with facts ascertainable by him with the help of appropriate expert advice which it would have been reasonable for him to seek. The test is therefore objective in that time may begin to run not from the date on which the damage was in fact discovered, but from the date when it could have been discovered. However, there is a subjective element since the court must consider when the plaintiff could reasonably have been expected to acquire the relevant knowledge. Differing criteria may apply to large organisations with plentiful resources, on the one hand, and individuals at the lower end of the housing market, on the other.[46]

Facts ascertainable with expert advice

In addition to knowledge of facts which the plaintiff could reasonably have been expected to observe for himself, the plaintiff will be fixed with knowledge of facts which were ascertainable by him with the help of appropriate expert advice which it would have been reasonable for him to seek. The stage at which it is reasonable to seek expert advice will be a question of fact in each case. However, where the loss in respect of which the plaintiff is claiming results from the negligence of an expert, there will be no expectation that he should have obtained independent advice in order to verify that the first expert has caused him no loss.[47] The obligation to consult a second expert will arise only once there has occurred some damage or other fact which would reasonably lead the plaintiff to suppose that the work of the first expert might have been defective in some way.

Trespass and false imprisonment

Three year limitation period

In an action for trespass to the person, the limitation period will be three years from the date on which the cause of action accrued, which, as trespass is actionable *per se*, will be the date of the trespass.[48] Where the plaintiff was unaware that damage had been suffered at the time of the tort, time will begin to run from the date when the plaintiff had the requisite knowledge.[49]

Continuing tort

An action for false imprisonment is actionable *per se*, and consequently the cause of action accrues upon the date of the imprisonment. However, for each day that the false imprisonment continues, a fresh cause of action will accrue.[50] The limitation period applicable is six years, rather than the shorter three years applicable in cases claiming damages for personal injury.

Defamation

Three year limitation period

In an action for defamation the limitation period is reduced to three years from the date of the accrual of the cause of action (section 4A Limitation Act 1980).[51] This date may differ

---

[46] See the comments of Lords Griffiths and Jauncey in *Smith* v. *Bush* [1990] 1 A.C. 831.

[47] See *Berg* v. *Glentworth Bulb Company Ltd.* July 25, 1988, C.A.; unrep.

[48] See *Letang* v. *Cooper* [1964] 2 All E.R. 929; *Stubbings* v. *Webb* [1991] 3 All E.R. 949, discussed in Chap. 6.

[49] Limitation Act 1980, s.14; in respect of the applicability of s.14 to actions for trespass to the person, see *Stubbings* v. *Webb* and Chap. 6.

[50] *Hardy* v. *Ryle* (1829) 9 B. & C. 603.

[51] This reduction was inserted by the Administration of Justice Act 1985, s.57(2), upon the recommendation of the Faulks Committee on Defamation Cmnd. 5909 (1975), and applies only to actions in defamation where the cause of action arose on or after December 30, 1985.

according to whether the action is in respect of libel or slander: the former is actionable without proof of damage and thus the cause of action accrues upon commission of the tort, *i.e.* on the publication of the libellous material. A new cause of action will accrue upon each publication.[52]

In most instances slander is actionable only upon proof of special damage,[53] and the cause of action will consequently accrue only once such damage has been sustained. However, in many cases the plaintiff will be unaware of the utterance of the slanderous statement and may not realise the damage which has been done to his reputation as a result thereof. Such ignorance will not prevent the running of time.

Discretionary extension

In order to assist the plaintiff against whom time has expired following publication of a defamatory statement of whose existence he was unaware, section 32A of the Act provides a discretionary extension of the three year time limit.[54] By section 32A(*a*) the extension will be one year from the earliest date on which the plaintiff knew all the facts relevant to the cause of action: but such an action may not be brought without the leave of the High Court.

In order to avail himself of this discretionary extension, the plaintiff must show that "all or any of the facts relevant to that cause of action did not become known to him until after the expiration of [the three year] period." The extension will be available only where the plaintiff discovered the cause of action after the expiry of the limitation period: if it is discovered a few days inside the limitation period, from the wording of the section there would be no room for exercise of the discretion.

There are as yet no reported cases on this section, but it is reasonable to suppose that the discretion will be exercised in those cases where the plaintiff became aware of the publication only once the limitation period had expired. The position is less clear in those situations where the plaintiff knew of the publication but failed to appreciate its defamatory nature: although there are no guidance provisions relating to the exercise of this discretion, as are provided in section 33, it is probable that, once it has been shown that the plaintiff knew of the existence of the publication and that it contained material which referred to him, the fact that he was either unaware of or failed to understand the defamatory nature of that publication will not be a "relevant fact" for the purposes of deciding whether or not to exercise the discretion. A more difficult situation will arise where the plaintiff becomes aware of the existence of a defamatory publication but, being confident that no damage has been caused, decides against incurring the expenditure involved

[52] *Duke of Brunswick* v. *Harmer* (1849) 14 Q.B. 185; on the question of what constitutes a publication for the purposes of the accrual of the cause of action, see *Clerk & Lindsell on Torts* (16th ed., 1989) at paras. 21–46 *et seq.*

[53] Slander will be actionable without proof of special damage where it imputes one of the following matters: a criminal offence punishable by a term of imprisonment, some disease which would have the effect of excluding the plaintiff from society, unchastity in a woman, or disparagement of the plaintiff in any office, profession, calling, trade or business held or carried on by him at the time of publication.

[54] This was again inserted by the Administration of Justice Act 1985, s.57(4), and as with s.4A, applies only in respect of actions where the cause of action accrued on or before December 30, 1985.

in a libel action. Some years later, without a fresh publication being made, the plaintiff may become aware that original publication has caused either financial loss or damage to reputation (for example, a job reference which has been kept on file by the original addressee, who acts on it only some years after receipt). In such a situation it may be argued that, since all the facts necessary for the bringing of an action were known to the plaintiff within the limitation period, the discretion should not be exercised, damage in this case not being a "relevant fact". Section 14A of the Act, as inserted by the Latent Damage Act 1986, would not assist the plaintiff here, as the section relates to latent damage caused by negligence.[55]

It is likely that the court will adopt a similar approach to that taken when exercising the discretionary exclusion of the time limit in respect of personal injuries or death[56] and conduct a balancing operation in order to determine the relative prejudice which would be suffered by the plaintiff if the extension were refused and by the defendant if it were granted.

Nuisance

A cause of action in nuisance will accrue once there has been an unlawful interference with the plaintiff's enjoyment of land; this interference may take the form of special damage to the structure of a building or disturbance by noise or smell. Where **Continuing tort** the nuisance continues over a period of time, a cause of action will accrue afresh on each day that the nuisance continues,[57] with damages being recoverable for all damage which has occurred within the six years prior to the issue of the writ. When calculating the damage caused by a disturbance such as smell, where part of the damage extends beyond the limitation period, it is submitted that the correct approach would be a mathematical one, with a certain amount being allowed in respect of each actionable year of damage. However, where **Calculation of** damage is to the structure of a building, the mathematical **damages** approach may prove to be inaccurate since the damage which is caused, for example by vibration, may be more substantial in the later years. In such a case, if the overall damage to a building over a period of 10 years amounts to £10,000, it may be permissible to award a sum considerably higher than the mere mathematical proportion of £6,000 since the damage which has occurred in each of the last six years may be considerably more than that which occurred in each of the first four years.[58]

Conversion

Conversion is "a wrongful interference with goods"[59] or "an act

---

[55] See further pp. 42 et seq.
[56] Limitation Act 1980, s.33; see further Chap. 7.
[57] *Masters* v. *Brent LBC* [1978] 1 Q.B. 841.
[58] See the method of calculation of damages for personal injury in *Berry* v. *Stone Manganese Marine Ltd*. [1972] 1 Lloyd's Rep. 182.
[59] Torts (Interference with Goods) Act 1977, s.1(*a*).

of deliberate dealing with a chattel in a manner inconsistent with another's right whereby that other is deprived of the use and possession of it."[60] By the Torts (Interference with Goods) Act 1977, conversion now includes all acts which would previously have been classified as detinue.[61] An infringement of copyright no longer amounts to conversion in English law.[62] The normal tortious limitation period of six years will apply and time will start to run from the date of the conversion.[63] However, in cases of conversion, it is necessary to read section 2 of the 1980 Act (which provides the six year period in tort actions) with sections 3 and 4, which provide special rules with regard to successive conversions and theft respectively.

Six year limitation period

Operation of the limitation period in conversion will serve to extinguish the plaintiff's title, not merely to bar his remedy.

Extinction of title

Section 3 of the 1980 Act provides that, where there have been successive conversions of the plaintiff's goods without the plaintiff recovering possession, time will not start to run afresh from the date of each subsequent conversion: subsequent converters may thus take advantage of the time which had run in favour of the previous converter. Thus, if Y converted X's goods in 1990, and in 1995 sold them to Z, Z would be guilty of conversion, but any action brought by X against Z would be time-barred in 1996, six years after the original conversion by Y.

Subsequent conversions

In the case of theft, special provisions apply. Theft is defined in section 4(5) in accordance with the Theft Act 1968[64] and will also include "any conduct outside England and Wales which would be theft if committed in England and Wales."[65] This is an important provision in the context of stolen goods, since in many instances the property will have been taken from its country of origin. The question of whether or not the original divesting of the owner of his property constituted theft is a question for the *lex fori*.[66] Section 4 of the 1980 Act has been described as "a paradigm of all that [is] wrong with domestic legislative drafting"[67]; it provides as follows:

Special provisions for theft

"(1) The right of any person from whom a chattel is stolen to bring an action in respect of the theft shall not be subject to the time limits under sections 2 and 3(1) of this Act, but if the title to the chattel is extinguished

---

[60] *Clerk & Lindsell on Torts* (16th ed., 1989), paras. 22–10 *et seq.*

[61] See *Howard E. Perry & Co.* v. *British Railways Board* [1980] 1 W.L.R. 1375.

[62] Section 18 of the Copyright Act 1956 has been repealed by the Copyright, Designs and Patents Act 1988, s.303, Sched. 8. However, in other common law jurisdictions where an infringement of copyright continues to constitute conversion, time will run from the date of marketing of infringing copies, not from the date of production or simple possession, see *Wham-O Manufacturing Co.* v. *Lincoln Industries Ltd.* [1985] R.P.C. 127, Court of Appeal (New Zealand).

[63] This will be so even though the plaintiff does not know the identity of the converter; the provisions of the Latent Damage Act 1986 are limited to actions in negligence and will not apply here. However, s.4 of the Limitation Act 1980 makes special provision in the case of theft.

[64] Under s.15(1) of the Theft Act 1968 a person is guilty of theft if he "dishonestly appropriates property belonging to another with the intention of permanently depriving the other of it."

[65] Limitation Act 1980, s.4(5)(*a*).

[66] See *Bumper Development Corp. Ltd.* v. *Commissioner of Police for the Metropolis* [1991] 4 All E.R. 638, C.A.

[67] [1980] *Current Law Statutes Annotated* c.58, Limitation Act 1980.

under section 3(2) of this Act he may not bring an action in respect of a theft preceding the loss of his title, unless the theft in question preceded the conversion from which time began to run for the purposes of section 3(2).

(2) Subsection (1) above shall apply to any conversion related to the theft of a chattel as it applies to the theft of a chattel; and, except as provided below, every conversion following the theft of a chattel before the person from whom it is stolen recovers possession of it shall be regarded for the purposes of this section as related to the theft.

If anyone purchases the stolen chattel in good faith neither the purchase nor any conversion following it shall be regarded as related to the theft."

Thief may not rely on limitation period

Section 4 reverses the previous law by providing that a thief may no longer rely on the limitation period in any action concerning theft of goods. Any person who subsequently acquires the stolen goods will be guilty of conversion as against the owner, and will similarly be unable to rely on the defence of limitation in an action brought by the owner of the goods.

Subsequent purchaser in good faith

However, an exception is made where the person who subsequently acquires the goods bought them in good faith, in which case the "chain" will be broken and the purchaser and subsequent converters may rely on the limitation period. In such a situation the limitation period will probably start to run in favour of the bona fide purchaser from the date of purchase, rather than any earlier date. The thief will never obtain the benefit of the limitation period and an action for the value of the goods will be possible even after they have been sold to a bona fide purchaser.

Some uncertainty exists as to whether the effect of the second part of section 4(1) is to preclude an action to recover the goods once title to the goods is considered to have expired under section 3(2), thereby limiting the owner to an action to recover the value of the goods from the thief or subsequent converter.[68] However, section 4(1) expressly states that the owner's "right" (which must logically include the right to recover the property) shall not be subject to the time limits laid down in sections 2 and 3(1): the six year limitation period simply does not apply, and the owner's right to recover the goods from the thief cannot be extinguished. It would be ridiculous if, for example, the owner of an extremely valuable old master, which he had refused to sell, could find his title to the painting extinguished by a theft, with his only remedy being an action to recover the value of the painting after the expiration of six years.

Right to recover goods from thief after six year period

Conversion followed by theft

Section 4(1) envisages a different scenario, one where the goods are originally converted in a non-theftuous manner (*i.e.* the converter deals with the goods in a manner inconsistent with the rights of the owner, but without a dishonest appropriation, intending permanently to deprive the owner) and are subsequently stolen without the owner regaining possession. Once six years have passed from the date of the conversion, the owner will lose his title to the goods to the converter (section

---

[68] See McGee, *Limitation Periods* (1990), pp. 183–184.

3(1) and 3(2)). Once title has been lost to the converter, there is clearly no title which can be asserted against the thief, unless the theft occurred prior to the conversion and thereby prevented title from being lost under section 3(2).

When considering the applicability of section 4, attention should be paid to the provisions of section 32(1)(*a*) and (*b*) which serve to postpone the running of time where the action is based upon the fraud of the defendant or where the defendant has deliberately concealed from the plaintiff any fact relevant to his right of action. In such a case, title to the goods will not be extinguished, and the period of limitation will not begin to run until the fraud or relevant facts are, or could reasonably have been, discovered.[69] In many cases, however, no relevant fact will have been concealed by the defendant so as to postpone the running of time, and the plaintiff's sole hope of recovery will be under section 4.[70]

Fraud and deliberate concealment

Breach of statutory duty

Tortious limitation period applies

The tortious limitation period will also apply in respect of actions for breach of statutory duty.[71]

Limitation periods imposed by statutes other than the Limitation Act

Defective Premises Act

The person who acquires a defectively constructed building will generally be unable to bring an action in tort against the builder in respect of the cost incurred in remedying the defects.[72] The Defective Premises Act 1972 provides an alternative form of action for householders (the statute does not protect the owners of non-residential buildings), but one in which the effective limitation period is considerably less generous than in tort. As in tort, the limitation period is six years, but unlike in a tort action, time will start to run against the plaintiff on the date when the dwelling was completed. Damage resulting from the defective work may not occur for some years after the completion of the dwelling, with the result that time may have expired under the Act before the plaintiff acquires a cause of action. The action will be available as against any "person taking on work for or in connection with the provision of a dwelling" and will include conversions and enlargements of dwellings.[73]

Six year limitation period

[69] *Eddis* v. *Chichester Constable* [1969] 2 Ch. 345, C.A.
[70] See *R.B. Policies at Lloyd's* v. *Butler* [1950] 1 K.B. 76, where the plaintiff was unsuccessful in an action to recover a stolen car; the plaintiff relied on the equivalent in the Limitation Act 1939 to s.32, but failed as the thief had not concealed any fact relevant to the plaintiff's cause of action.
[71] *Clarkson* v. *Modern Foundries Ltd.* [1957] 1 W.L.R. 1210.
[72] *Murphy* v. *Brentwood D.C.* [1990] 2 All E.R. 908; *D. & F. Estates* v. *Church Commissioners for England* [1988] 3 W.L.R. 368.
[73] Defective Premises Act 1972, s.1(1).

Consumer Protection Act 1987

By section 6(6) of and Schedule I to the Consumer Protection Act 1987, a new section 11A is inserted into the 1980 Act which has the effect of modifying the limitation periods which would normally apply in tort. Two new time limits now apply to all actions brought under Part I (which imposes strict liability in respect of damage caused by defective products) of the 1987 Act, with no distinction being made according to whether the damage suffered is property damage or personal injury.

No distinction property damage/ personal injury

Three year limitation period

Section 11A(4) imposes a three year limitation period in respect of actions seeking damages under the 1987 Act for either personal injury or property damage. Time will start to run from whichever is the later of two dates: first, the date on which the cause of action accrued or secondly, the date of knowledge of the injured person or, in the case of loss of or damage to property, the date of knowledge of the plaintiff or (if earlier) of any person in whom his cause of action was previously vested. The limitation period in respect of property damage is thus considerably reduced where the plaintiff seeks to rely on the 1987 Act.

"Knowledge"

Under section 14A, references to a person's date of knowledge are references to the date on which he first had knowledge of the following facts:

(a) such facts about the damage caused by the defect as would lead a reasonable person who has suffered such damage to consider it sufficiently serious to justify his instituting proceedings against a defendant who did not dispute liability and was able to satisfy a judgment; and

(b) that the damage was wholly or partly attributable to the facts and circumstances alleged to constitute the defect; and

(c) the identity of the defendant.

Ten year longstop

Section 11A(3) imposes a "longstop" limitation period of 10 years from the date when the defective product was supplied by the producer (or, in the case of electricity, the time at which it was generated, *i.e.* before it was transmitted or distributed), own-brander or importer,[74] the effect of which may be to time-bar an action before the cause of action has even accrued. The longstop starts to run on the date when the particular product which has caused the damage was supplied, not on the date when the producer ceased supplying products of that type. Where the longstop applies, it will not be possible to argue that the damage was not discoverable within the 10 years, or even that damage was suffered only once the 10 years had passed. In cases of damage caused by certain drugs or asbestos the plaintiff may be obliged to avail himself of the more generous limitation period allowed in an ordinary tort action,[75] where it will of course be necessary to establish fault on the part of the defendant, unlike an action under the 1987 Act.

The running of time under the Consumer Protection Act

---

[74] See s.4 of the Consumer Protection Act 1987.
[75] Limitation Act 1980, ss.11 and 14.

Fraud, concealment and mistake subject to longstop may be postponed where there had been fraud, concealment or mistake,[76] but not where this would have the effect of permitting an action to be brought more than 10 years after the product was supplied. Similarly, the court has a discretion to exclude the three year limitation period in respect of personal injuries, but again this will not be applied so as to defeat the longstop.

Carriage statutes

Shorter limitation periods Tortious actions brought in respect of personal injury or property damage incurred in the course of international transport, will be subject to the generally shorter limitation periods provided for by the relevant international convention.[77]

---

[76] *Ibid.* s.32(4A); see further Chap. 3.
[77] See Appendix I: Table of Limitation Periods. A limitation period of two years in respect of personal injury is laid down by the Maritime Conventions Act 1911 where the injury arises from a "collision between vessels". A jet-ski is not a vessel for these purposes (*Steadman* v. *Scholfield, The Times*, April 15, 1992) and neither is a sailing dinghy used on a reservoir for pleasure (*Curtis* v. *Wild* [1991] 4 All E.R. 172).

6 PERSONAL INJURY ACTIONS

The limitation period in respect of personal injury actions is three years: Limitation Act 1980, section 11(4). The usual time limits relating to actions in contract or tort do not apply here (*i.e.* the generally longer periods laid down in sections 2–10 of the 1980 Act).[1] However, it should be noted that in some instances a shorter limitation period may be applicable by virtue of statute.[2] The three year time limit is stated to apply: "to any action for damages for negligence, nuisance or breach of duty (whether the duty exists by virtue of a contract or of provision made by or under a statute or independently of any contract or any such provision)..."

Shorter limitation period

It was argued in *Letang* v. *Cooper*[3] that this wording did not cover an action for trespass to the person, and that the time-bar for such an action remained six years, as it was prior to the 1954 legislation. In the Court of Appeal Lord Denning M.R. pointed to the absurd consequences to which such a distinction would give rise, and stated that the words "breach of duty" will "cover not only a breach of a contractual duty, or a statutory duty, but also a breach of any duty under the law of tort ... [and] are wide enough to comprehend the cause of action for trespass to the person as well as negligence."[4]

Wide applicability of section 11

The question arose again in *Long* v. *Hepworth*[5] where, unlike *Letang* v. *Cooper* the injuries inflicted by the defendant were intentional rather than merely negligent. The plaintiff's contention that an intentional trespass to the person is not a breach of duty within the meaning of the provision was rejected by Cooke J. on the basis that neither of the authorities relied on by the defendant interpreted the term "breach of duty" so as to exclude an intentional trespass to the person.[6]

It is therefore clear that the period of limitation is three years in all personal injury actions other than those for which a shorter period is prescribed by statute.[7]

Definition of personal injury

Under section 38(1) of the Act the term "personal injuries" includes "any disease and any impairment of a person's physical

---

[1] Under the Limitation Act 1939 the period of limitation was six years in all actions founded "on tort", but the Law Reform (Limitation of Action, etc.) Act 1954 reduced this period to three years.
[2] Article 29(1) of Schedule I to the Carriage by Air Act 1961 provides that the right to damages under the Warsaw Convention as amended at The Hague is extinguished if an action is not brought within two years.
[3] [1965] 1 Q.B. 232; [1964] 2 All E.R. 929.
[4] [1965] 1 Q.B. 232 at 241; [1964] 2 All E.R. 929 at 933.
[5] [1968] 1 W.L.R. 1299; [1968] 3 All E.R. 248.
[6] See also *Billings* v. *Reed* [1945] K.B. 11; [1944] 2 All E.R. 415.
[7] The argument that the six year limitation period should apply in cases of trespass to the person was recently canvassed before the Court of Appeal in

or mental condition." In addition to physical injury and illness, the term will be interpreted as covering psychiatric illness and nervous shock.[8] Any action in respect of a tort or breach of contract which is alleged to have had such an effect must be brought within the three year period.

Cumulative injury Where personal injury has been suffered on a cumulative basis over a number of years (*e.g.* progressive deafness caused by an employer's failure to provide adequate protection for the hearing of his workers) with some of that time falling outside the limitation period, damage will be recoverable only in respect of that damage which can be shown to have occurred within the limitation period.[9]

Mental distress Damages may also be available in tort in respect of mental distress as distinct from nervous shock: the courts have awarded mental distress damages in actions for deceit,[10] for the negligent performance of a survey,[11] for wrongful repossession under a hire-purchase agreement,[12] for loss of a holiday following a road accident[13] and for negligent loss of goods by a bailee.[14] However, there is generally no right to recover damages in tort in respect of the grief and anguish suffered in respect of seeing a spouse or child injured or killed.[15]

In recent years damages have occasionally been awarded in contract to compensate for the mental distress and disappointment suffered by the plaintiff as a result of the defendant's breach. Such damages will be available only where the purpose of the contract was "to provide peace of mind or freedom from distress"[16] or to provide some form of enjoyment or entertainment[17] and will not generally be available where the contract is commercial in nature.[18]

Distinction between mental distress and personal injury While there is no authority on the point, the approach which the courts are likely to adopt in an action for damages for mental distress in both contract and tort is to consider that mental distress and disappointment fall outside the scope of personal injury. The limitation period in such cases, where there is no claim for other personal injury, is thus likely to be six rather than three years. Care will need to be taken in

Stubbings v. *Webb* [1991] 3 All E.R. 949, C.A. and was roundly rejected by Bingham L.J. at p. 952.

[8] For discussions of the definition of nervous shock, see *Clerk and Lindsell on Torts* (16th ed., 1989), pp. 437–443.

[9] *Berry* v. *Stone Manganese Marine Ltd.* [1971] 115 S.J. 966; [1972] 1 Lloyd's Rep. 182.

[10] See *Archer* v. *Brown* [1985] Q.B. 401; [1984] 2 All E.R. 267; *Shelley* v. *Paddock* [1980] Q.B. 348; [1980] 1 All E.R. 1009.

[11] *Perry* v. *Phillips (Sidney) & Son (A Firm)* [1982] 1 W.L.R. 1297. However, following the recent decision of the Court of Appeal in *Watts* v. *Morrow* (1991) 141 New L.J. 1331, the availability of damages for mental distress in such situations is now likely to be restricted.

[12] *Harris* v. *Lombard (New Zealand) Ltd.* [1974] 2 N.Z.L.R. 161.

[13] *Ichard* v. *Frangoulis* [1977] 1 W.L.R. 556; [1977] 2 All E.R. 461.

[14] *Graham* v. *Voigt* 89 A.C.T.R. 11.

[15] See, *inter alia, Dulieu* v. *White* [1901] 2 K.B. 669; *Hinz* v. *Berry* [1970] 2 Q.B. 40.

[16] *Bliss* v. *South East Thames Regional Health Authority* [1987] I.C.R. 700 at 718; see also *Heywood* v. *Wellers* [1976] Q.B. 446; and *Watts* v. *Morrow* [1991] 4 All E.R. 937.

[17] See *Jarvis* v. *Swans Tours Ltd.* [1973] Q.B. 233; *Jackson* v. *Horizon Holidays Ltd.* [1975] 1 W.L.R. 1468. See also *Ichard* v. *Frangoulis* (above, n. 13) for a discussion of the appropriate measure of damages where the defendant's tortious act causes the plaintiff to lose his holiday.

[18] *Hayes* v. *Dodd* [1990] 2 All E.R. 815, C.A.

determining whether the plaintiff's mental distress is indicative merely of disappointment and vexation or whether it should be classified as a form of mental illness.

Direct claims for compensation for personal injury

The three year limitation period applies only in respect of claims which directly seek compensation for personal injury. Where the plaintiff alleges that the defendant's breach of contract or negligent act has caused him to lose the right to obtain compensation for his injury from a third party, the normal limitation period will apply. Thus in *Ackbar* v. *C. F. Green & Co. Ltd.*[19] the plaintiff purchased a lorry and instructed the defendant insurance brokers to insure the lorry with cover for passenger liability. This they failed to do, unknown to the plaintiff, who was subsequently injured when travelling as a passenger in the lorry. He brought an action against the insurance brokers less than six years but more than three years after the date of the breach of contract. The defendants argued that the action was time-barred since it was an action for breach of duty where the damages claimed "consisted of or included damages for personal injuries" (see section 11(1) of the Act). It was held that, upon a proper construction of the relevant section, the only actions which are time-barred after a period of three years are those which seek damages for, in the sense of the defendant having caused the personal injuries. In this case, the plaintiff was seeking compensation in respect of the loss of the chance or the right to recover such compensation from the insurers. Section 11 was therefore not applicable and the limitation period was six years.

A similar result was reached in the Scots case of *McGahie* v. *Union of Shop, Distributive, and Allied Workers*[20] where a woman sued her trade union for failure to pursue a claim for compensation for personal injury against her employers on her behalf. It was held that, although the evaluation of the damages to be awarded in respect of the union's failure would necessarily include consideration of the nature and extent of the personal injuries suffered by the plaintiff, the real loss for which compensation was now sought was the loss of the chance to sue her employers in respect of the injury.

Employers and defective machinery

Where an employer brings an action in respect of loss of profit following personal injury to an employee caused by a defective piece of machinery, that action will be classified as an action claiming damages for personal injury, and the above cases will not apply.[21] The limitation period in respect of the employer's claim will be three years rather than six.

The running of time

In an action for personal injuries time begins to run from:

"(a) the date on which the cause of action accrued; or
(b) the date of knowledge (if later) of the person injured."
(Section 11(4))

---

[19] [1975] Q.B. 582.
[20] 1966 S.L.T. 74.
[21] *Howe* v. *David Brown Tractors (Retail) Ltd.* [1991] 4 All E.R. 30, C.A.

Accrual of the cause of action

Date of injury The cause of action will be held to have accrued on the date on which plaintiff has suffered personal injury beyond that which can be regarded as negligible, even when that injury is unknown to and cannot be discovered by the sufferer. Under the Limitation Act 1939 the plaintiff's action was time-barred upon the elapsing of the stipulated period (then six years), with no provision being made for those cases where the plaintiff could not have known of the existence of the damage until after the passing of the limitation period. The injustice of this rule was

Injustice of old rule recognised by the House of Lords in *Cartledge* v. *E. Jopling & Sons Ltd.*[22] where the plaintiff contracted pneumoconiosis as a result of the failure of his employers to provide effective ventilation in his workplace, a failure which constituted a breach of the Factories Act 1937. This breach ceased in 1950, by which time the plaintiff was already afflicted with the disease, although the symptoms had not yet made themselves felt. It was held that the action which he commenced more than three years after the cessation of the breach was time-barred since time, under the 1939 Act, could not be interpreted to run from the date when the plaintiff knew or ought to have known that he was suffering from pneumoconiosis, but must be read as running from the date on which material injury was in fact suffered, whether the plaintiff was aware of this fact or not. All the members of the House of Lords expressed their regret at being obliged to come to this conclusion and called for a speedy amendment of the law in this area.

Parliament reacted swiftly to this plea and enacted the Limitation Act 1963 which sought to remove the injustice of the situation which arose in *Cartledge* v. *Jopling*. Section 11(4)(*b*) of the 1980 Act is now the relevant provision where the plaintiff is unaware that he has suffered injury; it states that an action shall not be brought after the expiration of three years from the date of knowledge (if this is later than the date of accrual) of the person injured. It is therefore necessary to determine what precisely is meant by knowledge.

Knowledge on the part of the plaintiff

Definition of date of knowledge Section 14 defines the date of knowledge for the purpose of applying the three year limitation period in section 11. By subsection(1):

> "references to a person's date of knowledge are references to the date on which he first had knowledge of the following facts:
> (a) that the injury in question was significant; and
> (b) that the injury was attributable in whole or in part to the act or omission which is alleged to constitute negligence, nuisance or breach of duty; and
> (c) the identity of the defendant; and
> (d) if it is alleged that the act or omission was that of a person other than the defendant, the identity of that

[22] [1963] A.C. 758, H.L. See also *Archer* v. *Catton & Co. Ltd.* [1954] 1 W.L.R. 775.

person and the additional facts supporting the bringing
of an action against the defendant;
and knowledge that any acts or omissions did or did not, as
a matter of law, involve negligence, nuisance or breach of
duty is irrelevant."

Section 14(3) further defines knowledge, providing:

". . . a person's knowledge includes knowledge which he
might reasonably have been expected to acquire
(a) from facts observable or ascertainable by him; or
(b) from facts ascertainable by him with the help of medical
or other appropriate expert advice which it is reasonable
for him to seek;
but a person shall not be fixed under this subsection with
knowledge of a fact ascertainable only with the help of
expert advice so long as he has taken all reasonable steps to
obtain (and, where appropriate, act upon) that advice."

What the plaintiff should know   Before time starts to run against the plaintiff, he should be
aware of certain material facts: he must *know* that he has a
significant injury which was *attributable to some act or omission* of
the defendant. Lack of knowledge that the act or omission in
question did in fact constitute negligence or breach of duty is
clearly not now a circumstance to be taken into account when
deciding whether or not time has started to run.[23] The
knowledge in question may be actual or constructive, in that it
may be ascertainable only with the help of medical or other
expert advice (not including legal advice), where it is reasonable
to seek such advice.

The precise meaning to be given to the word "knowledge"
has been discussed in a number of cases. In *Davis* v. *Ministry of
Defence*[24] May L.J. stated: "Knowledge is an ordinary English
word with a clear meaning to which one must give full effect:
'reasonable belief' or 'suspicion' is not enough."

Belief is not sufficient   The fact that the plaintiff in *Davis* had believed strongly for
a period of some 10 years before the commencement of
proceedings that his dermatitis had been caused by his working
conditions and that he had a strong claim for damages against
his employers was not sufficient to bar his claim, since for some
time he did not *know* that this was the case. Similarly, in *Stephen*
v. *Riverside Health Authority*[25] it was held that even where the
plaintiff had some degree of professional knowledge which led
her to realise that damage may have been caused (she had
completed part of her training as a radiographer and was injured
by what she perceived at the time to be an overdose of X-rays),

[23] Certain older cases which were decided on this basis must now be held to have
been overruled by the current legislation; in particular *Skingsley* v. *Cape
Asbestos Co. Ltd.* [1968] 2 Lloyd's Rep. 201; *Newton* v. *Cammell Laird Ltd.*
[1969] 1 W.L.R. 415; and *Smith* v. *Central Asbestos Co. Ltd.* [1972] 1 Q.B. 244
where the House of Lords held by a majority that, given the somewhat
ambiguous wording of the former legislation, Parliament intended that the
plaintiff's ignorance of his legal rights should be treated in the same way as his
ignorance of any other material fact. The minority view (Lords Simon and
Salmon) that the fact the plaintiff has or does not have knowledge that he has a
cause of action for negligence or breach of duty is not a material fact, was
subsequently confirmed in the 1980 Limitation Act.
[24] *The Times*, August 7, 1985, C.A.
[25] *The Times*, November 29 and November 24, 1989, *per* Auld J.

the ensuing anxiety which she experienced could not amount to "knowledge" within the meaning of section 14(1) since all the doctors and consultants connected with her case assured her that her symptoms were not related to the allegedly negligent act.

Knowledge of particular act or omission

In order that time should start to run against the plaintiff, it is not enough that he should be aware that he has been injured and that his injury resulted from some act or omission of the defendant. He should know (section 14(1)(b)) "that the injury was attributable in whole or in part to the act or omission which is alleged to constitute negligence . . . or breach of duty." He should be in a position to point to a particular act or series of acts, and time will not start to run merely because he is aware that the defendant, by some aspect of his conduct, must have caused the injury.

"Attributable"

"Capable of being attributed to"

The term "attributable" should be read as meaning "capable of being attributed to" rather than "caused by".[26] The court requires the plaintiff to have knowledge of the likely or possible, rather than the actual, cause of his injury: to read "attributable" in this context as meaning "caused by" could have the result that, in certain difficult cases, time might not start to run until the actual judgment of the action itself![27] It is not even necessary that the act or omission at issue should be "reasonably likely" to have caused the injury:

> "interpreting the word 'attributable' as meaning 'capable of being attributed,' . . . that phrase means that attribution is merely possible, a real possibility and not a fanciful one. The act or omission of the defendant must be a possible cause as opposed to a probable cause of the injury. One is dealing here with knowledge, actual or imputed, and not with proof of liability."[28]

"The act or omission"

Degree of knowledge required

It is necessary that the plaintiff should be able to identify the particular act or omission which is alleged to constitute negligence or breach of duty. He should know that his injury was capable of being attributed in whole or in part to the very act or omission which his lawyers say in his eventual action constitutes negligence or breach of duty: there should be an identity between the act or omission of which the plaintiff has knowledge and that upon which his case in negligence or breach of duty is eventually brought.[29] However, this does not mean that time will not start running against him until such date as he has the precise knowledge which would enable him or his legal advisers to draft a fully and comprehensively particularised statement of claim.[30] In many cases the plaintiff will have a

---

[26] *Davis* v. *Ministry of Defence, The Times*, August 7, 1985, C.A.; *Wilkinson* v. *Ancliff (BLT) Ltd.* [1986] 3 All E.R. 427.

[27] See May L.J. in *Davis* v. *Ministry of Defence.*

[28] *Guidera* v. *NEI Projects (India)*, January 30, 1990, C.A.; unrep., *per* Sir David Croom-Johnson in a judgment with which Slade L.J. and Mann L.J. agreed.

[29] *Nash* v. *Eli Lilly* [1991] 2 Med LR 169.

[30] *Wilkinson* v. *Ancliff (BLT) Ltd.* [1986] 3 All E.R. 427 at 438, *per* May L.J.

rough idea of how his injury was caused, such that he will be justified in consulting a solicitor and other advisers, but the details of his claim will emerge only after investigation and correspondence with experts and the defendant himself. At what stage, then, in this gradual discovery of relevant facts, will time start to run?

Two categories of situation

When considering the question of the act or omission which is alleged to constitute negligence, a distinction may be drawn between two broad categories of case. On the one hand, there are those situations where the plaintiff has experienced injury unexpectedly: a car accident or an accident at work; here it is necessary only that the plaintiff has "broad knowledge" that his injury was due to the way in which the car was driven or to dangerous working conditions.[31] The alternative scenario is where the plaintiff is already ill or in some way injured and then suffers further injury following either a surgical operation or the ingestion of drugs. Here the plaintiff has consented to the general act which has caused the injury and consequently it is necessary that he should have more than a broad knowledge of what went wrong. The point was considered in some detail in *Davis* v. *City & Hackney Health Authority*[32] and *Nash* v. *Eli Lilly*.[33]

The specific act

In *Davis* the plaintiff was a younger twin; the elder twin had been born without any complications, but it was apparent that something had occurred either during or immediately before the birth of the plaintiff to cause him to become spastic. The plaintiff's mother, and through her, the plaintiff himself, had possessed this broad knowledge from the time of the birth, but did not know the precise nature of the act or omission of the hospital which caused the spasticity: it was only a considerable time later that it was revealed that the precise cause was an injection administered to the mother between the two births of a drug called Ovametrin. The judge held that the act or omission of which the plaintiff was required to have knowledge in order to start time running was in this case knowledge of the injection of the drug rather than knowledge that something had gone wrong in the handling of the birth.

In *Nash*, where the plaintiffs had suffered injury following the ingestion of the anti-arthritis drug Opren, Hidden J., after listening to considerable argument on both sides as well as conducting his own careful analysis of a number of other drugs and hospital cases,[34] concluded that, when considering the act of which knowledge is required: "there must be a degree of specificity and not a mere global or catch-all character about the act or omission." The act was not the putting into circulation a drug which was defective: knowledge of something more specific was required; however, it was not necessary that the plaintiffs should be able to list all the acts or omissions which were finally to be listed in the pleadings.

---

[31] See *Wilkinson* v. *Ancliff*. (See above, n. 26).
[32] *The Times*, January 27, 1989, *per* Jowitt J.
[33] [1991] 2 Med LR 169, *per* Hidden J.
[34] See, *inter alia*, *Driscoll-Varley* v. *Parkside Health Authority*, January 15, 1990; unrep., *per* Hidden J.; *Bentley* v. *Bristol & Western Health Authority*, *The Times*, December 6, 1990, *per* Hirst J.

Significance of the injury

Under section 14(2) an injury is "significant if the person whose date of knowledge is in question would reasonably have considered it sufficiently serious to justify his instituting proceedings against a defendant who did dispute liability and was able to satisfy a judgment."

Objective/ subjective test

The test is partly objective, in that it requires the conduct of the plaintiff to be judged as against what is considered to be reasonable, and partly subjective, in that the reasonableness of the plaintiff's conduct is to be judged according to the plaintiff's own particular circumstances.

The reasonable plaintiff

The plaintiff should not be judged as against a litigious person, someone who is ready to issue a writ for the slightest injury,[35] so that, although the damage to the plaintiff's health may have manifested itself on a particular date and may even have been sufficiently serious to have enabled the plaintiff to obtain damages in respect of it, time will not begin to run until the plaintiff would "reasonably have considered it sufficiently serious to justify his instituting proceedings." Once the injury is of a sufficiently serious level, time will start to run; however, the plaintiff's reluctance to sue in respect of a relatively minor, but clearly actionable, injury may be a factor which the court will take into account when considering whether or not to exercise its discretion to exclude the limitation period under section 33.[36]

Identity of the defendant

Hit and run accidents

Where the plaintiff is injured in an accident in which the identity of the perpetrator is unknown, *e.g.* a hit and run accident, time will not start to run in an action against the perpetrator until such time as he is identified or could reasonably have been identified.[37]

Harmful drugs

Similar considerations may arise in the case of harmful drugs where the defendant could be one of a number of manufacturers who had manufactured the drug in a given period.[38]

Corporate groups

Occasionally, in the case of corporate defendants, it may be difficult to ascertain the identity of a particular defendant within a group of companies.[39] In such a situation, provided the

---

[35] *Woods* v. *Att.-Gen.*, July 18, 1990; unrep., *per* McPherson J.; see also *Young* v. *G.L.C. and Massey*, December 19, 1986; unrep., *per* Owen J.

[36] See *McCafferty* v. *Metropolitan Police District Receiver* [1977] 2 All E.R. 756; and below, p. 83.

[37] However, where the victim of such a hit and run accident chooses instead to sue the Motor Insurers' Bureau under the Uninsured Drivers' Agreement, time will start to run immediately as the identity of the defendant, the M.I.B., is known. It is possible that where an action is ultimately brought against the M.I.B. after time has been spent in a reasonable but fruitless search for the perpetrator it may be a relevant circumstance under s.33 where the court is asked to exercise its discretion to exclude the three year limit.

[38] See, for example, the difficulties encountered by the plaintiffs injured by the drug diethylstilbestrol (DES), a synthetic hormone manufactured by hundreds of drugs companies in the United States and widely prescribed between 1947 and 1971 to pregnant women to prevent miscarriage, and which was subsequently found to cause internal deformities and, ultimately, cancer in the daughters of women who had taken the drug, described in Redmond-Cooper, "Product liability—Problems of the unknown defendant" (1986) S.J. 621.

[39] *Simpson* v. *Norwest Holst Southern Ltd.* [1980] 2 All E.R. 471.

plaintiff has done all that he reasonably could to identify the particular company responsible for his injury, time will not start to run against him. Where an action is commenced against a named company, and the plaintiff subsequently discovers that the company had gone into liquidation and consequently no longer exists, section 651 of the Companies Act 1985, as amended by section 141 of the Companies Act 1989, allows for an application to be made by any interested person (which includes the plaintiff in a personal injuries action) to ask the court to make an order declaring the dissolution to have been void. Upon the making of such an order, an action may be brought against the company in the normal manner. Such an order will not normally be made more than two years after the date of the dissolution of the company. However, an exception may be made in the case of a personal injuries action where section 33 of the Limitation Act 1980 may apply.[40]

Constructive knowledge

Subjective test of constructive knowledge

It is clear from section 14(3) that knowledge need not be actual, but may be constructive, since a person's knowledge includes facts which could have been ascertained with the help of medical advice, where it was reasonable for him to seek such advice. The test here is an objective one, but it was held in *Davis* v. *City & Hackney Health Authority*[41] that it must be applied to the kind of plaintiff in question, taking account of his disability, age, intelligence and circumstances. It has been stated that "you do not ask: at what date would a *reasonable person* have taken advice? You ask: at what date was it reasonable for *this man* to take it?"[42] and in answering that question the circumstances of the plaintiff's illness should be taken into account. Thus, in *Stubbings* v. *Webb*[43] where the plaintiff had been sexually abused as a child, but sought to bring an action in respect of the mental illness and psychological disturbance some nine years after attaining her majority, it was held that "mental impairment caused as this allegedly was almost necessarily produces a lack of insight" and that the plaintiff's failure to seek expert medical advice on the possible existence of a causal link should not be held against her since "unless she suspected such a link she could not reasonably be expected to do so."[44]

Failure to seek medical advice

Difficulties may arise where the court considers that the plaintiff has acted unreasonably in refusing to seek medical advice in respect of an illness or injury where he mistakenly believed both that his symptoms could not be alleviated and that the cause was natural. The imposition of a purely objective test in such circumstances may be unduly harsh towards the plaintiff, but at the same time it should be remembered that the primary purpose of enforcing limitation periods is to protect the defendant against stale claims. In order to ensure justice for both

---

[40] *Re Workvale Ltd.* [1992] 2 All E.R. 627, C.A.
[41] *The Times*, January 27, 1989, *per* Jowitt J.
[42] *Newton* v. *Cammell Laird Ltd.* [1969] 1 W.L.R. 415, *per* Lord Denning at p. 419.
[43] [1991] 3 All E.R. 949.
[44] *Per* Bingham L.J. at p. 955.

parties, the court may well prefer to declare such an action prima facie time-barred, but then proceed to consider the exercise of its discretion under section 33 to exclude the time limit where this would appear to be equitable.[45] It is perhaps useful at this stage to consider separately the issues of legal advice and medical advice, since differing factual matrices will apply in each case.

Legal advice

The fact that the plaintiff is not aware that the defendant's act or omission constituted negligence or a breach of duty is not a material circumstance when considering whether or not time has started to run against him.[46] A party's solicitor is not to be regarded as an expert within the meaning of section 14(3)(b).[47]

Limited relevance of legal advice

However, this does not mean to say that the taking of legal advice will never be relevant when determining the question of when time starts to run. In some instances the plaintiff may have only a vague idea of how his injury was caused, and in order to obtain the full facts it may be necessary to obtain discovery of certain documents—in such cases time may not start to run till the plaintiff has acquired the knowledge which discovery of those documents will give him. It is then necessary to consider at what stage it was appropriate for him to seek expert legal advice with a view to determining the precise cause of his injury.[48]

This question was considered in *Davis* v. *City & Hackney Health Authority*[49] where the negligence of the defendant at the time of the plaintiff's birth had caused him to be spastic. It was found that the plaintiff's mother was averse to him taking legal action and consequently it would not have been reasonable to expect him to seek such advice while he was still living with his parents and dependent upon their care and attention. Moreover, once he left the parental home to live in a centre for disabled people, the judge considered it necessary to take into account the problems which he undoubtedly experienced in settling in to the new environment. Thus, time did not start to run until such time as it was reasonable for the plaintiff, taking into account his personal circumstances, to take the legal advice which would enable him to know the cause of his accident.

It is possible that the plaintiff may have delayed seeking legal advice in the mistaken belief that no liability could arise since the defendant had prominently displayed at the scene of the accident a wide disclaimer clause (contrary to the Unfair Contract Terms Act 1977). In such a situation, time would probably continue to run, but the invalid disclaimer would constitute a strong factor to be taken into account under section 33 (see Chap. 7). Alternatively, the court may consider that the disclaimer operates as a deliberate concealment of the plaintiff's

Disclaimers and personal injury

[45] See below, Chap. 7.
[46] See above, n. 18.
[47] *Fowell* v. *N.C.B.*, *The Times*, May 28, 1986, C.A.
[48] In relation to the precise facts of which the plaintiff should have knowledge before time starts to run, see above, pp. 67–74.
[49] See above, n. 41.

cause of action, with the result that the running of time is postponed under section 32. (See further Chap. 3).

Medical advice

Taking of reasonable steps

Time will start to run against the plaintiff from the date on which he could, by taking appropriate medical advice, have ascertained the cause of his injury. However, it is clear from section 14(3) that time should not start to run against a plaintiff where he has taken all reasonable steps, including asking specific questions as to whether a previous accident could have caused the present injury, in seeking to obtain medical advice in respect of a fact which is ascertainable only with such help, if the advice given has, for some reason, failed to provide the plaintiff with the information necessary to found his action.[50] This would appear to be so whether the doctor negligently misinterprets the results of an X-ray or takes a conscious decision that the true state of the plaintiff's health should be kept from him.[51]

Criminal injuries compensation

Payments made by the Criminal Injuries Compensation Board are regulated by Schedule 7 to the Criminal Justice Act 1988. Paragraph 2(a) provides that, unless the circumstances of the case appear to them to be exceptional, the Board shall not determine a claim in respect of which they have not previously awarded compensation after the end of three years from the date of the incident giving rise to the injury. Where an award has previously been made by the Board in respect of an injury, the claim is not to be determined after a period of three years from the date of the notice relating to the award (paragraph 2(b)). However, where the Board has previously made an award specifically recognising that a particular medical condition may arise in the future as a result of the injury in question, paragraph 3 obliges the Board to determine a claim based upon such a condition whenever it may arise in the future.

---

[50] See the comments of Leggatt L.J. in *Newman* v. *Bevan Funnell Ltd.*, October 29, 1990, C.A.; unrep. See also *Young* v. *G.L.C. and Massey* (above, n. 33).
[51] It should be noted that the position is different in relation to negligent advice by a solicitor with regard to the bringing of the action: here time is considered to continue running against the plaintiff and a cause of action in negligence will lie against the solicitor: see *Donovan* v. *Gwentoys Ltd.* [1990] 1 W.L.R. 472; [1990] 1 All E.R. 1018.

7 JUDICIAL DISCRETION TO EXCLUDE THE LIMITATION PERIOD

Where the plaintiff in a personal injuries action is unable to establish that either the date of the accrual of the cause of action or the date of relevant knowledge came within the three year limit, section 33 of the Act provides a discretionary exclusion of the time limit if it appears equitable to allow the action to proceed. In deciding whether or not to exercise its discretion under this provision, the court should have regard to the

Balancing of prejudice to the plaintiff and to the defendant

prejudice which would be caused to the plaintiff by the three year limitation period and also to the prejudice which might be caused to the defendant by the exclusion of the limit.[1] The court must take into account all the relevant circumstances, affecting both parties, in order to determine whether or not it would be equitable to permit the action to proceed.[2]

Discretion of the court

Section 33(3) directs that, "the court shall have regard to all the circumstances of the case": it has been held that this wording gives the court "as wide a discretion as could well be imagined."[3] Consequently, any argument that the application of the section should be confined to either difficult or unusual cases will be rejected by the court.[4]

Unfettered discretion

The discretion conferred on the courts by section 33 is unfettered, and provided the judge has regard to all the circumstances of the case, in particular those enumerated in section 33(3),[5] the Court of Appeal will not interfere with the exercise of that discretion.[6]

However, if the judge baldly states that, as a matter of law, he has no jurisdiction to make an order under the section, this will not constitute an exercise of discretion and the matter should then be remitted to the judge for further consideration of whether or not it would be equitable to direct that the normal limitation period should not apply.[7] Where the judge has

---

[1] Limitation Act 1980, s.33(1)(a) and (b).
[2] *Pilmore* v. *Northern Trawlers* [1986] 1 Lloyd's Rep. 552.
[3] *Firman* v. *Ellis* [1978] 2 All E.R. 851, at p. 868, *per* Geoffrey Lane L.J.; confirmed by the House of Lords in *Thompson* v. *Brown Construction (Ebbw Vale) Ltd.* [1981] 1 W.L.R. 744; [1981] 2 All E.R. 296.
[4] *Firman* v. *Ellis* [1978] 2 All E.R. 851 at p. 868, *per* Geoffrey Lane L.J.
[5] See below, pp. 80–84.
[6] *Conry* v. *Simpson* [1983] 3 All E.R. 369, C.A.
[7] *Thompson* v. *Brown Construction* (see above, n. 3).

Circumstances in which Court of Appeal will intervene granted an extension, the Court of Appeal will interfere with this decision only where it is plainly wrong or constitutes an error in the exercise of the discretion.[8] It has been emphasised that, when considering whether or not to exercise his discretion under the Act, the trial judge must have regard to *all* the circumstances of the case, not merely those enumerated in section 33 itself.[9]

Guidance on exercise of discretion While the discretion conferred upon the judge by section 33 is wide and unfettered, some degree of guidance in the exercise of the discretion was given in *Walkley* v. *Precision Forgings Ltd.*[10] where Lord Diplock stated[11]:

> "In deciding how to exercise its discretion under [section 33], there are two matters to which the court must have regard and two matters only: first the degree to which the plaintiff is prejudiced by being prevented by [section 11 or 12] from starting his action after the expiry of the primary limitation period and, second, the degree to which the defendant would be prejudiced by allowing the action to be started after the expiry of the primary limitation period. There must always be some degree of prejudice to the defendant in allowing the action to proceed; he will be exposed to trouble, expense and risk of liability which he would otherwise be spared. So, to entitle the court to give a direction under [section 33] there must be *some* prejudice to the plaintiff and the cause of that prejudice must be the requirement that he should start his action before the expiry of the primary limitation period."

However, the House of Lords[12] and the Court of Appeal[13] have rejected requests to lay down a general set of guidelines for the exercise of the discretion under section 33.

The decision to exclude the three-year limitation period may be made only upon the general grounds laid down in section 33(1)(*a*), namely that "provisions of section 11 [or 11A] or 12 of this Act prejudice the plaintiff or any person whom he represents." The court is not entitled to have regard merely to any prejudice which might be suffered by the plaintiff following **Prejudice must be caused by sections 11–12 time-bar** a refusal to exclude, but must have regard only to prejudice which is caused by the operation of the time-bar in sections 11 or 12. Where the plaintiff has originally issued a writ within the three year limitation period, but then, through his own dilatoriness allows that writ to lapse and seeks to issue a second writ outside the three year period, although he will be

---

[8] *Bradley* v. *Hanseatic Shipping Co. Ltd.* [1986] 2 Lloyd's Rep. 34, C.A.
[9] *Taylor* v. *Taylor, The Times*, April 14, 1984, C.A.; see further p. 84.
[10] [1979] 2 All E.R. 548.
[11] *Ibid.* at p. 559.
[12] *Thompson* v. *Brown Construction (Ebbw Vale) Ltd.* [1981] 1 W.L.R. 744 at p. 752 where Lord Diplock stated: "I do not think that this House with its minimal experience of appeals which have involved directions under [s.33] ought to attempt itself to lay down guidelines for the High Court judges who are familiar with the typical kinds of circumstances in which applications are made. In matters of practice and discretion if guidelines are needed they are better laid down by the Court of Appeal."
[13] *Ramsden* v. *Lee* [1992] 2 All E.R. 204 at p. 209, C.A. where Dillon L.J. stated: "To my mind there is considerable danger in laying down guidelines where the need for guidelines has not been made entirely apparent. The risk is that then more and more cases will come which are treated as matters of law on the application not of the statute but of the guidelines."

prejudiced by a refusal to exclude the limitation period, that prejudice will arise not from the operation of section 11 but from his own failure to pursue the original action. In the view of Lord Diplock, the only circumstances in which a court would exercise its discretion under section 33 in favour of a plaintiff who had allowed an original writ to lapse would be where the plaintiff had been persuaded to abandon the earlier litigation following a misrepresentation or other improper conduct by the defendant.[14] The desire to protect the defendant is clearly paramount here, not so much because the claim is stale (the defendant will, after all, have been forewarned by the earlier writ) but because the defendant will be entitled to assume that upon expiry of the original writ he has nothing more to fear.

Relevance of principles established in Birkett v. James

The court may also exclude the limitation period in cases where a writ was originally issued within the three year limit, but not served within the one year allowed under R.S.C., Order 6, rule 8 and the plaintiff then issues a further writ outside the three-year limit.

The case of *Birkett* v. *James*[15] concerned an action for breach of contract, where the court had no discretion to exclude the six-year limitation period. The House of Lords held that an action will not normally be dismissed for want of prosecution where the limitation period has not expired, since the court would have no power to prevent the plaintiff from starting a fresh action within the limitation period.

In *Walkley* v. *Precision Forgings Ltd.*[16] the House of Lords considered the impact of the decision in *Birkett* v. *James* on actions for personal injuries and came to the conclusion that the

Birkett v. James not applicable in section 33 case

reasoning expounded in *Birkett* v. *James* has no application in such a case to any period after the primary limitation period has expired. This is because the plaintiff then, unlike in *Birkett* itself, no longer has an indefensible right to start a second action for the same cause of action. It is not, therefore, possible to argue that the existence of the discretionary exclusion of the limitation period under section 33 should equate with the situation in *Birkett* where the plaintiff had an absolute right to continue with his action. Once the primary limitation period has expired in a personal injuries action, the court is at liberty to direct that a subsequent action be struck out.

Similar considerations arose in *Chappell* v. *Cooper*,[17] where, rather than seeking leave to start a second action after the original writ had expired, the plaintiff was seeking leave to extend the validity of the original writ. The Court of Appeal held that a plaintiff who fails to serve his writ in time must comply with the established principles and practice for renewal

---

[14] *Ramsden* v. *Lee* [1992] 2 All E.R. 204, impliedly overruling on this point *Firman* v. *Ellis* [1978] 2 All E.R. 851.
[15] [1977] 2 All E.R. 801, [1978] A.C. 297; see Chap. 2.
[16] [1979] 2 All E.R. 548.
[17] [1980] 2 All E.R. 463.

of a writ if he wishes to obtain an extension of its validity under R.S.C. Order 6, rule 8(2). The plaintiff will not generally be permitted to avail himself of the provisions of section 33 in seeking to renew a writ after expiry of the period allowed for service.

Prejudice to the defendant

It is important to bear in mind in this context that one of the fundamental justifications for the imposition of strict limitation periods is to protect defendants from having to defend stale claims where memories may have become blurred and witnesses may be untraceable.[18] In addition, the court may take into account the prejudice which may be suffered by a defendant who may have difficulty in conducting his affairs with the prospect of an action hanging indefinitely over his head.[19] However, mere prejudice to the defendant will not of itself be a sufficient reason for refusing to apply the provisions of section 33: an exclusion of time will always be prejudicial. Even if the defendant has a good defence on the merits, he will be obliged to expend time, energy and money in establishing his case; if he has no defence, he will have everything to lose if the exclusion is granted.[20] In all cases the court must perform a balancing act in order to determine the relative prejudice suffered by the defendant if the order is made and the plaintiff if it is not.[21]

Relative prejudice

Relevance of negotiations

When considering the degree of potential prejudice to the defendant, the court will take into account any negotiations conducted between the parties prior to the issue of the writ which is asserted to be out of time. Where a writ is issued several years after an accident with little warning to the defendant, an argument of prejudice will be relatively easily sustained.[22] However, where the limitation period expires only after protracted negotiations between the parties it will usually be difficult for the defendant to show actual prejudice since there will be little difficulty in preparing his case.[23] The fact that negotiations have been proceeding between the parties will not prevent time from running under section 11; it is not possible to argue that service of a writ would have jeopardised sensitive negotiations and prevented a settlement.[24] In order to succeed in an argument that the running of time has been suspended in this way, it will be necessary for the plaintiff to point to a clearly expressed agreement to that effect.[25]

[18] In *Donovan* v. *Gwentoys Ltd.* [1990] 1 All E.R. 1018, Lord Griffiths stated at p. 1024: "The primary purpose of the limitation period is to protect a defendant from the injustice of having to face a stale claim, that is a claim with which he never expected to have to deal."

[19] *Biss* v. *Lambeth, Southwark and Lewisham Health Authority* [1978] 1 W.L.R. 382, [1978] 2 All E.R. 125, C.A.

[20] See *Thompson* v. *Brown Construction (Ebbw Vale) Ltd.* [1981] 1 W.L.R. 744 at p. 750, *per* Lord Diplock.

[21] See generally on this point, the judgment of Parker L.J. in *Hartley* v. *Birmingham City District Council* [1992] 2 All E.R. 213.

[22] *Donovan* v. *Gwentoys Ltd.* [1990] 1 All E.R. 1018.

[23] *Firman* v. *Ellis* [1978] 2 All E.R. 851 at p. 866, *per* Ormrod L.J.

[24] *Jones* v. *Jones* [1970] 2 Q.B. 576, [1970] 3 All E.R. 47; *Easy* v. *Universal Anchorage Co. Ltd.* [1974] 2 All E.R. 1105.

[25] *Adams Holden & Pearson* v. *Trent Regional Health Authority* (1989) 47 B.L.R. 34.

Prejudice to the plaintiff

The prejudice suffered by the plaintiff in the event of a refusal to exclude the time limit must result from the operation of the three-year limit laid down in section 11 or 12. Where the prejudice results from some other cause, *e.g.* the striking out of an earlier writ for want of prosecution, section 33 will not apply.[26]

Availability of action against plaintiff's solicitors — The availability of an action against the plaintiff's solicitors for failing to ensure that the action was brought within time may be a relevant factor when determining whether or not the plaintiff will suffer prejudice if the time limit is not excluded. If there is any doubt about the likely success of an action against the solicitor, then, all other things being equal, the discretion should be exercised in favour of the plaintiff. Even where there exists a cast-iron case against the solicitor in which the measure of damages would be no less than those that he would be able to recover against the defendant if the action were allowed to proceed, it is still open to the court to find that the plaintiff would be prejudiced by a refusal to exclude.[27] This is because the court is not concerned solely with financial prejudice to the plaintiff. It is prejudicial to be forced to start another set of proceedings against a party whom one does not particularly wish to sue and to be deprived of a good cause of action against the original tortfeasor. In starting new proceedings against the solicitor there will inevitably be further delay which may militate against the plaintiff. He will also incur a personal liability for the costs of the action up to the date of the court's refusal to give a direction under section 33. This prejudice will be further compounded by the fact that the plaintiff must change from an action against a tortfeasor who may know little or nothing of the weak points of his case, to an action against his solicitor, who will know a great deal about them.[28]

The prejudice of being forced to start a new action against the negligent solicitor who has caused the action to be started out of time will be a determining factor only where the prejudice which would be caused to the defendant by excluding the time limit is non-existent or minimal. This will be the case where the action is commenced very shortly after the expiry of the limitation period[29] or where the parties have been conducting negotiations from a date shortly after the accident for which it is sought to make the defendant liable, such that the defendant is aware that the action is forthcoming and has been able to prepare accordingly. The court is obliged to conduct a balancing exercise: the fact that the plaintiff has an available action against the solicitor may tip the scale where the defendant has been substantially prejudiced by the delay.[30]

---

[26] See above, p. 77, *Walkley* v. *Precision Forgings Ltd.* [1979] 1 W.L.R. 606; *Chappell* v. *Cooper* [1980] 1 W.L.R. 958.

[27] *Thompson* v. *Brown Construction* (above n. 20), *per* Lord Diplock at p. 301; *Firman* v. *Ellis, per* Ormrod L.J. at p. 865; *Ramsden* v. *Lee* [1992] 2 All E.R. 204 at p. 208, C.A.

[28] *Hartley* v. *Birmingham City District Council* [1992] 2 All E.R. 213 at p. 224, *per* Parker L.J.

[29] As in *Pheasant* v. *S.T.H. Smith (Tyres) Ltd.* [1978] 2 All E.R. 851 and *Hartley* v. *Birmingham City District Council* [1992] 2 All E.R. 213 where the actions were commenced one day after the expiry of the limitation period.

[30] *Firman* v. *Ellis* [1978] 2 All E.R. 851 at p. 863, *per* Lord Denning M.R.

Although, in deciding whether or not to exercise the discretion to exclude, the judge may take into account that there is no prospect of the plaintiff succeeding in his action,[31] the mere fact that the plaintiff is likely to have difficulty in establishing certain facts owing to the passage of time, should not constitute a reason for a refusal to exclude.[32]

Relevant circumstances

Section 33(3) provides that, in the exercise of its discretion under this section, the court shall have regard to "all the circumstances of the case . . ." As stated above, this gives the court an unfettered discretion in all cases to determine whether or not a particular personal injuries action, ostensibly started out of time, should be permitted to continue, regard being had to the prejudice which would be caused to the plaintiff by the operation of the three year limit. In addition to this general catch-all provision, section 33(3) lists a number of factors to which the court should pay particular regard. These will be examined in turn below.

(a) **The length of and the reasons for the delay on the part of the plaintiff.** Where the plaintiff, despite having acquired the knowledge that he has a cause of action against the defendant, has delayed commencing proceedings until after the expiration of the time limit, the court, in the exercise of its discretion as to whether or not to extend, must consider the length of and the reasons for the delay on the part of the plaintiff. If the delay is minimal (for example, in *Hartley* v. *Birmingham City District Council*[33] the writ was issued one day out of time, see also *Thompson* v. *Brown Construction*[34] where the delay was of 37 days, but where the damage had been fully considered by the defendants' solicitors at an early stage (Lord Griffiths in *Donovan* v. *Gwentoys Ltd.*[35] described the error of the plaintiff's solicitor in *Thompson* in issuing the writ 37 days out of time as "a totally unexpected windfall benefit for the defendants' insurers") the court will have little difficulty in holding that the defendant has not been prejudiced. Where the plaintiff has known for a considerable time that he has an action, and has simply chosen not to pursue it, the court is unlikely to be sympathetic.[36]

Minimal delay

There was at one time some confusion over whether the delay referred to in section 33(3)(*a*) was delay from the accrual of the cause of action or delay after the expiry of the primary limitation period.[37] It was held in *Donovan* v. *Gwentoys Ltd.*[38] that the relevant delay is that which falls after the expiry of the three year period. When considering the separate question of

Delay after expiry of limitation period

---

[31] *Napper* v. *National Coal Board*, March 1, 1990, C.A.; unrep.
[32] *Woods* v. *Att.-Gen.*, July 18, 1990; unrep., *per* McPherson J.
[33] [1992] 2 All E.R. 213.
[34] [1981] 1 W.L.R. 744; [1981] 2 All E.R. 296.
[35] [1990] 1 All E.R. 1018.
[36] See the comments of Hidden J. in *Nash* v. *Eli Lilly* [1991] 2 Med LR 169.
[37] See *Thompson* v. *Brown Construction (Ebbw Vale) Ltd.* (above, n. 20).
[38] [1990] 1 All E.R. 1018.

prejudice to the defendant, the court will take into account the time which passed prior to the expiry of the limit.

(b) The extent to which, having regard to the delay, the evidence is or is likely to be less cogent than if the action had been brought within the time allowed. Again, the delay referred to is the delay which has elapsed since the expiry of the limitation period. Where many years have passed since the incident giving rise to the action memories may have faded, documents may have been lost or destroyed and witnesses may have died.[39] Where a defendant seeks to rely on this in order to avoid the exclusion of time, it is not enough to point to the passage of years in order to show that evidence is less likely to be cogent: he must give reasons as to why this is so, for example, by showing that key witnesses have died or documents have been reasonably destroyed.[40]

Delay after expiry of limitation period

Evidence required from defendant

Although both parties may suffer from the passing of time, the defendant is more likely to be prejudiced since the action may be unexpected and he may be faced with the prospect of defending an action without the benefit of proper records; the plaintiff, conversely, will have been able to consider the availability and cogency of evidence before deciding to bring the action. It is unclear whether the court will place equal weight on reduced cogency in the evidence for the plaintiff and for the defendant. In *Thompson* v. *Brown Construction*[41] Lord Diplock expressed the view that the court should consider both aspects: in the case of the defendant it is clear that any decreased cogency will increase the degree of prejudice he will suffer if the action is allowed to be brought despite the delay; and in the case of the plaintiff, any diminished cogency will reduce his chances of establishing the cause of action. Recently in *Woods* v. *Attorney-General*[42] McPherson J. expressed the view that, if the plaintiff wishes to continue in full awareness of the fact that the evidence may be more difficult to establish after so many years "that is her funeral."

Often the question of cogency of evidence will arise where the defendant, particularly in the case of corporate or institutional defendants, has destroyed the files relating to the accident for which the plaintiff now seeks leave to bring an action out of time. Where negotiations have been proceeding between the parties and the defendant should have known that a writ was likely to be served, he will be unable to plead lack of cogent evidence where he destroyed files immediately upon expiry of the limitation period and the writ arrived some days later.[43] Where following negotiations within the limitation period, the claim has not been pursued, it will be open to the court to hold that the defendant has acted reasonably in destroying the files relating to the accident.[44] *A fortiori* where

---

[39] *Napper* v. *National Coal Board*, March 1, 1990, C.A.; unrep.
[40] *Nash* v. *Eli Lilly* [1991] 2 Med LR 169. *Conry* v. *Simpson* [1983] 3 All E.R. 369, C.A.
[41] [1981] 1 W.L.R. 744.
[42] July 18, 1990; unrep.
[43] *Thompson* v. *Brown Construction* (see above, n. 20); *Firman* v. *Ellis* (above n. 30).
[44] *Conry* v. *Simpson* [1983] 3 All E.R. 369.

there have been no preliminary negotiations and, more than three years after an accident, the injured person suddenly seeks to bring proceedings.

(c) The conduct of the defendant after the cause of action arose, including the extent (if any) to which he responded to requests reasonably made by the plaintiff for information or inspection for the purpose of ascertaining facts which were or might be relevant to the plaintiff's cause of action against the defendant. The court is required to take into account the defendant's actions from the moment the cause of action arose, not from the date of the plaintiff's relevant knowledge or from the date of the expiry of the limitation period.[45] Although this refers specifically to the defendant, it includes the conduct of his solicitors and insurers, since in many instances it is they, rather than the defendant, who will be dealing with the plaintiff and answering, or not answering his requests for information.[46] An obligation is placed on the defendant and his professional advisers and representatives not to be obstructive in enabling a potential plaintiff to obtain relevant information: they must respond honestly and within a reasonable time to reasonable requests for information from the plaintiff; however, they are not required to volunteer such information.

In many of the cases where paragraph (c) is being considered, the conduct of the defendant which is at issue will be in some way discreditable or at least unsatisfactory, for example he has deliberately attempted to protract negotiations such that the limitation period expires before a writ is issued. The court is not limited to a consideration of discreditable behaviour: all conduct is relevant where it has caused the plaintiff to conduct proceedings in a particular way with the result that the limitation period has passed. Therefore, the making of an interim payment may lead a reasonable plaintiff to assume that liability would not be contested and is consequently a circumstance to be taken into account under section 33(3)(c) even though it was a benevolent rather than a discreditable act.[47]

It has been stated that paragraph (c) "is concerned with purely procedural matters, where the forensic tactics of a defendant may lead to delay."[48] Conduct of the defendant which is totally unconnected with the conduct of the litigation will not be taken into account for the purposes of paragraph (c); for example, the giving of perjured evidence in a criminal trial relating to the same facts as those on which the later civil action was based.[49] However, the term "tactics" should be understood in a broad sense as encompassing all action which is connected with the progress of the proceedings, and need not necessarily be conduct which is deliberately designed to lead to delay. In *Marston* v. *British Railways Board*[50] it was held that the maintenance of an honest but erroneous defence constituted conduct which was relevant for the purpose of paragraph (c).

Margin notes:
Delay from date of incident

Solicitors and insurers included

All conduct relevant

---

[45] *Thompson* v. *Brown Construction* (see above, n. 20).
[46] *Ibid.* at p. 751.
[47] *Marshall* v. *Martin*, June 10, 1987, C.A.; unrep.
[48] *Per* Russell L.J. in *Halford* v. *Brookes* [1991] 3 All E.R. 559, at p. 567, C.A.
[49] *Ibid.*
[50] [1976] I.C.R. 124, *per* Croom-Johnson J.

(d) The duration of any disability of the plaintiff arising after the date of the accrual of the cause of action. Where the plaintiff is under a disability at the time when the cause of action arose, time will not start to run until the disability is removed (in the case of a child, upon attaining majority).[51] Where a disability arises in an adult after the date at the time when the cause of action arose, this will not serve to suspend the running of time. Instead, section 33(3)(*d*) provides that this is a relevant circumstance to be weighed against all other relevant factors in the case.

Legal disability   The term "disability" must be understood here in the sense of a legal disability: section 38(2) states that "[f]or the purposes of this Act a person shall be treated as under a disability while he is an infant, or of unsound mind." It is not, therefore, possible to argue that the court should exercise its discretion on the ground that the plaintiff has been suffering from some physical disability or illness which has made it more difficult for him to bring the action within the necessary time.[52] However, any illness or physical disability of the plaintiff which may make it understandable that he has been dilatory in bringing his action, may be taken into account when considering the date on which the plaintiff could have been expected to acquire the necessary knowledge in order to start time running against him: *Davis* v. *City & Hackney Health Authority*.[53]

Mere mental ill-health not sufficient   Section 38(3) states that a person is of unsound mind "if he is a person who, by reason of mental disorder within the meaning of the [Mental Health Act 1983], is incapable of managing and administering his property and affairs." The mere fact that a person is suffering from mental ill-health, or even that he has been invalided out of a job on the ground of mental ill-health does not necessarily lead to his being incapable of managing his own affairs.[54]

(e) The extent to which the plaintiff acted promptly and reasonably once he knew whether or not the act or omission of the defendant, to which the injury was attributable, might be capable at that time of giving rise to an action for damages. In some cases, a primary reason for the plaintiff's initial reluctance to commence proceedings, particularly in the case of an industrial accident, may be fear of jeopardising a relationship which exists with the defendant. The extent to which this should be regarded as a valid reason for postponing proceedings is uncertain. Where an injured employee defers pursuing a claim out of feelings of loyalty towards the employer or wishing to preserve good relations, it may be argued that the delay is understandable, and, in the absence of demonstrable prejudice to the defendant, the action should be permitted to proceed.[55] Although it has been held that a plaintiff who

Relevance of relationship with defendant

[51] Limitation Act 1980, s.28.
[52] *Pilmore* v. *Northern Trawlers Ltd.* [1986] 1 Lloyd's Rep. 552.
[53] *The Times*, January 27, 1989.
[54] *Dawson* v. *Spain-Gower*, October 18, 1988, C.A.; unrep.
[55] See *McCafferty* v. *Metropolitan Police District Receiver* [1977] 1 W.L.R. 1073; [1977] 2 All E.R. 756; *Buck* v. *English Electric Co. Ltd.* [1977] 1 W.L.R. 806; [1978] 1 All E.R. 271; *Newman* v. *Bevan Funnell Ltd.*, October 29, 1990, C.A.; unrep.

refrained from bringing an action as he feared that he would lose his job if he did so was not entitled to have the limitation period excluded,[56] this does not mean that insecurity of tenure should in all cases be automatically discounted as a relevant circumstance under this paragraph.[57]

(f) The steps, if any, taken by the plaintiff to obtain medical, legal or other expert advice and the nature of any such advice he may have received. The fact that the plaintiff has received defective legal advice will not prevent time from running against him, although the receipt of defective medical advice will prevent him from having the necessary knowledge within the meaning of section 14 of the Act.[58] However, under section 33(3)(*f*) the court is entitled to take into account any advice, whether legal, medical or otherwise, which may have convinced him that he had no cause of action.[59]

Other relevant circumstances   Other relevant circumstances which may be taken into account include the following: the fact that the plaintiff's case is weak,[60] or strong[61]; the fact that the plaintiff is legally aided and therefore the defendant will be unable to recover his costs[62]; the availability of an alternative action against the plaintiff's solicitors[63]; and, possibly, a change in judicial interpretation of the law which has the result that an action which, on the basis of the previous law, would not have succeeded, is now sustainable.[64]

Application of section 33 in multi-partite claims

Opren litigation   The principles laid down above apply equally to single party and multi-partite litigation. It was argued in the *Opren* litigation[65] that, where a defendant has permitted the bringing of a class action in circumstances where the individual plaintiffs would have experienced great difficulty in funding a single action, different criteria should be applied when determining whether or not to grant an exclusion of the time limit under section 33.

[56] *Miller* v. *London Electrical Manufacturing Co.* [1976] 2 Lloyd's Rep. 284.
[57] See *McCafferty* v. *Metropolitan Police Receiver* (see above, n. 55).
[58] See *Smith* v. *Central Asbestos Co. Ltd.* [1973] A.C. 518, H.L.
[59] *Waghorn* v. *Lewisham & North Southwark Health Authority*, June 23, 1987, Q.B.D.; unrep.
[60] *Napper* v. *National Coal Board* (see above n. 31).
[61] *Beer* v. *London Borough Waltham Forest*, December 16, 1987; unrep., *per* Hodgson J.
[62] *Lye* v. *Marks and Spencer plc*, *The Times*, February 15, 1988, C.A.
[63] *Donovan* v. *Gwentoys* see above, p. 79.
[64] This point has not been considered in relation to s.33, but arose before the Employment Appeals Tribunal in the context of sexual discrimination: *Foster* v. *South Glamorgan Health Authority* [1988] I.C.R. 526, where the plaintiff, a female nurse, was obliged to retire at the age of 60; more than three months after her retirement but within three months of the judgment of the European Court of Justice in *Marshall* v. *Southampton & South-West Hampshire Health Authority* [1986] Q.B. 401, she started a claim for damages for unlawful sexual discrimination. It was held that, as she did not have a cause of action until the judgment in *Marshall*, she had made her claim within the relevant three-month limitation period.
[65] *Nash* v. *Eli Lilly* [1991] 2 Med. LR 169, *per* Hidden J.

In such a situation, where the potential number of plaintiffs is very large, defendants could be prejudiced by the application of the normal rules since they would be left in an uncertain position not knowing how many more plaintiffs might materialise and have their claims allowed under section 33: therefore, the multi-partite nature of the litigation should be one of the relevant circumstances to be taken into account under section 33. However, Hidden J. rejected the strenuous arguments of counsel for Eli-Lilly that a liberal interpretation of section 33 by the court would remove certainty and would consequently remove the incentive on defendants to settle, and held that there should be no general presumption in multi-plaintiff litigation against disallowing the limitation period except in exceptional circumstances.

8 ADVERSE POSSESSION

Distinction between limitation and prescription

With land actions, the concepts of limitation and prescription must be distinguished. Limitation is a statutory creation which serves to extinguish the rights of action of an owner of land (and with it his rights in the land[1] at the expiration of the given period of time). Prescription, is a common law notion which serves to create rights in one person over the land of another.[2] It has been said that[3]: "the essential difference between prescription and limitation is that in the former case title can be acquired only by possession as of right. That is the antithesis of what is required for limitation, which perhaps can be described as possession as of wrong." In this chapter the concept of adverse possession, the acquisition of title to land of another, will be discussed; prescription, the acquisition of rights over the land of another, will be discussed in the following chapter.

General matters

In respect of an action to recover land,[4] to redeem land in possession of a mortgagee[5] or to recover any principal money secured by a mortgage or other charge or the proceeds of sale of

Twelve-year limitation period

land[6] the limitation period will generally be 12 years. "Land" is defined as including corporeal hereditaments, tithes and rentcharges and any legal or equitable interest therein, including an interest in the proceeds of sale of land held on trust for sale.[7]

Future interests

Account must be taken, not only of the interest of the legal owner of the land in question, but also of any future, equitable interests in the land held by remaindermen or reversioners. Section 15(2) protects these interests in the following terms:

> "Subject to the following provisions of this section, where—
> (a) the estate or interest claimed was an estate or interest in reversion or remainder or any other future estate or interest and the right of action to recover the land accrued on the date on which the estate or interest fell into possession by the determination of the preceding estate or interest; and
> (b) the person entitled to the preceding estate or interest (not being a term of years absolute) was not in possession of the land on that date;
> no action shall be brought by the person entitled to the succeeding estate or interest after the expiration of twelve years from the date on which the right of action accrued to

---

[1] See the Limitation Act 1980, s.17.
[2] See Megarry and Wade, *The Law of Real Property* (5th ed., 1984).
[3] *Buckinghamshire County Council* v. *Moran* [1989] 2 All E.R. 225, at p. 238, *per* Nourse L.J.
[4] Limitation Act 1980, s.15(1).
[5] *Ibid.* s.16.
[6] *Ibid.* s.20(1).
[7] *Ibid.* s.38(1).

the person entitled to the preceding estate or interest or six years from the date on which the right of action accrued to the person entitled to the succeeding estate or interest, whichever period last expires."

Thus, while the right of action of the first owner, X, may be extinguished upon the expiration of the 12-year period, the interests of any future owner, Y, will not be in danger of being extinguished while these remain future interests. The limitation period will begin to run anew against Y only once those future interests fall into possession. The right of action of the person(s) entitled to the future interests will be barred on the later of two alternative dates: either 12 years from the date on which the preceding owner was dispossessed or six years from the date on which his own interest falls into possession. For example, where land is held by X for life with remainder to Y in fee simple and before his death X is dispossessed, Y will have either 12 years from the date of dispossession or six years from the date of X's death in which to bring his action. If the dispossession occurs ~~more than 12 years before X's death, Y will have the shorter~~ six-year period from the date of death. If the dispossession occurs less than six years before the death, Y may avail himself of the 12-year limitation from the date of dispossession.

Thirty-year limitation period   A 30-year limitation period applies in relation to actions where the plaintiff is the Crown or any spiritual[8] or eleemosynary corporation sole.[9] The term eleemosynary charity covers all charities directed to the relief of individual distress, whether due to poverty, age, sickness or other similar individual afflictions.[10]

Sixty-year limitation period   Where the action concerns land which is classified as foreshore,[11] the limitation period for recovery by the Crown will be 60 years from the date of accrual of the cause of action.[12] Where the land in question has ceased to be foreshore, the action may be brought at any time before the expiration of either 60 years from the date of accrual of the cause of action or 30 years from the date when the land ceased to be foreshore, whichever period first expires.[13]

In the case of mines owned by the National Coal Board, no title can be gained by adverse possession.[14]

General principles of adverse possession   The principle that, at the end of a certain period, title to land should pass from the owner to the squatter comes from the general desire to prevent injustices which would arise following attempts to resurrect and enforce dormant claims. However, in deference to the importance attached to rights over land, the limitation period is generally extended to 12 years, rather than the more usual six. It will be necessary to determine whether, in addition to the passing of the 12-year period, all the factors

---

[8] Certain holders of office in the Church of England are classified as spiritual corporations sole, *e.g.* archbishops, bishops and vicars.

[9] See the Limitation Act 1980, s.15(7) and Pt. II of Sched. 1.

[10] *Re Armitage dec'd* [1972] 1 Ch. 438, *per* Goulding J. at p. 445.

[11] That is, land which is overflowed by the sea at mean high tide, but not at mean low tide: see *Fowley Marine (Elmsworth) Ltd.* v. *Gafford* [1968] 2 Q.B. 618, C.A.

[12] See the Limitation Act 1980, Pt. II of Sched. 1, para. 11(1).

[13] *Ibid.* Pt. II of Sched. 1, para. 11(2)(*a*) and (*b*).

[14] Coal Industry Nationalisation Act 1946, s.49(3).

necessary to constitute adverse possession have been established. These factors will include the question of whether or not there has been discontinuance or dispossession, whether or not the possession is adverse, the intention of both the owner and the squatter and the date on which time begins to run.

Requirements for acquisition of title by limitation

Acquisition of possession

Section 15 of the Limitation Act 1980 provides for a general 12-year limitation period in respect of actions to recover land, with Schedule 1 of the Act giving further details concerning the accrual of the cause of action. Paragraph 1 of Part I of Schedule 1 provides:

> "Where the person bringing an action to recover land, or some person through whom he claims, has been in possession of the land, and has while entitled to the land been dispossessed or discontinued his possession, the right of action shall be treated as having accrued on the date of the dispossession or discontinuance."

Requirement that there be possession followed by discontinuance or dispossession

Title to land may be acquired only where the true owner was formerly in possession and has either been dispossessed or has discontinued his possession. Concurrent possession with the true owner will be insufficient.[15] Dispossession is "where the squatter comes in and drives out the true owner from possession"[16] and discontinuance occurs where "the true owner goes out of possession and is followed in by the squatter."[17]

Discontinuance

Discontinuance occurs where the true owner goes out of possession and is followed in by the squatter. In deciding what amounts to discontinuance in a particular case, it is necessary to look at the nature of the property[18]: if the land is not capable of use and enjoyment, it will be difficult to argue that an absence of use by the owner amounts to discontinuance.[19] If the owner has been doing all that he could in the circumstances to use the land, he will not be considered to have discontinued his possession.[20] It has been said that "the smallest act would be sufficient to show that there was no discontinuance",[21] for example, repairing

Nature of the property

---

[15] *Treloar* v. *Nute* [1977] 1 All E.R. 230, C.A.

[16] *Buckinghamshire County Council* v. *Moran* [1989] 2 All E.R. 225, at p. 239, *per* Nourse L.J.; see also Fry J. in *Rains* v. *Buxton* (1880) 14 Ch.D. 537 at p. 539.

[17] *Ibid.*

[18] *Leigh* v. *Jack* (1879) 5 Ex.D. 264 at p. 274, *per* Cotton L.J. See also *Williams Bros. Direct Supply Ltd.* v. *Raftery* [1958] 1 Q.B. 159.

[19] *Leigh* v. *Jack* (1879) 5 Ex.D. 264 at p. 274, *per* Cotton L.J. See also *Tecbild Ltd.* v. *Chamberlain* (1969) 20 P. & C.R. 633.

[20] *Williams Bros. Direct Supply Ltd.* v. *Raftery* [1958] 1 Q.B. 159 at p. 167, *per* Hodson L.J.

[21] *Leigh* v. *Jack* (1879) 5 Ex.D. 264, *per* Bramwell L.J. at p. 272.

a fence[22] or, possibly, dumping rubbish on the property in question.[23]

Whilst it was previously the case that a mere formal entry onto land would not serve to establish possession of the land,[24] no similar restriction has been reproduced in the Limitation Act 1980.[25] This should not necessarily be interpreted as meaning that an absent owner may protect his title by the making of occasional formal visits to the land: in all cases the question of whether there has been factual discontinuance should be considered.

Where the owner of the land has unilaterally granted the occupier a licence to remain on the land, whether or not the occupier has accepted that licence, there can be no question of discontinuance by the owner.[26] The situation may be different where the occupier expressly rejects the terms of the licence proposed by the owner.

Dispossession

The fact that it is not possible to establish discontinuance by the owner will not necessarily prevent adverse possession from being obtained by the possessor: dispossession may have occurred.[27]

Possession is a question of fact — Whether or not a person has taken possession of land is a question of fact depending on all the particular circumstances.[28]

It has been said that[29]: "In order to defeat a title by dispossessing the former owner, acts must be done which are inconsistent with his enjoyment of the soil for the purposes for which he intended to use it."

Future development — In *Leigh* v. *Jack*[30] it was held that, where the intention of the owner of the land was neither to cultivate nor to build upon the land but to devote it to public use at some future date, there was no dispossession by the defendant by reason of his blocking the land to vehicles. There will similarly be no dispossession where the possessor has merely used for recreational purposes rough, uncultivated land intended by the owner for future development.[31]

Relevance of squatter's intention — The fact that an absent owner has retained a piece of land with a view to its utilisation in the future for a specific purpose does not in itself indicate that he can never be dispossessed. If the squatter is able to establish a firm and obvious intention to dispossess, he must succeed notwithstanding that his acts cannot

[22] *Leigh* v. *Jack* (1879) 3 Ex.D. 264, *per* Bramwell L.J. at p. 272.
[23] *Williams Bros. Direct Supply Ltd.* v. *Raftery* [1958] 1 Q.B. 159.
[24] Limitation Act 1939, s.13; for the distinction between a mere formal entry and one indicating possessory rights, see *Randall* v. *Stevens* (1853) 2 E. & B. 641; see also *Solling* v. *Broughton* [1893] A.C. 556, P.C.
[25] Section 13 of the Limitation Act 1939 was repealed by the Limitation Amendment Act 1980.
[26] *B.P. Properties Ltd.* v. *Buckler* [1987] 2 E.G.L.R. 168, C.A.
[27] See *Buckinghamshire County Council* v. *Moran* [1989] 2 All E.R. 225, at p. 232 where it was found that the council (the owner of the land) had never discontinued its possession but had been dispossessed by the defendant.
[28] *Treloar* v. *Nute* [1976] 1 W.L.R. 1295 C.A., *per* Sir John Pennycuick.
[29] *Leigh* v. *Jack* (1879) 5 Ex.D. 264 at p. 273, *per* Bramwell L.J. See also *Williams* v. *Usherwood* (1983) 45 P. & C.R. 235, C.A.
[30] *Ibid.*
[31] *Tecbild Ltd.* v. *Chamberlain* (1969) 20 P. & C.R. 633.

be said to have inconvenienced the owner. In *Buckinghamshire County Council* v. *Moran*[32] the plaintiff council had acquired in 1955 a plot of land adjacent to some houses with a view to implementing a road diversion at some time in the future. The owners of a house abutting onto this plot gradually started to treat it as part of their garden, trimming the hedges and mowing the grass. Thereafter the road surveyor's department ceased maintaining the plot, and restricted itself to merely cursory inspections, usually from a car window. The defendant acquired the house in question in 1971, and was aware at that time, on the one hand, of the council's title to the land and of the intention to build a road diversion thereon, and, on the other, of the fact that the vendors had acquired or were in the course of acquiring a possessory title to the plot. It was argued by the council that the rule in *Leigh* v. *Jack*[33] prevented the acquisition of a possessory title in circumstances such as these: the land had been acquired for a specific purpose and the acts of the defendant were not inconsistent with that purpose. This argument was rejected by the Court of Appeal on the ground that dispossession may occur despite the lack of inconvenience to the owner if two conditions had been fulfilled: firstly, the defendant could show the required *animus possidendi*[34] and secondly, the acts relied on by the defendant were not trivial in nature.[35]

Acts which have been held to constitute factual possession

Possession of land for the purposes of the Limitation Act requires an appropriate degree of physical control of the land and, when seeking to determine whether particular acts suffice to establish possession, it is necessary to take into account the

Necessary to take into account the nature of the land

nature of the land and the manner in which land of that nature would commonly be used.[36] Therefore, even though a particular act has been held to constitute possession in one case, it will not necessarily serve as authority for a subsequent case where the nature of the land is different. Where the land is of little

Waste land

practical use to anyone and the squatter makes use of it in the only way possible, this may be held to constitute possession. In *Red House Farms (Thorndon) Ltd.* v. *Catchpole*[37] it was held that the shooting of pigeons over a piece of land of no agricultural value could amount to possession. Similarly, in *Cadija Umma* v. *S. Don Manis Appu*[38] the cutting and selling of wild grass was treated as possession of a piece of swamp land on which lotus and wild grass were growing.[39]

[32] [1989] 2 All E.R. 225 at p. 234, *per* Slade L.J.
[33] (1879) 5 Ex.D. 264.
[34] See below, at p. 94.
[35] See below, "Acts which have been held to constitute taking of possession".
[36] *Powell* v. *McFarlane* (1977) 38 P. & C.R. 452 at pp. 470–471, *per* Slade J. See also *West Bank Estates Ltd.* v. *Arthur* [1967] A.C. 665 at pp. 678–679, P.C., *per* Lord Wilberforce.
[37] (1977) E.G.D. 798, C.A.
[38] [1939] A.C. 136, P.C.
[39] It should be noted that the decision of the Privy Council attached particular weight to the opinion of the local courts in Ceylon as to the conditions of life and habits and ideology of the people.

Shared driveways

In a more suburban setting, disputes have arisen between the owners of houses between which an originally shared driveway had been appropriated to the use of one of the houses to the exclusion of the other. In *Williams* v. *Usherwood*[40] shared land between two houses was used as a driveway by only one of the houses and a fence was erected on the land of the other. It was held that this enclosure, together with the parking of cars on the land and crazy paving the surface of the land constituted possession.

Trivial acts

Trivial acts performed on land for which the owner has no immediate use will not generally be held to amount to possession. Permitting children to play and tethering ponies on land which is ultimately to be developed has been held not to constitute possession.[41] Claims were similarly rejected where the claimant relied simply on the erection of a rough fence coupled with dumping of poultry manure[42] or on the putting up of compost pens, having bonfires, keeping free range chickens and planting of trees and shrubs[43]: it has been doubted whether the planting of flowers on land could ever amount to possession.[44]

When is possession adverse?

In order for time to run in favour of the occupier of another's land, it is necessary not only that he should have possession of the land, but also that his possession should be adverse to the owner. Possession will be adverse where the owner has the right to bring an action against the squatter for recovery of the land; it is not necessary that the owner's right to recovery should be absolute and unqualified.[45]

Permission of the owner

No adverse possession if with permission

Possession will not be adverse if it can be referred to a lawful title, for example, the permission of the owner.[46] The effect of a lawful title is to prevent the owner from bringing any action to evict the person in possession without determining the licence. The fact that the person who is in possession is unaware that he is on the land lawfully is irrelevant.[47]

In *Hughes* v. *Griffin*[48] the original owner of the property, G,

[40] (1983) 45 P. & C.R. 235, C.A.
[41] *Tecbild Ltd.* v. *Chamberlain* (1969) 20 P. & C.R. 633.
[42] *Basildon District Council* v. *Manning* (1975) 237 E.G. 878.
[43] *Bills* v. *Fernandez-Gonzalez* (1982) 132 New L.J. 66.
[44] *Ellett-Brown* v. *Tallishire Ltd.*, March 29, 1990, C.A.; unrep.
[45] For example, where a tenant has failed to pay rent over a period of time, the right of the landlord to recover land to which the Rent Acts apply is subject to the discretion of the court. The landlord does, however, retain the right to bring the action, even though recovery might be refused by the court: *Moses* v. *Lovegrove* [1952] 1 All E.R. 1279 at p. 1284, C.A.; *Jessamine Investment Co.* v. *Schwartz* [1976] 3 All E.R. 521, C.A.
[46] Hence the development of the (now discredited) implied licence theory in cases such as *Wallis's Cayton Bay Holiday Camp Ltd.* v. *Shell-Mex and BP Ltd.* [1975] Q.B. 94, in an attempt to prevent owners of land from being divested of their title in circumstances where they were unaware that the land was being used by another. For an account of this theory, see below, at p. 93.
[47] *B.P. Properties Ltd.* v. *Buckler* [1987] 2 E.G.L.R. 168, C.A.
[48] [1969] 1 W.L.R. 23, C.A.

conveyed that property to his nephew, but was permitted by him to stay in the house. It was held that G remained there by virtue of a licence and consequently time did not run in his favour. The result of this was that G's widow, who claimed through him, was unable to establish adverse possession.

Time will run only from express revocation of permission

Where the squatter originally went onto the land with the permission of the owner, he will remain as a licensee of the owner until such time as the permission is expressly revoked.[49] The question of which acts will amount to revocation of the licence will depend on the circumstances of the case. Whilst a demand for the return of keys will generally constitute an effective revocation, so that time would begin to run in favour of the squatter, this will not be sufficient where a person has relied on the licence in order to obtain possession and to justify retention of the keys. In *Hyde* v. *Pearce*[50] the plaintiff had agreed in 1958 to purchase a property and, prior to completion and without the consent of the vendor, he went into occupation. It was subsequently discovered that the vendor had previously conveyed to a third party a piece of the ground which was to have been conveyed to the plaintiff and a dispute arose between them as to the *quantum* of the abatement to which the plaintiff was entitled. The vendor requested the return of the keys, but the plaintiff refused, maintaining that he wished to continue on the basis of the contract and was concerned only with the question of the abatement. Despite repeated requests, the keys were never returned and the dispute was never settled. In 1972 the vendor contracted to sell the property to the defendant, who taking advantage of the plaintiff's absence from the property during a stay in prison, had demolished the house and had built a new one. The plaintiff claimed possession and damages, arguing that the vendor had either discontinued possession or had been dispossessed by the plaintiff in 1958 when he went into occupation. It was held by the Court of Appeal that the plaintiff had never expressly rescinded the contract of sale and that his explanation, for remaining on the premises after the return of the keys had been demanded, would have been that he was a purchaser in possession awaiting ascertainment of the purchase price. Having relied on the existence of the contract in order to obtain possession, the plaintiff could not rely on the doctrine of adverse possession and effectively repudiate the contract with hindsight.

Tenancy agreements

Adverse possession following termination of tenancy

Where land is occupied under a periodic oral tenancy, the lease will be treated as being determined at the expiration of the stipulated period (subject to any rent being paid), and possession will be adverse if the tenant remains, without permission from the landlord, after this time.[51] Possession will be adverse even where the landlord has, for his own reasons, chosen not to demand payment from the occupier. In *Hayward* v. *Challoner*[52]

---

[49] *Powell* v. *McFarlane* (1977) 38 P. & C.R. 452 at p. 469.
[50] [1982] 1 W.L.R. 560, C.A.
[51] See *Moses* v. *Lovegrove* [1952] 1 All E.R. 1279, C.A.; *Jessamine Investment Co.* v. *Schwartz* [1976] 3 All E.R. 521, C.A.
[52] [1968] 1 Q.B. 107, C.A.

the plaintiffs' predecessors in title had rented a piece of land to the rector of the village church. Rent was paid for only a short time, but the plaintiffs forebore to request payment, on the ground that they did not wish to force the church to pay. Some 14 years after the last payment of rent, the rector sought to sell this land for use as a coach park, claiming that he had acquired a title by virtue of adverse possession. The Court of Appeal expressed considerable reservations as to the propriety of the defendant's actions, but held (Lord Denning dissenting) that the tenancy was determined on the date of the last payment of rent, and the possession of the defendant thereafter became adverse.

Implied licence

Implied licence theory now discredited

In the mid-1970s the Court of Appeal sought to extend the statement of principle in *Leigh* v. *Jack*[53] to provide that where the defendant's use of the plaintiff's land was not inconsistent with the plaintiff's intended use of the property, such use would be by virtue of an implied licence and consequently the defendant would be unable to plead adverse possession since the possession of a licensee cannot be adverse.[54] The more traditional viewpoint was stated in *Treloar* v. *Nute*[55]:

> "... if a squatter takes possession of land belonging to another and remains in possession for twelve years to the exclusion of the owner, that represents adverse possession and accordingly at the end of the twelve years the title of the owner is extinguished. That is the plain meaning of the statutory provisions."

The *Treloar* v. *Nute* approach was endorsed by the Law Reform Committee,[56] and it is now provided by paragraph 8(4) of Schedule 1 of the 1980 Act so that:

No implied licence merely because possession not inconsistent with owner's use

> "For the purpose of determining whether a person occupying any land is in adverse possession of the land it shall not be assumed by implication of law that his occupation is by permission of the person entitled to the land merely by virtue of the fact that his occupation is not inconsistent with the latter's present or future enjoyment of the land."

The provision does not exclude the finding of an implied licence in circumstances in which such a finding is justified on the facts of the case. It is submitted that such an implied licence should not be found where the owner of the land is unaware of the presence of the squatter.

Certainty paramount

The current prevailing attitude is that certainty is to be paramount: therefore, where the defendant has been in possession for 12 years, his claim should not be defeated simply because his use of the land did not inconvenience the owner.

---

[53] (1879) 5 Ex.D. 264, see above at p. 89.
[54] See *Wallis's Cayton Bay Holiday Camp Ltd.* v. *Shell-Mex and B.P. Ltd.* [1975] 1 Q.B. 94 and *Gray* v. *Wykeham-Martin*, 1977, Supreme Court Library, Transcript No. 10A.
[55] [1977] 1 All E.R. 230 at pp. 234–235, *per* Sir John Pennycuick.
[56] Law Reform Committee Twenty First Report, Cmnd. 6293 at para. 3.52.

Adverse possession is mixed question of fact and law

The question whether a squatter has proved adverse possession for the purpose of the Limitation Act is one of mixed fact and law.[57] It will be necessary to have regard to the intention of the owner in relation to the land,[58] to the acts which the squatter has performed on the land,[59] to any facts which may point to his having permission to be on the land (in which case his possession cannot be adverse),[60] and to his intention in occupying the land.

The intention of the squatter: animus possidendi

Possession of land will be adverse where the use made by the squatter is inconsistent with ownership of any other person.[61] In addition, it is necessary to show a mental element on the part of the squatter: the *animus possidendi*, *i.e.* the intention to possess. The precise scope of the intention which must be proved in order to establish adverse possession is a little blurred and subject to some controversy, but there are some common themes.

Necessity of mental element on part of possessor

Relevance of fencing: who is being excluded?

Intention of excluding all comers

Where the squatter has erected fencing around the disputed land with the intention of excluding all comers, including the true owner, possession will clearly be adverse.[62] However, the fencing of the disputed property will not be conclusive evidence that the possession was adverse[63]: it has been held in a number of cases that time will not start to run against the owner unless the squatter can establish that his acts of fencing land or locking gates were done with the intention of excluding the owner as well as the general public.[64] The requirement of such a general intention has been criticised[65] and was not adopted in the leading Privy Council case in this area.[66]

An intention to do what?

It has been said that what is required for this purpose is not an intention to own, or even an intention to acquire ownership, but

---

[57] *Williams* v. *Usherwood* (1983) 45 P. & C.R. 235, C.A.; *West Bank Estates Ltd.* v. *Arthur* [1967] 1 A.C. 665, H.L.
[58] See below, p. 95.
[59] See above, p. 91.
[60] *Ibid.*
[61] *Seddon* v. *Smith* (1877) 36 L.T. 168.
[62] *Buckinghamshire County Council* v. *Moran* [1989] 2 All E.R. 225; in *Seddon* v. *Smith* (1877) 36 L.T. 168 at p. 169 Cockburn C.J. stated: "Enclosure is the strongest possible evidence of adverse possession". See also *Colchester Borough Council* v. *Smith* [1992] 2 All E.R. 561, C.A.; *Marsden* v. *Miller, The Times,* January 23, 1992, C.A.
[63] *Tecbild Ltd.* v. *Chamberlain* (1969) 20 P. & C.R. 633.
[64] *Littledale* v. *Liverpool College* [1900] 1 Ch. 19; *George Wimpey & Co.* v. *Sohn* [1966] 1 All E.R. 232; *Powell* v. *McFarlane* (1979) 38 P. & C.R. 452.
[65] See Dockray, "Adverse Possession and Intention" (1982) Conv. 256.
[66] *Ocean Estates Ltd.* v. *Pinder* [1969] 2 A.C. 19; see also *Paradise Beach and Transportation Company Ltd.* v. *Price-Robinson* [1968] A.C. 1072.

Intention to possess the land to the exclusion of all comers

an intention for the time being to possess the land to the exclusion of all others, including the owner.[67] It is not, therefore, necessary for the squatter to establish that he had a long term plan to acquire ownership of the land by adverse possession: ignoring the title of the paper owner and treating the land as his own may serve to demonstrate the requisite *animus possidendi*.[68]

Possession by child

Where the squatter was a minor at the start of the purported period of adverse possession, time may still run in his favour.[69] However, his age may be relevant when considering whether the necessary intention was present[70]: it will be more difficult to show that the acts of a child in relation to a disputed piece of land were accomplished with the intention of possessing the land to the exclusion of all others.

The intention of the owner

Owner who intends to use land in future may be dispossessed

The Court of Appeal has recently stated[71] that the decision in *Leigh* v. *Jack*[72] should not be taken as authority for the proposition that an owner who retains a piece of land with a view to its future utilisation for a specific purpose can never be dispossessed. Where the acts of the squatter are trivial in nature and do not reveal a clear intention to dispossess, it will be relevant to take into account the owner's intended use of the land; but where the squatter has demonstrated a firm and obvious intention to dispossess, time may run in his favour.[73]

Accrual of the cause of action

Dispossession and discontinuance

In an action to recover land, "the right of action shall be treated as having accrued on the date of the dispossession or discontinuance."[74] Discontinuance will be the date when the owner of the property effectively abandoned all rights over it: this will be difficult to establish unless the owner has left the property taking all his belongings with him, and has committed no acts in the intervening period which might be interpreted as acts of ownership. It has been said that "the smallest act would be sufficient to show that there was no discontinuance."[75] Such acts would include any repairs done on the property, any entry

---

[67] *Buckinghamshire County Council* v. *Moran* [1989] 2 All E.R. 225 at 238, *per* Slade L.J.

[68] *Colchester Borough Council* v. *Smith* [1992] 2 All E.R. 561, C.A.

[69] See *Willis* v. *Earl of Howe* [1893] 2 Ch. 545.

[70] *Powell* v. *McFarlane* (1977) 38 P. & C.R. 452, where the plaintiff was 14 years of age when he started to use the defendant's land for the purpose of grazing the family cow and for cutting and taking hay.

[71] *Buckinghamshire County Council* v. *Moran* [1989] 2 All E.R. 225 at p. 234, *per* Slade L.J.

[72] (1879) 5 Ex.D. 264.

[73] *Buckinghamshire County Council* v. *Moran* [1989] 2 All E.R. 225; see also *Powell* v. *McFarlane* (1977) 38 P. & C.R. 452. See further above, "When is possession adverse?"

[74] Limitation Act 1980, Sched. 1, para. 1.

[75] *Leigh* v. *Jack* (1879) 5 Ex.D. 264 at p. 272, *per* Bramwell L.J.; see further, above.

onto the land for the purposes of inspection, storage or removal of goods or even, it would seem, the dumping of rubbish.[76]

The owner will have 12 years from the date on which he first had a cause of action against the squatter. "Action" is defined in section 38 of the 1980 Act as "any proceeding in a court of law, including an ecclesiastical court." Time will not run against the owner where it is certain that his action will fail.[77] Where tenants have ceased paying rent and may be considered to be in adverse possession, the court have a discretion as to whether or not to grant repossession to the owner: time will continue to run against the owner since he has the right to bring the action even though the decision is at the discretion of the court.[78]

Acknowledgment of owner's title

An acknowledgment by the squatter of the owner's title after time has started to run but before the limitation period has expired, will serve to postpone the commencement of the running of time.[79] An offer by the squatter to purchase the land constitutes an acknowledgment that the offeree's title is better than that of the squatter and, while it may not constitute an acknowledgment that the offeree has a marketable title, it will serve to postpone the running of time.[80] Similarly, an offer to pay rent will be regarded as an acknowledgment of the better title of the other party.[81]

Once the limitation period has expired, a subsequent acknowledgment by the squatter of the rights of the former owner, whether express or implied (for example, in the form of payment of rent) will not serve to revive the title of the owner.[82] However, if the squatter enters into a tenancy agreement with the owner after the latter's title has been extinguished by the squatter's adverse possession, and, under that tenancy agreement he acknowledges that his previous possession was by licence and consent of the owner, he will not be entitled to go back on that contractual acknowledgment and assert that by virtue of his previous occupation he had obtained title by adverse possession. The owner's title to the land will be revived by the contractual acknowledgment and the squatter will be estopped from denying its truth.[83]

A judgment or possession order made against the occupier in favour of the owner will serve to restart the running of time: the owner will have a further six years before his title is

---

[76] *Williams Bros. Direct Supply Ltd.* v. *Raftery* [1958] 1 Q.B. 159.
[77] *Warren* v. *Murray* [1894] 2 Q.B. 648, C.A. where a 99-year lease had been agreed between the parties, but had not been executed. It was held that time did not run against the owner since an order for specific performance of the lease would be granted if the owner sought to recover the land before the expiry of the lease.
[78] *Moses* v. *Lovegrove* [1952] 1 All E.R. 1279, C.A.; *Jessamine Investment Co.* v. *Schwartz* [1976] 3 All E.R. 521, C.A.
[79] Limitation Act 1980, s.29(2).
[80] *Edginton* v. *Clark* [1964] 1 Q.B. 367.
[81] *R.* v. *Secretary of State for the Environment, ex p. Davies* [1991] 1 P.L.R. 78, C.A.
[82] *Nicholson* v. *England* [1926] 2 K.B. 93.
[83] *Colchester Borough Council* v. *Smith* [1992] 2 All E.R. 561, C.A. As to estoppel by convention in general, see *Amalgamated Investment and Property Co. Ltd.* v. *Texas Commerce International Bank Ltd.* [1981] 3 All E.R. 577. See *Chitty on Contracts* (26th ed., 1989), paras. 221–225.

extinguished.[84] This will be so even where the action to recover the land was commenced at the very end of the initial limitation period with the result that the 12-year period expires whilst proceedings are pending.[85]

Leases and tenancies

Action for arrears of rent: six-year limitation period
An action to recover arrears of rent or damages in respect of arrears of rent may not be brought after the expiration of six years from the date on which those arrears fell due: section 19 of the Limitation Act 1980. However, where the title of the owner of the land has been extinguished by virtue of adverse possession, no action will be possible to recover rent which fell due during the period of such adverse possession.[86]

Land subject to periodic tenancy agreement
In the case of an action to recover land which was subject to a tenancy agreement, regard must be had to Schedule 1 of the 1980 Act which provides that a tenancy from year to year or other period, without a lease in writing, shall be treated as being determined at the expiration of the first year or other period,[87] the cause of action will therefore accrue on this date. But, if rent is received after such deemed determination, the right of action will be deemed to have accrued on the date of the last receipt of rent.[88]

Effect of expiry of time

The effect of the expiry of time will differ according to whether the land in question is registered or unregistered, and whether it is freehold or leasehold.

Unregistered land
In the case of unregistered land, once the limitation period has expired as against the owner of land, by virtue of there having been continuous adverse possession for the requisite period, the owner's title to that land is extinguished together with his right of action to recover the land.[89] The squatter then holds a new estate in the land based on his adverse possession.[90]

Registered land
The provisions of the Limitation Act 1980 apply to registered land[91] in the same way as non-registered except that in the case of registered land, the estate of the person registered as proprietor is not extinguished, but is held in trust for the person who has acquired title by virtue of adverse possession.[92] The

---

[84] It should be noted that the time limit for an action to enforce a judgment was formerly 12 years under the Limitation Act 1939. It was reduced to six by the Limitation Amendment Act 1980.

[85] See *B.P. Properties Ltd.* v. *Buckler* [1987] 2 E.G.L.R. 168, C.A.; it should be noted that this case was decided under the limitation Act 1939 where the longer limitation period of 12 years for enforcement of a judgment was permitted.

[86] *Re Jolly, Gathercole* v. *Norfolk* [1900] 2 Ch. 616.

[87] Limitation Act 1980, Sched. 1, para. 5(1).

[88] *Ibid.* Sched. 1, para. 5(2). See also *Hayward* v. *Challoner* [1968] 1 Q.B. 107, C.A.

[89] Limitation Act 1980, s.17.

[90] However, in respect of settled land and land held on trust, see *ibid.* s.18 and Chap. 11.

[91] See further Ruoff and Roper, *Registered Conveyancing* (5th ed., 1986), Chap. 32.

[92] Land Registration Act 1925, s.75(1). See *Bridges* v. *Mees* [1957] Ch. 475.

person who has acquired title can then apply to be registered as the proprietor of the land.[93]

No recovery of rent or damages

The owner's right to recover rent owing for the period of adverse possession is extinguished once the limitation period has expired.[94] Similarly, his right to recover damages from the person who has dispossessed him is extinguished with the expiry of the limitation period.[95]

Leasehold land

Where the land is leasehold rather than freehold land, the situation is more complicated. After 12 years' adverse possession, the leaseholder's title will be extinguished as against the possessor. However, the landlord's (freeholder's) title is unaffected by this adverse possession and time will not start to run against the freeholder until the date of determination of the lease.[96] Since title to land is relative rather than absolute, the leaseholder's title may remain good against the freeholder or landlord even though it has been extinguished as against the squatter. The landlord will not be able to bring an action for possession against the squatter until the determination of the leaseholder's lease.

Unregistered leasehold land

In *Fairweather* v. *St. Marylebone Property Co.*[97] the House of Lords held that, if, in respect of unregistered land, the leaseholder surrendered his title to the land to the freeholder after time had run against him in favour of the possessor, the surrender would take effect as a determination of the lease and the landlord would acquire an immediate right to bring an action for possession against the possessor.[98]

Registered leasehold land

The position regarding acquisition by adverse possession of title to registered leasehold land was considered in *Spectrum Investment Co.* v. *Holmes*[99] where the defendant had acquired by adverse possession the title of registered leasehold land and had been registered as proprietor under section 75 of the Land Registration Act 1925. Following this new registration, the former leaseholder purported to surrender her lease to the plaintiff (the freeholder), thereby seeking to benefit from the decision in *Fairweather*. The plaintiff claimed possession of the land from the defendant, and the former leaseholder, who was joined as the second plaintiff, claimed rectification of the register by the cancellation of the defendant's possessory title and the restoration of her own. It was held that, while the Land Registration Act 1925 was not intended to alter substantive rights relating to land, it undoubtedly was intended to alter the manner in which such rights were to be established and transferred. Since the second plaintiff was not registered as the leasehold owner at the time of the purported surrender, that surrender could not have the effect of transferring rights to the

---

[93] Land Registration Act 1925, s.75(1).
[94] *Re Jolly, Gathercole* v. *Norfolk* [1990] 2 Ch. 616.
[95] *Mount Carmel Investments Ltd.* v. *Peter Thurlow Ltd.* [1988] 3 All E.R. 129.
[96] *Fairweather* v. *St. Marylebone Property Co. Ltd.* [1963] A.C. 510.
[97] [1963] A.C. 510.
[98] The decision has been criticised (the Supreme Court of Ireland declined to follow it: *Perry* v. *Woodfarm Homes Ltd.* [1975] I.R. 104), but the Law Reform Committee in its Final Report on Limitation of Actions, Cmnd. 6923 at paras. 3.44–3.45, was of the opinion that although a statutory reversal of the decision might produce a more logical situation, it would not resolve all the difficulties and could be circumvented by a carefully drawn covenant.
[99] [1981] 1 W.L.R. 221.

landlord. Moreover, even if the surrender had been effected prior to the registration of the defendant as leaseholder, it would have been ineffective since it was not effected by the only means authorised by the Land Registration Act 1925 for the disposal of a registered leasehold interest by act of the parties. The evasory tactics permitted in *Fairweather* will not aid a dispossessed leaseholder of registered land unless the surrender is effected in accordance with the procedure laid down in the Land Registration Act.

No privity of estate with landlord

A transfer of title by adverse possession in relation to leasehold land will not serve to substitute the squatter for the leaseholder for all purposes. Whilst he may be entitled to be registered as the leaseholder, he does not enter into privity of estate with the landlord, who consequently cannot sue him for rent or require him to observe any covenants in the lease which existed between the landlord and the dispossessed leaseholder.[1] However, in the event that covenants contained in the lease are not performed, the landlord may exercise his rights of re-entry, and the squatter may suffer forfeiture.[2] Where the disputed covenants run with the land, the squatter, or anyone claiming through him, will be bound by them.[3]

Squatter bound by covenants running with the land

---

[1] *Tichborne* v. *Weir* (1892) 67 L.T. 735, C.A.
[2] *Tickner* v. *Buzzacott* [1965] Ch. 426.
[3] *Re Nisbet and Potts' Contract* [1906] 1 Ch. 386.

9 PRESCRIPTION

Acquisition of an easement

Title is not the only right over land which may be acquired by virtue of the running of time: an easement may also be acquired, although the conditions for acquisition of an easement are rather different from those pertaining to the acquisition of land by adverse possession. It has been said that adverse possession "extinguishes old titles, whereas prescription has the effect of generating new rights. Limitation thus has a negative and extinctive effect, whereas prescription is positive and creative in its mode of operation."[1] An action for trespass against a person who has acquired an appropriate easement will not lie once the necessary period of limitation has expired.

An easement is a right attached to the land in ownership of one person to use land belonging to another in a particular manner (which does not involve the taking of soil or the natural produce of that land).[2] An easement may be created in one of three ways: by an express grant from the owner of the servient tenement, by statute or by prescription. This chapter is concerned with the third of these methods.

Creation of an easement

An easement over the land of another may be acquired by prescription in one of the following ways:

(a) by prescription at common law;
(b) by the doctrine of the lost modern grant;
(c) under the Prescription Act 1832.

Easement to commit a nuisance

The requisite period of prescription may also serve to permit the owner of land to commit what would otherwise be an actionable nuisance. However, in practice, such a claim is unlikely to succeed mainly because some important aspect of either the plaintiff's or the defendant's user of the land will have changed during the 20-year prescription period. An assertion of a prescriptive right to commit a nuisance will fail where the plaintiff (or his predecessor in title) was not in a position to complain about the defendant's activity for the requisite period, for example, when the plaintiff's property has only recently been built close to the source of noise or smell.[3] The defendant may also fail where he cannot establish that the nuisance in respect of which his neighbours are suing has continued for the whole of the 20-year period at the same level of intensity: if matters have deteriorated in any way over the course of the period relied on, there will be no prescriptive right.[4]

Right to light

An action claiming a prescriptive right to light is in essence an action in nuisance which will succeed only where it can be shown that:

---

[1] Gray, *Elements of Land Law* (1989) at p. 679. See also Goodman, "Adverse Possession or Prescription? Problems of Conflict" (1968) 32 Conv.(N.S.) 270.

[2] The acquisition of *profits à prendre* (*i.e.* the right to enter land belonging to another and to take from it some profit from the soil or a portion of the soil itself) is governed by the same principles as acquisition of easements.

[3] *Sturges* v. *Bridgman* (1879) 11 Ch.D. 852, C.A.; *Miller* v. *Jackson* [1977] Q.B. 966.

[4] For a more general discussion of limitation periods in nuisance, see Chap. 5.

> (a) the defendant has obstructed (or proposes so to do) the light falling through the claimant's windows;
>
> (b) that, as a result of this obstruction, the claimant now has (or will have) insufficient light for the comfortable enjoyment of his premises; and
>
> (c) that the premises had previously enjoyed sufficient light for the requisite 20-year period.

The right to light is discussed more fully at the end of this chapter.

Common conditions of acquisition

Certain conditions are common to all three forms of acquisition and these are considered next; the individual conditions for each of the three forms will be detailed at the end of this chapter.[5] It should be noted that these conditions do not apply to the acquisition of rights to light under section 3 of the Prescription Act 1832.

Continuity of user

Question of continuity depends on nature of the right

In all cases, the claimant must show that there has been sufficient continuity of user throughout the period in question. This will be a question of fact, and will depend on the nature of the right claimed over the land.[6] If the land has been used just a few times a year, but for certain specific purposes, e.g. vehicular access for the sowing of seeds and harvesting in spring and autumn this may constitute sufficient continuity of user.[7] But where the claimant needed to use the land only once every 10 to 12 years, this was held not to constitute sufficient continuity of user for the purposes of prescription.[8]

User must be "as of right"

Use must be consistent with presumption of grant

It is not enough for the claimant to show merely that he has used the land on a continuous basis for the required number of years: he must also show that his use of the land was consistent with the presumption that a grant of an easement had been granted. If the claimant's use is inconsistent with such a presumption, he cannot assert the existence of a prescriptive easement. The Latin maxim *nec vi, nec clam, nec precario* (without force, without secrecy and without permission) is generally used in order to illustrate the nature of the user which the claimant must establish.

---

[5] The existence of three methods of establishing an easement by prescription was criticised by the Court of Appeal in *Tehidy Minerals Ltd.* v. *Norman* [1971] 2 Q.B. 528 on the grounds that it results in much unnecessary complication and confusion.

[6] *Hollins* v. *Verney* (1884) 13 Q.B.D. 304.

[7] See *Diment* v. *N.H. Foot Ltd.* [1974] 1 W.L.R. 1427 at p. 1430 where it was stated that a user of land limited to no more than six to 10 occasions a year was sufficient in extent and regularity to be capable of creating a right of way.

[8] *Hollins* v. *Verney* (1884) 13 Q.B.D. 304.

No prescription if force has been used

(a) **Force.** If the claimant exerted some degree of force in order to use the land, he clearly cannot show that this is consistent with a presumption of a grant. Force will include physical violence (for example, the breaking down of a fence or forcing of a lock), any dispute with the servient owner as to the claimant's right to use the land[9] or where the user relied on to establish the easement is illegal.[10]

No prescription if land used secretly

(b) **Secrecy.** The dominant owner's claim may be defeated on the ground of secrecy not only where he has acted by stealth or in the night,[11] but also where he has acted openly but the circumstances of the case are such that the servient owner would not normally be expected to have been aware of his use even if he had exercised diligence in the protection of his interests over the land.[12]

Absence of secrecy is required, not in order to establish any state of mind on the part of the claimant, but because the acquisition of the easement should be consistent with the presumption of a grant. The vital factor is, therefore, some form of acquiescence, whether actual or implied: if the user has been "secret", the servient owner cannot be said to have had an opportunity to acquiesce and therefore the right cannot be established.[13] Acquiescence involves knowledge on the part of the servient owner of the acts being done by the dominant owner and power to stop those acts or to sue[14] in respect of them.[15] Acquiescence should not, however, be interpreted as having a meaning wider than mere tolerance without objection.[16]

No prescription if permission given

(c) **Permission.** Where the claimant enjoys the land under some form of permission or licence from the servient owner, this will again be inconsistent with the presumption of a grant of an easement over the land.[17] If any payment is made by the claimant for the use of the land, the claim will be defeated.[18] At common law, permission of any kind, whether oral or in writing, would suffice to defeat a claim to an easement; this rule has been modified by the Prescription Act 1832.[19]

The mistaken belief on the part of the claimant that he had

---

[9] *Eaton* v. *Swansea Waterworks Co.* (1851) 17 Q.B. 267; *Dalton* v. *Angus* (1881) 6 App.Cas. 740 at p. 786.

[10] *Cargill* v. *Gotts* [1981] 1 W.L.R. 441.

[11] See *Dawson* v. *Duke of Norfolk* (1815) 1 Price 246; *Liverpool Corp.* v. *Coghill* [1918] 1 Ch. 307.

[12] *Union Lighterage Co.* v. *London Graving Dock Co.* [1902] Ch. 557, C.A.; *Diment* v. *N. H. Foot* [1974] 1 W.L.R. 1427.

[13] The importance of acquiescence was stressed by Fry L.J. in *Dalton* v. *Angus* (1881) 6 App.Cas. 740 at p. 773: "the whole law of prescription and the whole law which governs the presumption or inference of a grant or covenant rest upon acquiescence."

[14] If the land is in the possession of a tenant, the owner may not be able to sue: see *Pugh* v. *Savage* [1970] 2 Q.B. 373. If the act of the claimant does not amount to trespass or other actionable wrong, again, the owner will not be able to sue: *Liverpool Corp.* v. *Coghill* [1918] 1 Ch. 307; *Sturges* v. *Bridgman* (1879) 11 Ch.D. 852, C.A.

[15] *Dalton* v. *Angus* (1881) 6 App.Cas. 740 at p. 774; see also *Diment* v. *N.H. Foot* [1974] 1 W.L.R. 1427 at p. 1433; *Mills* v. *Silver* [1991] 2 W.L.R. 324.

[16] *Mills* v. *Silver* [1991] 2 W.L.R. 324.

[17] For a recent example under the Prescription Act 1832, see *Jones* v. *Price, The Independent*, January 16, 1992, C.A.

[18] *Gardner* v. *Hodgson's Kingston Brewery Co. Ltd.* [1903] A.C. 229.

[19] See n. 20.

an express grant of a right of way over the land in question will not prevent his use being as of right so as to enable him to establish a prescriptive action.[20]

User against whom?

Claim must be asserted against fee simple owner

Since the basis of any claim to the establishment of an easement by prescription resides in the presumption of a grant, the user relied on by the dominant owner must be asserted against the fee simple owner of the land, since only he has the capacity to make such a grant. Consequently, if at the start of the user, the land is in the occupation of someone other than the fee simple owner, the claim will fail. However, a subsequent letting of the servient tenement will not destroy the claim, since the grant could have been made.[21]

Fee simple owner of dominant tenement must be different from fee simple owner of servient tenement

It is always necessary that the fee simple owner of the dominant tenement is different from the fee simple owner of the servient tenement: a tenant, even on a long lease, cannot acquire an easement by prescription against land held by his landlord.[22] This will be so whether the claim is made under the Prescription Act 1832, at common law or on the basis of a lost modern grant.[23] This can have the somewhat impractical consequence that in a street where some houses are held in fee simple and others on very long leases, only the former can acquire easements by prescription over the land of a neighbour.

User by whom?

Claim by fee simple owner of dominant tenement or someone claiming through him

The claim may be made by either the fee simple owner of the dominant tenement or, on his behalf, by some person occupying the land through him. It is not necessary that the claimant should himself have been in occupation of the dominant tenement for the entire period of prescription; he may claim where the land has been leased to a tenant or where he has acquired the fee simple in the land from a former owner in whose favour the period of prescription had started to run.

Nature of the right acquired

Right limited by nature of user

A prescriptive right of way will be limited by the nature of the user which has arisen.[24] Where the right acquired is to use land as a right of way, exercise of the right may be limited to pedestrian access or may include bridle or vehicular use, depending on the use which was made during the period of acquisition.

The claimant will be entitled to repair the way when necessary (for example by filling in ruts[25]), but not to carry out improvements which would change its nature.[26]

---

[20] *Bridle v. Ruby* [1988] 3 All E.R. 64. The same is true where the claimant believed he had an effective express grant of a right to light: *Newham v. Lawson* (1971) 115 S.J. 446; (1971) 22 P. & C.R. 852.

[21] *Pugh v. Savage* [1970] 2 Q.B. 373.

[22] *Kilgour v. Gaddes* [1904] 1 K.B. 457; *Derry v. Sanders* [1919] 1 K.B. 233, C.A.; recently confirmed by the Court of Appeal in *Simmons v. Dobson* [1991] 1 W.L.R. 720.

[23] *Simmons v. Dobson* [1991] 1 W.L.R. 720.

[24] *Wimbledon and Putney Commons Conservators v. Dixon* (1875) 1 Ch.D. 362, C.A.

[25] *Taylor v. Whitehead* (1781) 2 Doug. K.B. 744.

[26] *Mills v. Silver* [1991] 2 W.L.R. 324.

Common law prescription

Time immemorial test

Common law prescription was based upon a presumed grant, but this could be presumed only where the appropriate user had continued from time immemorial, that is 1189.[27] Clearly, in most cases, it was impossible to satisfy this test. Claims in respect of rights of light were particularly vulnerable to such a rebuttal, since, although the dominant owner may establish an uninterrupted flow of light for a period of many years, there can be no user from time immemorial if the building receiving the light was erected after 1189.

The lost modern grant

Fictitious presumption

In order to mitigate the harshness of the common law rule under which a claim would fail if it could be shown that the enjoyment of the right claimed did not date from time immemorial, the courts evolved the doctrine of the lost modern grant. Here there is a fictitious presumption which arises out of long usage that an easement had in fact been granted at some time since 1189, but that the grant has been lost.[28]

Where there has been sufficient use of the land at some time in the past to warrant the application of the doctrine, discontinuance of use will not defeat that grant or amount to an abandonment of the right and in an action brought against him for trespass, the defendant may rely on a continuous period of user by his predecessors in title, notwithstanding that he himself has not exercised the right with continuity during his period of ownership of the dominant tenement.[29]

The Prescription Act 1832

Supplementary basis for claim

The statute provides a supplementary basis for a claim to an easement by prescription: it does not replace the above forms of prescription, indeed, a claimant is entitled to rely on all three.[30] The statute provides differing rules according to whether the easement asserted relates to a right of light or to any other form of easement.

Forms of easement other than rights of light

Two limitation periods

Two periods of prescription are provided for by the Act: a shorter 20-year period, which is subject to a number of conditions, and a 40-year period subject to fewer conditions.

---

[27] 1189 was the date fixed by the Statute of Westminster the First as the limit of legal memory; any right which could be shown to have existed at that date could not be challenged.

[28] The doctrine was approved by the House of Lords in *Dalton* v. *Henry Angus & Co.* (1881) 6 App. Cas. 740.

[29] *Mills* v. *Silver* [1991] 2 W.L.R. 324.

[30] *Pugh* v. *Savage* [1970] 2 Q.B. 373; *Healey* v. *Hawkins* [1968] 1 W.L.R. 1967.

(a) **Twenty years user.** Section 2 of the Prescription Act 1832 removes the barrier to many common law claims by providing that no claim to an easement which may lawfully be made at common law shall be defeated simply by showing that the land was first enjoyed at any time prior to the 20-year period. However, the claim may be defeated if any of the other conditions necessary to support a common law claim are not fulfilled (*i.e.* that the user was not of right as outlined above, *e.g.* because there was some form of permission, whether oral or in writing).

Twenty-year period subject to conditions

No interruption
It is necessary that the user be for the full period without interruption: interruption in this context does not mean suspension of user by the claimant, but some interruption by the owner of the land or a third party which prevents the claimant's user (*e.g.* barring access to the land). Entry onto the servient tenement of a tenant will not be classed as an interruption.[31]

For an interruption to operate so as to interrupt the running of time in the claimant's favour, it is necessary he should acquiesce in it for at least one year after he had notice of its existence.[32] Consequently the barring access to land 19 years after the commencement of the user by the claimant may be useless to prevent him acquiring an easement by prescription if he issues a writ more than 20 years after commencement of the user, but less than one year after the barring.[33]

Acquiescence for one year

Where an action is brought more than a year after the interruption, the burden will be on the plaintiff to prove that he had not acquiesced or submitted to the interruption[34] and that he had effectively communicated his opposition to the defendant.[35]

Where a claim based on the Prescription Act 1832 fails on the ground that there has been an interruption of more than one year, there may still be a valid claim on the basis of a lost modern grant.[36]

Twenty-year period must be immediately preceding
In order to rely on the Act, the claimant must show that the necessary user took place over the 20 years before the action was brought, *i.e.* the 20 years immediately prior to the issue of the writ. It would seem that any absence or intermission of use in those 20 years will defeat a claim under the Act.[37]

Suspension of running of time
The running of the period of user may be suspended in certain circumstances and the period before suspension may then be added to the period following it, so that it is not necessary for the claimant to restart the running of time.[38] Section 7 of the Prescription Act 1832 provides for deductions to be made from the period of user to allow for periods where the appropriate person to resist the claim was a minor or under a disability or was a tenant for life.

[31] *Pugh* v. *Savage* [1970] 2 Q.B. 373.
[32] Prescription Act 1832, s.4.
[33] *Flight* v. *Thomas* (1840) 11 A. & E. 688.
[34] *Presland* v. *Bingham* (1888) 41 Ch.D. 268.
[35] *Dance* v. *Triplow, The Times,* December 4, 1991, C.A.: the facts concerned acquiescence in an interruption to a right to light, but the principle will be the same in respect of other easements.
[36] *Ward (Helston) Ltd.* v. *Kerrier District Council* (1984) 24 R.V.R. 18.
[37] See *Mills* v. *Silver* [1991] 2 W.L.R. 324 where this was held to be so at first instance but was not dealt with by the Court of Appeal.
[38] *Pugh* v. *Savage* [1970] 2 Q.B. 373.

Forty-year period subject to fewer conditions

(b) Forty years user. Section 2 of the Prescription Act 1832 also provides an alternative period of prescription of 40 years. If the claimant can show the necessary enjoyment for the full period of 40 years next before his action[39] his right "shall be deemed absolute and indefeasible, unless it shall appear that the same was enjoyed by some consent or agreement expressly given or made for that purpose by deed or writing." Whereas a claim under the 20-year period will, like a common law claim, fail if there has been any permission, whether oral or in writing, for the user, a claim under the 40-year period will not fail if the consent has been given only orally at the beginning of the period. Such a claim will be defeated by consent in writing or by periodic consent, whether oral or in writing.

Relevance of consent

Deductions

Deductions will be made in respect of any period where the land was occupied by a tenant for life or by a tenant under a lease exceeding three years. However, no deduction will be made in respect of disability.

Easements of light

Section 3 of the Prescription Act 1832 provides a simpler method for the acquisition of rights of light than that which exists at common law. It provides that:

Twenty years without interruption

"when ... the ... use of light to ... any dwelling house, workshop or other building shall have been actually enjoyed ... for the full period of twenty years without interruption, the right thereto shall be deemed absolute and indefeasible ... unless ... the same was enjoyed by some consent ... given for that purpose by deed or writing."

Many of general rules do not apply

The right acquired under the section is an easement for the access of light to a building and not to a particular room within it.[40] Many of the rules outlined above in relation to the general acquisition of easements will consequently not apply: the claim will not be defeated where the claimant is a tenant claiming an easement of light against his landlord or against another tenant of the same landlord; the user need not be of right, but consent in writing will defeat the claim.

The rules relating to interruption[41] apply to the rights of light,[42] as it does to other easements under the Act[43]; as does the requirement that the 20-year period be immediately prior to the action.[44]

An action claiming a prescriptive right to light is an action in nuisance, even where it is claimed under the Prescription Act 1832.[45] It must, therefore, be shown that there has been such a substantial interference with the use and enjoyment of the claimant's property that it constitutes an actionable nuisance.[46]

[39] *Pugh* v. *Savage* [1970] 2 Q.B. 373.
[40] *Price* v. *Hilditch* [1930] 1 Ch. 500 at p. 508.
[41] *Ibid.*
[42] See also the Rights of Light Act 1959, which provides that a legal fiction of interruption may be created, so preventing the claimant from acquiring an absolute right to light, by registering a notice in the local land charges register.
[43] Prescription Act 1832, s.4; see also *Dance* v. *Triplow*, *The Times*, December 4, 1991, C.A.
[44] *Hyman* v. *Van den Bergh* [1908] 1 Ch. 167.
[45] *Higgins* v. *Betts* [1905] 2 Ch. 210.
[46] *Carr-Saunders* v. *Dick McNeil Associates Ltd.* [1986] 2 All E.R. 888.

Test is how much light is left

The test is not how much light has been taken and whether that amount has materially lessened the enjoyment and use of the property, but how much is left and whether that is enough for the comfortable use and enjoyment of the property according to the ordinary requirements of mankind.[47] The court must take into account the nature of the premises and the use to which the reasonable owner might put them. Such a use may well include internal, structural alterations, which will themselves affect the amount of light reaching a room from a particular window. In the case of a large, open room receiving light from windows on two or more sides, the owner may well be acting reasonably in dividing that space into smaller units, with the result that one or more of those units receives light from only one side. If the window on that side is then obstructed, the defendant cannot show that part of the premises was originally partially lit from the window on the other side of the building.[48]

Sensitive plaintiff

Where the light which remains is of such a level as to permit the owner to enjoy the premises in an ordinary manner, he will not be permitted to defeat an otherwise acceptable obstruction if, by reason of his activities, he requires light of a higher level than normal. He will probably also fail where the nature of his windows is such that they require a higher level of light than usual in order to light the premises.[49] It may be argued, though, that an ancient, semi-opaque window has acquired a right to a particular level of light which should be protected by the rules of prescription.

---

[47] *Carr-Saunders* v. *Dick McNeil Associates Ltd.* [1986] 2 All E.R. 888 at p. 215. See also *Colls* v. *Home and Colonial Stores Ltd.* [1904] A.C. 179.

[48] *Carr-Saunders* v. *Dick McNeil Associates Ltd.* [1986] 2 All E.R. 888.

[49] For example, stained glass windows as in *Newham* v. *Lawson* (1971) 22 P. & C.R. 852, *per* Plowman J. at p. 859.

10 ADMINISTRATIVE AND EUROPEAN COMMUNITY LAW

English administrative law

An application for judicial review is governed by the provisions of section 31 of the Supreme Court Act 1981 and Order 53 of the Rules of the Supreme Court. Order 53, rule 4(1) provides[1]:

Three-month limit for judicial review

> "An application for judicial review shall be made promptly and in any event within three months from the date when grounds for the application first arose unless the Court considers that there is good reason for extending the period within which the application shall be made."

The imposition of such a short time limit emphasises the fact that, in matters of judicial review, prompt action is vital since[2]:

> "the public interest in good administration requires that public authorities and third parties should not be kept in suspense as to the legal validity of a decision the authority has reached in purported exercise of decision-making powers for any longer period than is absolutely necessary in fairness to the person affected by the decision."

Section 31(6) Supreme Court Act further provides:

No relief if undue delay

> "Where the High Court considers that there has been undue delay in making an application for judicial review, the court may refuse to grant—(a) leave for the making of the application; or (b) any relief sought on the application, if it considers that the granting of the relief sought would be likely to cause substantial hardship to, or substantially prejudice the rights of, any person or would be detrimental to good administration."

Two-stage procedure

A two-stage procedure is required by Order 53: the applicant must first obtain leave through an *ex parte* application to apply for judicial review and then, if such leave is granted, the application will be heard by a Divisional Court. The three-month time limit laid down in Order 53 relates to the *ex parte* application, rather than to the substantive application.[3]

Limit not absolute

The three-month limit is not absolute either with regard to

[1] There is now a uniform time limit of three months for orders of mandamus, prohibition and certiorari. In the case of certiorari, this replaces the former time limit of six months. However, the court now has discretion to extend this limit where there is good reason, unless the granting of relief would cause substantial hardship, as laid down in section 31(6) of the Supreme Court Act 1981.

[2] *O'Reilly* v. *Mackman* [1983] 2 A.C. 238 at pp. 280–281.

[3] *R.* v. *Stratford-upon-Avon District Council, ex p. Jackson* [1985] 1 W.L.R. 1319, C.A.

the applicant or the public authority. Leave to apply may be refused even within the three-month period if the applicant has not acted promptly.[4]

Substantial hardship

Moreover, the time limit laid down in Order 53 must be read in conjunction with the provisions in section 31(6) of the Supreme Court Act 1981 relating to substantial hardship or prejudice caused by undue delay. The result is that, although the judge hearing the application for leave to apply for judicial review may determine that an extension to the three-month time limit is appropriate on the grounds that the delay arose through no fault of the applicant, the relief in the main application may be refused on the grounds of the undue delay and the hardship which would be caused.[5]

European Community law

When seeking to determine the time within which an action must be commenced in matters falling under the jurisdiction of the European Court of Justice in Luxembourg, regard must be had to the Treaty of Rome (which established the European Economic Community) and lays down a number of basic time limits which are supplemented by provisions in both the Court of Justice Protocol (which is appended to the Treaty of Rome) and the Rules of Procedure of the European Court of Justice.[6]

Documents containing time limits

The Treaty of Rome lays down time limits within which certain types of action must be brought: under article 173(3) proceedings challenging the legality of an act of the Council or the Commission (other than recommendations or opinions) must be[7] "instituted within two months of the publication of the measure or its notification to the plaintiff, or in the absence thereof, of the day on which it came to the notice of the latter." This two-month time limit for bringing an action for annulment applies to all proceedings, whether they are brought by a Member State, the Council, the Commission or a natural/legal person.

Two-month limit for action for annulment

Complaint of failure to act

A complaint that either the Council or the Commission has, in infringement of the Treaty, failed to act, must first be addressed to the institution concerned; if within two months of being so called upon to act, the institution has not defined its position, the action may be brought within a further period of two months.[8]

---

[4] The question of whether or not the applicant has acted promptly will depend on the circumstances of the case.
[5] *R*. v. *Stratford-upon-Avon District Council, ex p. Jackson* [1985] 1 W.L.R. 1319, C.A. It would seem that the reason for this inconsistency arises from an oversight in the drafting of the Supreme Court Act: see Wade, *Administrative Law*. See also *R*. v. *Dairy Produce Quota Tribunal for England and Wales, ex p. Caswell* [1990] 2 A.C. 738; [1990] 2 W.L.R. 1320.
[6] [1991] 3 C.M.L.R. 745.
[7] The time limit for an action for annulment under the European Coal and Steel Community (ECSC) Treaty is one month: art. 33(3). Under the Euratom Treaty it is two months: art. 146(3).
[8] Treaty of Rome, art. 175(2).

Contractual and tortious liability of Community

The contractual liability of the European Communities and their institutions is governed by the law applicable to the contract[9]; the limitation period will be that of the applicable law.[10] In the case of non-contractual (*e.g.* tortious) liability, article 43 of the Court of Justice Protocol provides for a five-year limitation period running from the occurrence of the event giving rise to such liability. Further time limits are laid down in a number of Community measures.

Periods of grace

In addition to the basic time limits laid down by the Treaty or relevant EC legislation, the Rules of Procedure of the European Court of Justice provide for periods of grace based on considerations of distance from the seat of the Court in Luxembourg.[11] In the case of United Kingdom residents, the period of grace is 10 days: all time limits are extended accordingly.

Directives not yet implemented

Where a Directive according rights to individuals has not been implemented into national law, EC law will preclude the Member State from relying on an individual's delay in instituting proceedings under the Directive, and any period laid down by national law within which proceedings must be initiated will not apply.[12] This is because of the state of uncertainty as to the extent of rights which exists as long as the Directive is not implemented. In such a situation, time can run only from the date when the situation of uncertainty is remedied, *i.e.* the date of implementation of the Directive.[13]

Nature and policy of EC time limits

Legal certainty

It has been stressed on a number of occasions that the time limits for instituting proceedings before the European Court of Justice have the objective of ensuring legal certainty.[14] Such time limits are consequently mandatory in nature, and are not subject to the discretion of either the parties or of the Court.[15] Unlike English law, it is not necessary for the defendant to raise the limitation point; since such limits constitute a matter of public interest, the Court may take the point of its own motion.[16] The time limits for instituting proceedings before the European Court of Justice are governed exclusively by Community law and are not subject to national rules of the Member States in relation

---

[9] European Economic Community (EEC) Treaty, art. 215.

[10] On the question of the applicable law, see the Contracts (Applicable Law) Act 1990, discussed in Chap. 1.

[11] The relevant "periods of grace" are set out in Annex II to the rules and are as follows: nothing for Luxembourg; two days for Belgium; six days for the European territory of France, Germany and the Netherlands; 10 days for the European territory of Denmark, Greece, Ireland, Italy, Spain, Portugal (excepting the Azores and Madeira for which the period of grace is three weeks); two weeks for other European countries and territories; one month for other countries, departments and territories.

[12] *Emmott* v. *Minister for Social Welfare* [1991] I.R.L.R. 387, E.C.J.

[13] *Cannon* v. *Barnsley Metropolitan Borough Council, The Times,* June 24, 1992.

[14] See Case 24/69 *Nebe* v. *Commission of the European Communities* [1970] E.C.R. 145; Joined Cases 122 and 123/79 *Schiavo* v. *Council of the European Communities* [1981] E.C.R. 473.

[15] Joined Cases 122 and 123/79 *Schiavo* v. *Council of the European Communities, ibid.*

[16] Case 33/72 *Gunnella* v. *Commission of the European Communities* [1973] E.C.R. 475.

to either the running of time or the interpretation of provisions.[17]

If no time limit, indefinite delay not permitted

Where there is no limitation period laid down for instituting proceedings (as, for example, in matters concerning the implementation of competition policy) the fundamental requirement of legal certainty will prevent the Commission from indefinitely delaying the exercise of its power to impose fines.[18] However, it has been held that two years from the date of infringement is too short a time to justify the idea that the right to take action in this area has been renounced by implication.[19] Presumably the question of what constitutes a reasonable limitation period in a given area will depend on the complexity of the issues involved and the time which would reasonably be considered necessary in order to investigate sufficiently before instituting proceedings.

Time limit extended for unforeseeable circumstances

Although legal certainty is paramount in this area, justice to the individual plaintiff is also vital; it is therefore provided that "no right shall be prejudiced in consequence of the expiry of a time limit if the party concerned proves the existence of unforeseeable circumstances or of *force majeure*."[20] The precise meaning to be given to the term *force majeure* will vary according to the facts of the case.[21] Generally, however, it will be interpreted narrowly and will not be available to extend the limitation period where the plaintiff has merely experienced undue difficulty in instituting proceedings.[22] It will not be limited to cases of absolute impossibility, but will apply where the plaintiff can show the existence of unusual circumstances beyond his control which could not reasonably have been avoided by him.[23] The fact that the plaintiff alleges that he could not find a lawyer to take his case within the time allowed because the action arose during the legal vacation will not constitute *force majeure*: he must show that it was impossible to find a lawyer.[24] Internal problems of communication within a company or group of companies which prevent the action from being commenced in time will not constitute *force majeure*.[25] Where, with individuals employed by the Community institutions, an employee did not have available to him an official text of the Staff Regulations in his own language, this will not constitute a case of unforeseeable circumstances or *force majeure*.[26] Similarly, the hazards of the postal service cannot normally be invoked as constituting unforeseeable circumstances or *force majeure*. However, the plaintiff will be entitled to rely on unforeseeable circumstances where the delay is caused, not by

[17] Case 209/83 *Ferriera Valsabbia SpA* v. *Commission of the European Communities* [1984] E.C.R. 3089.
[18] Case 48/69 *Imperial Chemical Industries Ltd.* v. *Commission of the European Communities* [1972] E.C.R. 619.
[19] *Ibid.*
[20] Court of Justice Protocol, Art. 42(2).
[21] Case 4/68 *Schwarzwaldmilch* v. *Einfuhr* [1968] E.C.R. 377.
[22] Case 209/83 *Ferriera Valsabbia SpA* v. *Commission of the European Communities* [1984] E.C.R. 3089.
[23] Case 11/70 *Internationale Handelsgesellschaft* v. *Einfuhr* [1970] E.C.R. 1125.
[24] *Ibid.*
[25] Case 42/85 *Cockerill-Sambre SA* v. *Commission of the European Communities* [1985] E.C.R. 3749.
[26] Case 276/85 *Cladakis* v. *Commission of the European Communities* [1987] E.C.R. 495.

the postal services, but by the fact that a registered letter containing the plaintiff's claim was not collected by the appropriate department of the Court until several days after its arrival in Luxembourg.[27]

The running of time

Time will start to run from the day following receipt by the person concerned of the notification of the measure or, where the measure is published, from the fifteenth day following publication in the Official Journal of the contested measure.[28] Where the plaintiff had knowledge of the measure prior to publication, he will still benefit from the time limit running from the fifteenth day following publication.[29]

Notification to registered office of company
In the case of a company, notification will be deemed to be received at the registered office, notwithstanding that the company has asked that notice be given at another address.[30] Receipt of notification by a subsidiary within the Community which has no authority from the parent (situated outside the Community) to accept such notification and which has no obligation to bring that notification to the attention of the parent company, will be valid.[31]

The calculation of time

Day complaint arose to be disregarded but not day of lodging complaint
When calculating the period of time available to the plaintiff in which to start proceedings, the day on which the cause of action arose will be ignored, regardless of the hour of day when the measure in question was notified.[32] The day on which the plaintiff's complaint is lodged at the European Court of Justice will not, however, be disregarded: in order for the complaint to be admissible, that date must fall within the limitation period.[33] Consequently, where the period of time for commencing proceedings is expressed in calendar months, a period will expire at the end of the day which, in the month of expiry, bears the same number as the day on which time was set running, *i.e.* the date of notification.[34] Thus, in the case of a measure which was notified to a natural or legal person residing in Luxembourg on March 2, 1992 and which was subject to a two-month time limit, any complaint must be lodged at the Court on or before May 2, 1992. In a case of a similar notification to a person residing in the United Kingdom, the 10-day period of grace would extend the limitation period to May 12, 1992. The running of time will include official holidays, Saturdays and Sundays and will not be

---

[27] Joined Cases 25 and 26/65 *Società Industriale Metallurgica di Napoli (Simet) & Acciairie e Ferriere di Roma (Feram)* v. *High Authority of the E.C.S.C.* [1967] E.C.R. 33.

[28] Rules of Procedure of the European Court of Justice, Art. 81(1).

[29] Case 88/76 *Société pour l'exportation de sucres SA* v. *Commission of the European Communities* [1977] E.C.R. 709.

[30] Case 42/85 *Cockerill-Sambre SA* v. *Commission of the European Communities* [1985] E.C.R. 3749.

[31] Case *Imperial Chemical Industries Ltd.* v. *Commission of the European Communities* [1972] E.C.R. 619.

[32] Rules of Procedure of the European Court of Justice, Art. 80(1)(*a*).

[33] Case 152/85 *Misset* v. *Council of the European Communities* [1987] E.C.R. 223.

[34] *Ibid.*

suspended during the judicial vacations.[35] Where the limitation period would otherwise end on a Saturday, Sunday or official holiday, it will be extended until the end of the first following working day.[36]

[35] Rules of Procedure of the European Court of Justice, Art. 80(1).
[36] *Ibid.* art. 80(2).

11 EQUITY, TRUSTS AND DEATH

Equity

Usual time limits not applicable

Where the claim is for specific performance of a contract, an injunction or other equitable relief, section 36 of the Limitation Act 1980 renders inapplicable the normal time limits laid down in sections 2 (tort), 5 (simple contract), 7 (actions to enforce awards where the submission is not by an instrument under seal), 8 (specialities), 9 (actions to recover a sum recoverable by virtue of any enactment) and 24 (actions to enforce a judgment). However, the running of time is not irrelevant in such actions: equitable relief may be refused where there has been either acquiescence or laches. It has been said that "acquiescence primarily means conduct from which it can be inferred that a party has waived his rights"[1] and that "laches essentially consists of a substantial lapse of time coupled with the existence of circumstances which make it inequitable to enforce the claim."[2] Delay will consequently constitute a bar in equity where it is of such a length as to indicate either that the plaintiff has impliedly agreed to the action of the defendant or that the defendant's chances of a fair trial will be prejudiced.

Acquiescence and laches

Statutory periods for some equitable claims

The following equitable claims now have statutory limitation periods laid down in the Limitation Act 1980, and laches and acquiescence will not apply:

(a) claims by beneficiaries to recover trust property or in respect of a breach of trust[3];
(b) claims to the personal estate of a deceased person[4];
(c) claims to redeem mortgaged land[5];
(d) claims to foreclose mortgages of real or personal property.[6]

With such claims delay short of the limitation period cannot bar the claim.

Application of limitation period by analogy

In some situations where statute did not previously provide for a limitation period, the relevant statutory limitation period would be applied by analogy to a similar equitable claim.[7] The

---

[1] *Snell's Equity* (29th ed., 1990), at p. 655; see also *Duke of Leeds* v. *Earl of Amherst* (1846) 2 Ph. 117 at p. 123. When considering whether or not there has been acquiescence, the length of time which has elapsed will be a significant factor: *Rundell* v. *Murray* (1821) Jac. 311.
[2] *Snell's Equity* (29th ed., 1990), p. 35; *Tottenham Hotspur Football and Athletic Co. Ltd.* v. *Princegrove Publishers Ltd.* [1974] 1 W.L.R. 113 at p. 122.
[3] Limitation Act 1980, s.21; see below, pp. 115–116.
[4] *Ibid.* s.22; see below, pp. 118–119.
[5] *Ibid.* s.16.
[6] *Ibid.* ss.15, 20(2) and 20(4).
[7] For example, a six-year limitation period corresponding to the limitation period applicable to actions for money had and received was applied by the courts to a case where one beneficiary brought an action against another beneficiary to recover trust property wrongly paid to the latter by the trustee: *Re Robinson, McLaren* v. *Public Trustee* [1911] 1 Ch. 502.

Limitation Act 1980 is unlikely to be applied by analogy to those equitable claims which still fall outside its provisions since these omissions must generally be regarded as deliberate.[8]

Trusts

Six year time limit

An action against a trustee by a beneficiary to recover trust property or in respect of a breach of trust[9] will generally be time-barred six years from the date on which the cause of action accrued.[10] The cause of action will accrue on the date when the breach occurred rather than the date on which the beneficiary suffered damage. However, where the beneficiary's interest is a future interest, the cause of action will not accrue until the interest falls into possession.[11]

Who is a trustee?

The term "trustee" has the same meaning as in section 68(17) of the Trustee Act 1925.[12] It will, therefore, include implied or constructive trustees and personal representatives (subject to the longer limitation period applicable in relation to actions claiming the personal estate of a deceased person[13]); the provisions will apply regardless of whether or not the trustee has a beneficial interest in the trust property. It has been held that the term will apply to the director of a company,[14] a mortgagee who has realised his security[15] and an auditor entrusted with money by the company.[16] It does not apply to a trustee in bankruptcy[17] or to the liquidator of a company in voluntary liquidation.[18] The six year period will not apply to an action by the Attorney-General to enforce a charitable trust, as in such circumstances there is no relevant beneficiary.[19]

No limitation period in case of fraud

There is no limitation period in an action against a trustee where there has been any fraud or fraudulent breach of trust to which the trustee was a party to privy.[20] It may also be argued that there will similarly be no limitation period in an action against a person who has acquired the trust property which is the subject of the action other than as a bona fide purchaser for value.[21]

---

[8] See *Snell's Equity* (29th ed., 1990), p. 34.

[9] On the question of the definition of a breach of trust, see *Tito* v. *Waddell (No. 2)* [1977] Ch. 106 at pp. 247–249.

[10] Limitation Act 1980, s.21(3).

[11] *Ibid.*

[12] *Ibid.* s.38(1).

[13] *Ibid.* s.22.

[14] *Re Lands Allotment Co.* [1894] 1 Ch. 616.

[15] *Thorne* v. *Heard* [1895] A.C. 495.

[16] *G.L. Baker Ltd.* v. *Medway Building and Supplies Ltd.* [1958] 1 W.L.R. 1216.

[17] *Re Cornish, ex p. Board of Trade* [1896] 1 Q.B. 99, C.A.

[18] *Re Windsor Steam Coal Co. (1901) Ltd.* [1928] Ch. 609.

[19] *Att.-Gen.* v. *Cocke* [1988] Ch. 414.

[20] Limitation Act 1980, s.21(1)(*a*). On fraud and limitations generally, see further Chap. 3.

[21] Trustees Act 1888, s.8(1) provided for the imposition of a limitation period: "in any action . . . against a trustee or any person claiming through him, except where the claim is founded upon any fraud or fraudulent breach of trust to which the trustee was party or privy . . ." That wording has not been reproduced in subsequent legislation, and it is consequently arguable as to whether or not the acquirer of trust property (other than for value) should be entitled to rely on the limitation period in an action to recover that property. See the decision of Danckwerts J. in *G.L. Baker Ltd.* v. *Medway Building and Supplies Ltd.* [1958] 1 W.L.R. 1216 at p. 1222.

In order that the trustee should be liable under this provision, he should have been a party or privy to the fraud or fraudulent breach of trust. Where the trustee is unaware of the fraud of his agent or employee, he will not be held to be a party to it, even though he may have been negligent in failing to identify it.[22]

No limitation period for proceeds in possession of trustee

There will similarly be no limitation period in respect of an action to recover from the trustee trust property or the proceeds of trust property in the possession of the trustee or previously received by the trustee and converted to his use.[23] A trustee who occupies property belonging to the trust[24] or a husband who seizes and retains property belonging to his wife, thereby becoming a trustee of that property,[25] will be unable to rely on the limitation period laid down in the Act.

Problems of limitation may also arise where the trustee is also a beneficiary under the trust and has divided the trust property (or its proceeds) amongst all those beneficiaries whom he believed to be entitled. If, after the expiry of the six year limitation period, it transpires that one or more further beneficiaries should have received property or proceeds from the trust fund, the previously unidentified beneficiary will not be

Unidentified beneficiaries

entitled to rely on section 21(1)(b) to recover from the trustee in possession of part of the trust property the full amount of his share of the property. Section 21(2) provides that the trustee's liability in such a case, providing he acted honestly and reasonably in making the distribution, will be limited to the excess over his proper share. Consequently, in a situation where the trustee honestly but mistakenly believed that there were only four beneficiaries to the trust property, including himself, if the fifth beneficiary makes a claim against the trustee more than six years after his right accrued, his right of recovery will be limited to the additional amount which the trustee himself received as a result of the mistake. In this case, the trustee has received 5/20 of the trust property instead of 4/20: the additional beneficiary will be entitled to recover the 1/20 which represents the difference.

Time running against one but not another beneficiary

Section 21(4) of the 1980 Act protects the trustee in those situations where time may have run against one beneficiary, but where another beneficiary, against whom time has not run, seeks to bring an action which would incidentally confer some benefit on a time-barred beneficiary; the time-barred beneficiary will not be entitled to take the benefit of this later action.

Death

Death may affect the running of the limitation period in a number of ways: the plaintiff may die as a result of injuries inflicted on him by the defendant, or he may die at a time when a cause of action unconnected with his death has accrued against

---

[22] *Thorne* v. *Heard* [1895] A.C. 495.
[23] Limitation Act 1980, s.21(1)(b).
[24] *Re Howlett* [1949] Ch. 767.
[25] *Wassell* v. *Leggatt* [1896] 1 Ch. 554.

the defendant. Alternatively, the defendant may die following the accrual of the cause of action against him. Limitation periods may also arise in relation to the distribution of the estate of a deceased person.

Death caused by the defendant

Action on behalf of dependants and actions on behalf of estate

Where the death constitutes the cause of action, a distinction must be drawn between actions which claim damages for the benefit of the dependants of the deceased, and those which claim damages on behalf of the estate of the deceased. Actions brought by and on behalf of dependants[26] are governed by the Fatal Accidents Act 1976 and sections 12 and 13 of the Limitation Act 1980, whereas those claiming damages on behalf of the estate are subject to the Law Reform (Miscellaneous Provisions) Act 1934. Damages may be sought under both Acts, but double recovery for loss of earnings is not possible.[27]

No action if time-barred at death

No action may be brought by the dependants of the deceased under the 1976 Act if, at the time of death, the deceased's right of action in respect of his injuries was already time-barred, regardless of the possibility that the three year time limit might have been excluded under section 33.[28] Provided that the injured person died within the three year period,[29] the dependants will benefit from a fresh three year limitation period running from the date of death or the date of knowledge of the person for whose benefit the action is brought.[30] Where there is more than one person on whose behalf an action under the 1976 Act is to be brought, there will be a separate limitation period in respect of each dependant, running from the date of his knowledge. By section 28 of the Limitation Act 1980, if a particular dependant is either a minor or of unsound mind at the

Disability

date of death, time will not run until such time as he is no longer under that disability.[31] The court may also exercise its discretion

Exclusion of the time limit

under section 33 so as to permit the time limit to be excluded.[32] This will be so whether or not the injured person died after the expiry of the three year limit. In such a case the court shall have regard to any delay on the part of the deceased in respect of commencing his own action[33] and the circumstances, listed in section 33(3) which the court shall have regard to when deciding whether or not to exercise its discretion in relation to each dependant.[34]

Damages for estate

An action under the Law Reform (Miscellaneous Provisions) Act 1934 claiming damages on behalf of the estate following personal injuries caused by the defendant, will be

[26] The term "dependant" is defined in section 1(3) of the Fatal Accidents Act, and includes the spouse or former spouse or a person who was living with the deceased as a spouse for the two years preceding the death, parents and others ascendants, children and grandchildren.

[27] Administration of Justice Act 1982, s.4.

[28] Limitation Act 1980, s.12.

[29] Or any other shorter period laid down by other legislation.

[30] Limitation Act 1980, s.12

[31] *Ibid.* s.12(8).

[32] *Ibid.* For an example of the exercise of judicial discretion in such a situation, see *Halford* v. *Brookes* [1991] 1 W.L.R. 428; [1991] 3 All E.R. 559.

[33] Limitation Act 1980, s.33(4).

[34] *Ibid.* s.33(5); see Chap. 7.

subject to a three year time limit running from the date of death or the date of knowledge[35] (if later) of the personal representative, provided that the deceased's own cause of action was not time-barred at the date of his death.[36] The "knowledge" of the personal representative will include knowledge acquired before and after he became the personal representative.[37] Where there is more than one personal representative and their dates of knowledge are different, the earliest date will be applicable for the purpose of the running of time.[38]

"Knowledge"

Death of plaintiff following accrual of independent cause of action against defendant

Survival of causes of action

By section 1 of the Law Reform (Miscellaneous Provisions) Act 1934, on the death of a person all causes of action (other than in defamation) vested in him shall survive for the benefit of his estate. Time will continue to run following the death, even though there may be an interval between the death and the grant of administration.[39]

Death of defendant

Time runs without interruption

Most claims against a tortfeasor or debtor will survive his death[40] and the running of time will not be interrupted: the plaintiff must bring his action against the estate within the normal limitation period starting from the date on which the cause of action accrued against the deceased.[41] Where a creditor subsequently becomes an administrator of the estate, the running of time is suspended,[42] but not where he becomes an executor.[43]

Actions claiming personal estate of a deceased person

Twelve year limit

Section 22 of the 1980 Act lays down the limitation period applicable to claims to any share or interest in the estate of a deceased (12 years) and to actions to recover arrears of interest in respect of any legacy or damages in respect of such arrears (six years). These time limits are expressly made subject to section 21(1) and (2) of the Act: there will be no limitation period where the personal representative of the deceased person has acted fraudulently in relation to the estate or has converted any part of it to his own use. If the personal representative is a beneficiary under the will of the deceased or under the intestacy rules and he has honestly but mistakenly omitted another beneficiary when distributing the estate, as with a trustee who is also a beneficiary, he will, after the expiry of the limitation period, be required to repay only the excess over his proper share.[44]

---

[35] On the question of the date of knowledge, see pp. 67–74.
[36] Limitation Act 1980, s.11(5).
[37] *Ibid.* s.11(6).
[38] *Ibid.* s.11(7).
[39] *Penny* v. *Brice* (1865) 18 C.B.N.S. 393.
[40] Law Reform (Miscellaneous Provisions) Act 1934, s.1; the Proceedings Against Estates Act 1970, s.1.
[41] *Rhodes* v. *Smethurst* (1846) 6 M. & W. 351.
[42] *Ibid.*
[43] *Bowring-Hanbury's Trustee* v. *Bowring-Hanbury* [1943] Ch. 104, C.A.
[44] See above, p. 116.

Another result of making the provisions relating to personal representatives subject to the provisions relating to trustees is **Personal** that in those cases where the personal representative may be **representative may** considered to be a trustee,[45] the shorter limitation period of six **be a trustee** years will be available, rather than the 12 year period which normally applies to personal representatives.

Date from which Under section 22, time will run from the "date on which **time will run** the right to receive the share or interest accrued." This will normally be the date of death[46] whether the share or interest falls due under a will or upon the intestacy of the deceased. Where the personal representative has no assets with which to satisfy the claim, time will not start to run until such time as he has such assets.[47] Similarly, where the share or interest is to be paid out of a reversionary fund, time will run from the date when the reversion falls in.[48] An action against a beneficiary who has been overpaid or some other person who has been wrongly paid will also fall within section 22.[49]

Where the personal representative has distributed the assets of the deceased without first identifying and satisfying the **Action by** creditors, an action can be brought by the latter on the ground **creditors** that a loss of assets has been caused by the former's breach of the duty. Such a breach of duty is known as *devastavit* and is subject to a six year limitation period. This action is probably tortious in nature and time will run from the date of the wrongful distribution rather than the date of death.[50]

---

[45] See the Trustee Act 1925, s.68(17) and *Re Oliver, Theobald* v. *Oliver* [1927] 2 Ch. 323.
[46] *Hornsey Local Board* v. *Monarch Investment Building Society* (1889) 24 Q.B.D. 1. This is so notwithstanding the fact that the personal representative may postpone the distribution of the estate for one year following death: Administration of Estates Act 1925, s.44.
[47] *Prior* v. *Horniblow* (1836) 2 Y. & C. Ex. 200.
[48] *Earle* v. *Bellingham (No. 2)* (1857) 24 Beav. 448.
[49] *Re Diplock, Diplock* v. *Wintle* [1948] 1 Ch. 465, C.A.; aff'd by H.L., [1951] A.C. 251.
[50] *Re Gale* (1883) 22 Ch. D. 820; *Re Blow* [1914] 1 Ch. 233.

APPENDIX 1

Table of limitation periods

Arbitration	The provisions of the Limitation Act 1980 and any other limitations enactments apply equally to arbitrations: section 34.
Carriage of goods and persons	
Carriage by road	**passengers**—in the case of actions for death or personal injury: three years from date of knowledge of injury, subject to longstop of five years from date of accident; other actions—one year: Carriage of Passengers by Road Act 1974. **goods**—one year, or three years where there has been wilful misconduct: Carriage of Goods by Road Act 1965.
Carriage by rail	**passengers**—three years from the day after the accident. Dependants of passengers five years from the day after the passenger's death. **goods**—one year, usually running from the date of delivery, or two years where cash on delivery has been charged or where there has been wilful misconduct: International Transport Conventions Act 1983.
Carriage by sea	**passengers**—in the case of international carriage a two year time limit applies: Merchant Shipping Act 1979. In the case of personal injury arising from a collision between vessels, a two year time limit applies. **goods**—one year from the date of delivery or the date on which goods should have been delivered: Carriage of Goods by Sea Act 1971.

Carriage by air	**passengers**—two years from date of arrival or date of accident: Carriage by Air Act 1961, asamended by Carriage by Air and Road Act 1979. goods—two years from date of arrival at the destination or the date on which the aircraft should have arrived or the date on which the carriage stopped (if these dates do not coincide, the latest applies): Carriage by Air Act 1961.
Concealment	Time will start to run only when deliberate concealment could reasonably have been discovered: section 32; pp. 22–29.
Contract	Six years from the date of breach in the case of a simple contract: section 5; 12 years in the case of a specialty: section 8; pp. 31–33.
Contribution	The right to recover contribution from a person who is jointly liable is subject to a limitation period of two years from the date of judgment or agreement: section 10; p. 17.
Conversion	Six years from the date of conversion: section 2; where there have been successive conversions, time will run from the first conversion: section 3. In the case of theft, time will not run, except where the goods have subsequently been purchased in good faith, where the limitation period will be six years from (probably) the date of purchase: section 4.
Death	Actions on behalf of the estate—three years from date of death or date of knowledge of personal representative: Law Reform (Miscellaneous Provisions) Act 1934. Actions on behalf of dependants—three years from date of death, provided death occurred within three years from the date of injury: Fatal Accidents Act 1976, and Limitation Act 1980, sections 11 and 12. Actions claiming personal estate of deceased person—generally 12 years from death or such time as the personal representative has the assets with which to satisfy the claim.

Deceit	Time will not start to run until the plaintiff has discovered the deceit or could with reasonable diligence have discovered it: section 32.
Defamation	Three years from date of publication if actionable *per se* (*i.e.* libel and certain types of slander), three years from date of damage otherwise: section 4A; subject to one year extension where publication not known to plaintiff: section 32A.
Disability	The commencement of the running of time will be suspended where the plaintiff is under a disability (*i.e.* he is a minor or is a person of unsound mind within the meaning of the Mental Health Act 1983) on the date of accrual of the cause of action: sections 28 and 38.
Easements and profits	Usually 20 or 40 years user: Prescription Act 1832.
Equitable claims	Claims by beneficiaries to recover trust property or in respect of a breach of trust—six years: section 21. Claims to the personal estate of a deceased person—12 years: section 22. Claims to redeem mortgaged land—12 years: section 16. Claims to foreclose mortgages of real or personal property—12 years: sections 15, 20(2) and 20(4). In the case of other equitable claims, no time limit is laid down but actions will be subject to the equitable doctrines of acquiescence and laches: see pp. 114–115.
Estate, action on behalf of or against	See above, Death.

European Community law	Two month time limit for action for annulment: Article 173(3) Treaty of Rome, plus 10 day period of grace for U.K. residents: Annex II to the Rules of Procedure of the European Court of Justice. Contractual liability of EC institutions is governed by the law applicable to the contract in question. For non-contractual liability there is a five year limitation period running from the date of the event giving rise to such liability.
False imprisonment	Six year time limit with the cause of action accruing from day to day as the imprisonment continues: section 2; p. 56.
Foreign limitations	A foreign limitation period is now to be regarded as a substantive matter rather than a procedural one: Foreign Limitation Periods Act 1984; pp. 5–7.
Fraud	Time (presumably six years) will start to run only when the fraud could reasonably have been discovered: section 32; pp. 25–29.
Injunction	No limitation period fixed by statute, but a claim will be defeated where there has been delay such as to amount to acquiescence or laches; see pp. 114–115.
Judgment, action upon	Six year limitation period from the date on which the judgment became enforceable: section 24 (*N.B.* the limitation period was previously 12 years).
Judicial review	Three month time limit: Rules of the Supreme Court, Order 53, rule 4(1); see pp. 108–109.
Land, adverse possession	Generally 12 years from the date when the adverse possession commenced: section 15. A 30 year limitation period applies where the plaintiff is the Crown or any spiritual or eleemosynary corporation sole and a 60 year period where the land is classified as foreshore.

Latent damage	The normal six year limitation period running from the date of negligently caused damage is supplemented by an alternative three year period running from the date when the plaintiff had the necessary knowledge to bring an action: section 14A, subject to a longstop of 15 years: section 14B.
Libel	See Defamation, above.
Loan	A contract of loan will be subject to the normal limitation periods for contracts (see above, Contract) unless the contract of loan in question does not provide for repayment of the debt on or before a fixed date or make the obligation to repay conditional on a demand. In such a case, the cause of action to recover the debt will accrue on the date on which a demand is made, and the normal six year limitation period will start to run: section 6.
Mistake	Time will start to run only when the mistake could reasonably have been discovered: section 32; pp. 25–29. In order for this provision to apply, the action must be based on mistake.
Mortgages	12 year limitation period in respect of an action by a mortgagor to redeem land in the possession of a mortgagee: section 16. 12 year limitation period in respect of mortgagee's right to recover any principal sum secured by a mortgage or other charge on property, or to recover the proceeds of the sale of the land: section 20. Six year limitation period to recover arrears of interest on a mortgage: section 20.

Negligence	The normal limitation period is six years from the date of damage: section 2; pp. 45 *et seq.* Where the damage could not reasonably have been discovered within this time, the provisions of the Latent Damage Act 1986, asincorporated into the Limitation Act 1980, sections 14A and 14B, may apply giving an alternative limitation period of three years from the date of reasonable discoverability (subject to 15 year longstop); see pp. 52–56. In the case of personal injury, the limitation period is three years from the date of injury or from the date of knowledge: sections 11 and 14; pp. 67–74.
Nuisance	Six years from the date when the nuisance was actionable: section 2.
Personal injury	Three year limitation period in respect of all actions claiming damages for personal injury, time running from date of damage or date of knowledge, whichever is later: sections 11 and 14; pp. 67–74. Limitation period may be excluded: section 33.
Slander	See above, Defamation.
Specialty	12 years from the date of breach: section 8; see pp. 31–33.
Specific performance	No time limit provided for the legislation, but a claim will be defeated by delay which is such as to amount to acquiescence or laches; see pp. 114–115.
Tort	Six years from the date of accrual of the cause of action: section 2.
Trespass	Generally six years from the date of trespass: section 2, but three years in the case of trespass to the person: section 11.
Trusts	Six year limitation period to recover trust property or in respect of any breach of trust: section 21. No time limit where the trustee is party or privy to any fraud or fraudulent breach of trust or to recover from the trustee trust property or the proceeds of trust property in his possession: section 21.

APPENDIX 2

Limitation Act 1980 (as amended)

PART I
ORDINARY TIME LIMITS FOR DIFFERENT CLASSES OF ACTION

Time limits under Part I subject to extension or exclusion under Part II

Time limits under Part I subject to extension under Part II

1.—(1) This Part of this Act gives the ordinary time limits for bringing actions of the various classes mentioned in the following provisions of this Part.

(2) The ordinary time limits given in this Part of this Act are subject to extension or exclusion in accordance with the provisions of Part II of this Act.

Time limit for actions founded on tort

2. An action founded on tort shall not be brought after the expiration of six years from the date on which the cause of action accrued.

Time limit in case of successive conversions and extinction of title of owner of converted goods

3.—(1) Where any cause of action in respect of the conversion of a chattel has accrued to any person and, before he recovers possession of the chattel, a further conversion takes place, no action shall be brought in respect of the further conversion after the expiration of six years from the accrual of the cause of action in respect of the original conversion.

(2) Where any such cause of action has accrued to any person and the period prescribed for bringing that action has expired and he has not during that period recovered possession of the chattel, the title of that person to the chattel shall be extinguished.

Special time limit in case of theft

4.—(1) The right of any person from whom a chattel is stolen to bring an action in respect of the theft shall not be subject to the time limits under sections 2 and 3(1) of this Act, but if his title to the chattel is extinguished under section 3(2) of this Act he may not bring an action in respect of a theft preceding the loss of his title, unless the theft in question preceded the conversion from which time began to run for the purposes of section 3(2).

(2) Subsection (1) above shall apply to any conversion related to the theft of a chattel as it applies to the theft of a chattel; and, except as provided below, every conversion following the theft of a chattel before the person from whom it is stolen recovers

possession of it shall be regarded for the purposes of this section as related to the theft.

If anyone purchases the stolen chattel in good faith neither the purchase nor any conversion following it shall be regarded as related to the theft.

(3) Any cause of action accruing in respect of the theft or any conversion related to the theft of a chattel to any person from whom the chattel is stolen shall be disregarded for the purpose of applying section 3(1) or (2) of this Act to his case.

(4) Where in any action brought in respect of the conversion of a chattel it is proved that the chattel was stolen from the plaintiff or anyone through whom he claims it shall be presumed that any conversion following the theft is related to the theft unless the contrary is shown.

(5) In this section "theft" includes—

(a) any conduct outside England and Wales which would be theft if committed in England and Wales; and

(b) obtaining any chattel (in England and Wales or elsewhere) in the circumstances described in section 15(1) of the Theft Act 1968 (obtaining by deception) or by blackmail within the meaning of section 21 of that Act;

and references in this section to a chattel being "stolen" shall be construed accordingly.

Time limit for actions for libel or slander

4A. The time limit under section 2 of this Act shall not apply to an action for libel or slander, but no such action shall be brought after the expiration of three years from the date on which the cause of action accrued.

Added by Administration of Justice Act 1985, s.57.

Time limit for actions founded on simple contract

5. An action founded on simple contract shall not be brought after the expiration of six years from the date on which the cause of action accrued.

Special time limit for actions in respect of certain loans

6.—(1) Subject to subsection (3) below, section 5 of this Act shall not bar the right of action on a contract of loan to which this section applies.

(2) This section applies to any contract of loan which—

(a) does not provide for repayment of the debt on or before a fixed or determinable date; and

(b) does not effectively (whether or not it purports to do so) make the obligation to repay the debt conditional on a demand for repayment made by or on behalf of the creditor or on any other matter;

except where in connection with taking the loan the debtor enters into any collateral obligation to pay the amount of the debt or any part of it (as, for example, by delivering a promissory note as security for the debt) on terms which would exclude the application of this section to the contract of loan if they applied directly to repayment of the debt.

(3) Where a demand in writing for repayment of the debt under a contract of loan to which this section applies is made by or on behalf of the creditor (or, where there are joint creditors, by or on behalf of any one of them) section 5 of this Act shall thereupon apply as if the cause of action to recover the debt had accrued on the date on which the demand was made.

(4) In this section "promissory note" has the same meaning as in the Bills of Exchange Act 1882.

Time limits for actions to enforce certain awards

7. An action to enforce an award, where the submission is not by an instrument under seal, shall not be brought after the expiration of six years from the date on which the cause of action accrued.

Time limit for actions on a specialty

8.—(1) An action upon a specialty shall not be brought after the expiration of twelve years from the date on which the cause of action accrued.

(2) Subsection (1) above shall not affect any action for which a shorter period of limitation is prescribed by any other provision of this Act.

Time limit for actions for sums recoverable by statute

9.—(1) An action to recover any sum recoverable by virtue of any enactment shall not be brought after the expiration of six years from the date on which the cause of action accrued.

(2) Subsection (1) above shall not affect any action to which section 10 of this Act applies.

Special time limit for claiming contribution

10.—(1) Where under section 1 of the Civil Liability (Contribution) Act 1978 any person becomes entitled to a right to recover contribution in respect of any damage from any other person, no action to recover contribution by virtue of that right shall be brought after the expiration of two years from the date on which that right accrued.

(2) For the purposes of this section the date on which a right to recover contribution in respect of any damage accrues to any person (referred to below in this section as "the relevant date") shall be ascertained as provided in subsections (3) and (4) below.

(3) If the person in question is held liable in respect of that damage—

(a) by a judgment given in any civil proceedings; or
(b) by an award made on any arbitration;

the relevant date shall be the date on which the judgment is given, or the date of the award (as the case may be).

For the purposes of this subsection no account shall be taken of any judgment or award given or made on appeal in so far as it varies the amount of damages awarded against the person in question.

(4) If, in any case not within subsection (3) above, the person in question makes or agrees to make any payment to one or more persons in compensation for that damage (whether he admits any liability in respect of the damage or not), the relevant date shall be the earliest date on which the amount to be paid by him is agreed between him (or his representative) and the person (or each of the persons, as the case may be) to whom the payment is to be made.

(5) An action to recover contribution shall be one to which sections 28, 32 and 35 of this Act apply, but otherwise Parts II and III of this Act (except sections 34, 37 and 38) shall not apply for the purposes of this section.

Special time limit for actions in respect of personal injuries

11.—(1) This section applies to any action for damages for negligence, nuisance or breach of duty (whether the duty exists by virtue of a contract or of provision made by or under a statute or independently of any contract or any such provision) where the damages claimed by the plaintiff for the negligence, nuisance or breach of duty consist of or include damages in respect of personal injuries to the plaintiff or any other person.

(2) None of the limits given in the preceding provisions of this Act shall apply to an action to which this section applies.

(3) An action to which this section applies shall not be brought after the expiration of the period applicable in accordance with subsection (4) or (5) below.

(4) Except where subsection (5) below applies, the period applicable is three years from—

(*a*) the date on which the cause of action accrued; or
(*b*) the date of knowledge (if later) of the person injured.

(5) If the person injured dies before the expiration of the period mentioned in subsection (4) above, the period applicable as respects the cause of action surviving for the benefit of his estate by virtue of section 1 of the Law Reform (Miscellaneous Provisions) Act 1934 shall be three years from—

(*a*) the date of death; or
(*b*) the date of the personal representative's knowledge;

whichever is the later.

(6) For the purposes of this section "personal representative" includes any person who is or has been a personal representative of the deceased, including an executor who has not proved the will (whether or not he has renounced probate) but not anyone appointed only as a special personal representative in relation to settled land; and regard shall be had to any knowledge acquired by any such person while a personal representative or previously.

(7) If there is more than one personal representative, and their dates of knowledge are different, subsection (5)(*b*) above shall be read as referring to the earliest of those dates.

Actions in respect of defective products

11A.—(1) This section shall apply to an action for damages by virtue of any provision of Part I of the Consumer Protection Act 1987.

(2) None of the time limits given in the preceding provisions of this Act shall apply to an action to which this section applies.

(3) An action to which this section applies shall not be brought after the expiration of the period of ten years from the relevant time, within the meaning of section 4 of the said Act of 1987; and this subsection shall operate to extinguish a right of action and shall do so whether or not that right of action had accrued, or time under the following provisions of this Act had begun to run, at the end of the said period of ten years.

(4) Subject to subsection (5) below, an action to which this section applies in which the damages claimed by the plaintiff consist of or include damages in respect of personal injuries to the plaintiff or any other person or loss of or damage to any property, shall not be brought after the expiration of the period of three years from whichever is the later of—

(a) the date on which the cause of action accrued; and
(b) the date of knowledge of the injured person or, in the case of loss of or damage to property, the date of knowledge of the plaintiff or (if earlier) of any person in whom his cause of action was previously vested.

(5) If in a case where the damages claimed by the plaintiff consist of or include damages in respect of personal injuries to the plaintiff or any other person the injured person died before the expiration of the period mentioned in subsection (4) above, that subsection shall have effect as respects the cause of action surviving for the benefit of his estate by virtue of section 1 of the Law Reform (Miscellaneous Provisions) Act 1934 as if for the reference to that period there were substituted a reference to the period of three years from whichever is the later of—

(a) the date of death; and
(b) the date of the personal representative's knowledge.

(6) For the purposes of this section "personal representative" includes any person who is or has been a personal representative of the deceased, including an executor who has not proved the will (whether or not he has renounced probate) but not anyone appointed only as a special personal representative in relation to settled land; and regard shall be had to any knowledge acquired by any such person while a personal representative or previously.

(7) If there is more than one personal representative and their dates of knowledge are different, subsection (5)(b) above shall be read as referring to the earliest of those dates.

(8) Expressions used in this section or section 14 of this Act and in Part I of the Consumer Protection Act 1987 have the same meanings in this section or that section as in that Part; and section 1(1) of that Act (Part I to be construed as enacted for the purpose of complying with the product liability Directive) shall apply for the purpose of construing this section and the following provisions of this Act so far as they relate to an action by virtue of any provision of that Part as it applies for the purpose of construing that Part.

Added by Consumer Protection Act 1987, Sched. 1.

Special time limit for actions under Fatal Accidents legislation

12.—(1) An action under the Fatal Accidents Act 1976 shall not be brought if the death occurred when the person injured could no longer maintain an action and recover damages in respect of the injury (whether because of a time limit in this Act or in any other Act, or for any other reason).

Where any such action by the injured person would have been barred by the time limit in section 11 of this Act, no account shall be taken of the possibility of that time limit being overridden under section 33 of this Act.

(2) None of the time limits given in the preceding provisions of this Act shall apply to an action under the Fatal Accidents Act 1976, but no such action shall be brought after the expiration of three years from—

(*a*) the date of death; or

(*b*) the date of knowledge of the person for whose benefit the action is brought;

whichever is the later.

(3) An action under the Fatal Accidents Act 1976 shall be one to which sections 28, 33 and 35 of this Act apply, and the application to any such action of the time limit under subsection (2) above shall be subject to section 39; but otherwise Parts II and III of this Act shall not apply to any such action.

Operation of time limit under section 12 in relation to different dependants

13.—(1) Where there is more than one person for whose benefit an action under the Fatal Accidents Act 1976 is brought, section 12(2)(*b*) of this Act shall be applied separately to each of them.

(2) Subject to subsection (3) below, if by virtue of subsection (1) above the action would be outside the time limit given by section 12(2) as regards one or more, but not all, of the persons for whose benefit it is brought, the court shall direct that any person as regards whom the action would be outside that limit shall be excluded from those for whom the action is brought.

(3) The court shall not give such a direction if it is shown that if the action were brought exclusively for the benefit of the person in question it would not be defeated by a defence of limitation (whether in consequence of section 28 of this Act or an agreement between the parties not to raise the defence, or otherwise).

Definition of date of knowledge for purposes of sections 11 and 12

14.—(1) Subject to subsection (1A) below. In sections 11 and 12 of this Act references to a person's date of knowledge are references to the date on which he first had knowledge of the following facts—

(*a*) that the injury in question was significant; and

(*b*) that the injury was attributable in whole or in part to the act or omission which is alleged to constitute negligence, nuisance or breach of duty; and

(c) the identity of the defendant; and
(d) if it is alleged that the act or omission was that of a person other than the defendant, the identity of that person and the additional facts supporting the bringing of an action against the defendant;

and knowledge that any acts or omissions did or did not, as a matter of law, involve negligence, nuisance or breach of duty is irrelevant.

(1A) In section 11A of this Act and in section 12 of this Act so far as that section applies to an action by virtue of section 6(1)(a) of the Consumer Protection Act 1987 (death caused by defective product) references to a person's date of knowledge are references to the date on which he first had knowledge of the following facts—

(a) such facts about the damage caused by the defect as would lead a reasonable person who had suffered such damage to consider it sufficiently serious to justify his instituting proceedings for damages against a defendant who did not dispute liability and was able to satisfy a judgment; and
(b) that the damage was wholly or partly attributable to the facts and circumstances alleged to constitute the defect; and
(c) the identity of the defendant;

but, in determining the date on which a person first had such knowledge there shall be disregarded both the extent (if any) of that person's knowledge on any date of whether particular facts or circumstances would or would not, as a matter of law, constitute a defect and, in a case relating to loss of or damage to property, any knowledge which that person had on a date on which he had no right of action by virtue of Part I of that Act in respect of the loss or damage.

(2) For the purposes of this section an injury is significant if the person whose date of knowledge is in question would reasonably have considered it sufficiently serious to justify his instituting proceedings for damages against a defendant who did not dispute liability and was able to satisfy a judgment.

(3) For the purposes of this section a person's knowledge includes knowledge which he might reasonably have been expected to acquire—

(a) from facts observable or ascertainable by him; or
(b) from facts ascertainable by him with the help of medical or other appropriate expert advice which it is reasonable for him to seek;

but a person shall not be fixed under this subsection with knowledge of a fact ascertainable only with the help of expert advice so long as he has taken all reasonable steps to obtain (and, where appropriate, to act on) that advice.

Subs. (1A) added by Consumer Protection Act 1987, Sched. 1.

Special time limit for negligence actions where facts relevant to cause of action are not known at date of accrual

14A.—(1) This section applies to any action for damages fornegligence, other than one to which section 11 of this Act applies, where the starting date for reckoning the period of limitation under subsection (4)(*b*) below falls after the date on which the cause of action accrued.

(2) Section 2 of this Act shall not apply to an action to which this section applies.

(3) An action to which this section applies shall not be brought after the expiration of the period applicable in accordance with subsection (4) below.

(4) That period is either—

(*a*) six years from the date on which the cause of action accrued; or

(*b*) three years from the starting date as defined by subsection (5) below, if that period expires later than the period mentioned in paragraph (*a*) above.

(5) For the purposes of this section, the starting date for reckoning the period of limitation under subsection (4)(*b*) above is the earliest date on which the plaintiff or any person in whom the cause of action was vested before him first had both the knowledge required for bringing an action for damages in respect of the relevant damage and a right to bring such an action.

(6) In subsection (5) above "the knowledge required for bringing an action for damages in respect of the relevant damage" means knowledge both—

(*a*) of the material facts about the damage in respect of which damages are claimed; and

(*b*) of the other facts relevant to the current action mentioned in subsection (8) below.

(7) For the purposes of subsection (6)(*a*) above, the material facts about the damage are such facts about the damage as would lead a reasonable person who had suffered such damage to consider it sufficiently serious to justify his instituting proceedings for damages against a defendant who did not dispute liability and was able to satisfy a judgment.

(8) The other facts referred to in subsection (6)(*b*) above are—

(*a*) that the damage was attributable in whole or in part to the act or omission which is alleged to constitute negligence; and

(*b*) the identity of the defendant; and

(*c*) if it is alleged that the act or omission was that of a person other than the defendant, the identity of that person and the additional facts supporting the bringing of an action against the defendant.

(9) Knowledge that any acts or omissions did or did not, as a matter of law, involve negligence is irrelevant for the purposes of subsection (5) above.

(10) For the purposes of this section a person's knowledge includes knowledge which he might reasonably have been expected to acquire—

(*a*) from facts observable or ascertainable by him; or
(*b*) from facts ascertainable by him with the help of appropriate expert advice which it is reasonable for him to seek;

but a person shall not be taken by virtue of this subsection to have knowledge of a fact ascertainable only with the help of expert advice so long as he has taken all reasonable steps to obtain (and, where appropriate, to act on) that advice.

Added by Latent Damage Act 1986, s.1.

Overriding time limit for negligence actions not involving personal injuries

14B.—(1) An action for damages for negligence, other than one to which section 11 of this Act applies, shall not be brought after the expiration of fifteen years from the date (or, if more than one, from the last of the dates) on which there occurred any act or omission—

(*a*) which is alleged to constitute negligence; and
(*b*) to which the damage in respect of which damages are claimed is alleged to be attributable (in whole or in part).

(2) This section bars the right of action in a case to which subsection (1) above applies notwithstanding that—

(*a*) the cause of action has not yet accrued; or
(*b*) where section 14A of this Act applies to the action, the date which is for the purposes of that section the starting date for reckoning the period mentioned in subsection (4)(*b*) of that section has not yet occurred;

before the end of the period of limitation prescribed by this section.

Added by Latent Damage Act 1986, s.1.

Time limit for actions to recover land

15.—(1) No action shall be brought by any person to recover any land after the expiration of twelve years from the date on which the right of action accrued to him or, if it first accrued to some person through whom he claims, to that person.

(2) Subject to the following provisions of this section, where—

(*a*) the estate or interest claimed was an estate or interest in reversion or remainder or any other future estate or interest and the right of action to recover the land accrued on the date on which the estate or interest fell into possession by the determination of the preceding estate or interest; and
(*b*) the person entitled to the preceding estate or interest (not being a term of years absolute) was not in possession of the land on that date;

no action shall be brought by the person entitled to the succeeding estate or interest after the expiration of twelve years from the date on which the right of action accrued to the person entitled to the preceding estate or interest or six years from the

date on which the right of action accrued to the person entitled
to the succeeding estate or interest, whichever period last
expires.

(3) Subsection (2) above shall not apply to any estate or
interest which falls into possession on the determination of an
entailed interest and which might have been barred by the
person entitled to the entailed interest.

(4) No person shall bring an action to recover any estate or
interest in land under an assurance taking effect after the right
of action to recover the land had accrued to the person by whom
the assurance was made or some person through whom he
claimed or some person entitled to a preceding estate or interest,
unless the action is brought within the period in which the
person by whom the assurance was made could have brought
such an action.

(5) Where any person is entitled to any estate or interest in
land in possession and, while so entitled, is also entitled to any
future estate or interest in that land, and his right to recover the
estate or interest in possession is barred under this Act, no
~~action shall be brought by that person, or by any person~~
claiming through him, in respect of the future estate or interest,
unless in the meantime possession of the land has been
recovered by a person entitled to an intermediate estate or
interest.

(6) Part I of Schedule 1 to this Act contains provisions for
determining the date of accrual of rights of action to recover
land in the cases there mentioned.

(7) Part II of that Schedule contains provisions modifying the
provisions of this section in their application to actions brought
by, or by a person claiming through, the Crown or any spiritual
or eleemosynary corporation sole.

Time limit for redemption actions

16.—When a mortgagee of land has been in possession of any
of the mortgaged land for a period of twelve years, no action to
redeem the land of which the mortgage has been so in possession
shall be brought after the end of that period by the mortgagor or
any person claiming through him.

Extinction of title to land after expiration of time limit

17.—Subject to—

(a) section 18 of this Act; and
(b) section 75 of the Land Registration Act 1925;

at the expiration of the period prescribed by this Act for any
person to bring an action to recover land (including a
redemption action) the title of that person to the land shall be
extinguished.

Settled land and land held on trust

18.—(1) Subject to section 21(1) and (2) of this Act, the
provisions of this Act shall apply to equitable interests in land,
including interests in the proceeds of the sale of land held upon
trust for sale, as they apply to legal estates.

Accordingly a right of action to recover the land shall, for the purposes of this Act but not otherwise, be treated as accruing to a person entitled in possession to such an equitable interest in the like manner and circumstances, and on the same date, as it would accrue if his interest were a legal estate in the land (and any relevant provision of Part I of Schedule 1 to this Act shall apply in any such case accordingly).

(2) Where the period prescribed by this Act has expired for the bringing of an action to recover land by a tenant for life or a statutory owner of settled land—

(a) his legal estate shall not be extinguished if and so long as the right of action to recover the land of any person entitled to a beneficial interest in the land either has not accrued or has not been barred by this Act; and

(b) the legal estate shall accordingly remain vested in the tenant for life or statutory owner and shall devolve in accordance with the Settled Land Act 1925;

but if and when every such right of action has been barred by this Act, his legal estate shall be extinguished.

(3) Where any land is held upon trust (including a trust for sale) and the period prescribed by this Act has expired for the bringing of an action to recover the land by the trustees, the estate of the trustees shall not be extinguished if and so long as the right of action to recover the land of any person entitled to a beneficial interest in the land or in the proceeds of sale either has not accrued or has not been barred by this Act; but if and when every such right of action has been so barred the estate of the trustees shall be extinguished.

(4) Where—

(a) any settled land is vested in a statutory owner; or

(b) any land is held upon trust (including a trust for sale);

an action to recover the land may be brought by the statutory owner or trustees on behalf of any person entitled to a beneficial interest in possession in the land or in the proceeds of sale whose right of action has not been barred by this Act, notwithstanding that the right of action of the statutory owner or trustees would apart from this provision have been barred by this Act.

Time limit for actions to recover rent

19.—No action shall be brought, or distress made, to recover arrears of rent, or damages in respect of arrears of rent, after the expiration of six years from the date on which the arrears became due.

Time limit for actions to recover money secured by a mortgage or charge or to recover proceeds of the sale of land

20.—(1) No action shall be brought to recover—

(a) any principal sum of money secured by a mortgage or other charge on property (whether real or personal); or

(b) proceeds of the sale of land;

after the expiration of twelve years from the date on which the right to receive the money accrued.

(2) No foreclosure action in respect of mortgaged personal property shall be brought after the expiration of twelve years from the date on which the right to foreclose accrued.

But if the mortgagee was in possession of the mortgaged property after that date, the right to foreclose on the property which was in his possession shall not be treated as having accrued for the purposes of this subsection until the date on which his possession discontinued.

(3) The right to receive any principal sum of money secured by a mortgage or other charge and the right to foreclose on the property subject to the mortgage or charge shall not be treated as accruing so long as that property comprises any future interest or any life insurance policy which has not matured or been determined.

(4) Nothing in this section shall apply to a foreclosure action in respect of mortgaged land, but the provisions of this Act relating to actions to recover land shall apply to such an action.

(5) Subject to subsections (6) and (7) below, no action to recover arrears of interest payable in respect of any sum of money secured by a mortgage or other charge or payable in respect of proceeds of the sale of land, or to recover damages in respect of such arrears shall be brought after the expiration of six years from the date on which the interest became due.

(6) Where—

(a) a prior mortgagee or other incumbrancer has been in possession of the property charged; and

(b) an action is brought within one year of the discontinuance of that possession by the subsequent incumbrancer;

the subsequent incumbrancer may recover by that action all the arrears of interest which fell due during the period of possession by the prior incumbrancer or damages in respect of those arrears, notwithstanding that the period exceeded six years.

(7) Where—

(a) the property subject to the mortgage or charge comprises any future interest or life insurance policy; and

(b) it is a term of the mortgage or charge that arrears of interest shall be treated as part of the principal sum of money secured by the mortgage or charge;

interest shall not be treated as becoming due before the right to recover the principal sum of money has accrued or is treated as having accrued.

Time limits for actions in respect of trust property

21.—(1) No period of limitation prescribed by this Act shall apply to an action by a beneficiary under a trust, being an action—

(a) in respect of any fraud or fraudulent breach of trust to which the trustee was a party or privy; or

(b) to recover from the trustee trust property or the proceeds of trust property in the possession of the trustee, or previously received by the trustee and converted to his use.

(2) Where a trustee who is also a beneficiary under the trust receives or retains trust property or its proceeds as his share on a distribution of trust property under the trust, his liability in any action brought by virtue of subsection (1)(b) above to recover that property or its proceeds after the expiration of the period of limitation prescribed by this Act for bringing an action to recover trust property shall be limited to the excess over his proper share.

This subsection only applies if the trustee acted honestly and reasonably in making the distribution.

(3) Subject to the preceding provisions of this section, an action by a beneficiary to recover trust property or in respect of any breach of trust, not being an action for which a period of limitation is prescribed by any other provision of this Act, shall not be brought after the expiration of six years from the date on which the right of action accrued.

For the purposes of this subsection, the right of action shall not be treated as having accrued to any beneficiary entitled to a future interest in the trust property until the interest fell into possession.

(4) No beneficiary as against whom there would be a good defence under this Act shall derive any greater or other benefit from a judgment or order obtained by any other beneficiary than he could have obtained if he had brought the action and this Act had been pleaded in defence.

Time limit for actions claiming personal estate of a deceased person

22.—Subject to section 21(1) and (2) of this Act—

(a) no action in respect of any claim to the personal estate of a deceased person or to any share or interest in any such estate (whether under a will or on intestacy) shall be brought after the expiration of twelve years from the date on which the right to receive the share or interest accrued; and

(b) no action to recover arrears of interest in respect of any legacy, or damages in respect of such arrears, shall be brought after the expiration of six years from the date on which the interest became due.

Time limit in respect of actions for an account

23.—An action for an account shall not be brought after the expiration of any time limit under this Act which is applicable to the claim which is the basis of the duty to account.

Time limit for actions to enforce judgments

24.—(1) An action shall be brought upon any judgment after the expiration of six years from the date on which the judgment became enforceable.

(2) No arrears of interest in respect of any judgment debt shall be recovered after the expiration of six years from the date on which the interest became due.

Administration to date back to death

26.—For the purposes of the provisions of this Act relating to actions for the recovery of land and advowsons an administrator of the estate of a deceased person shall be treated as claiming as if there had been no interval of time between the death of the deceased person and the grant of the letters of administration.

Cure of defective disentailing assurance

27.—(1) This section applies where—

(a) a person entitled in remainder to an entailed interest in any land makes an assurance of his interest which fails to bar the issue in tail or the estates and interests taking effect on the determination of the entailed interest, or fails to bar those estates and interests only; and

(b) any person takes possession of the land by virtue of the assurance.

(2) If the person taking possession of the land by virtue of the assurance, or any other person whatsoever (other than a person entitled to possession by virtue of the settlement) is in possession of the land for a period of twelve years from the commencement of the time when the assurance could have operated as an effective bar, the assurance shall thereupon operate, and be treated as having always operated, to bar the issue in tail and the estates and interests taking effect on the determination of the entailed interest.

(3) The reference in subsection (2) above to the time when the assurance could have operated as an effective bar is a reference to the time at which the assurance, if it had then been executed by the person entitled to the entailed interest, would have operated, without the consent of any other person, to bar the issue in tail and the estates and interests taking effect on the determination of the entailed interest.

PART II
EXTENSION OR EXCLUSION OF ORDINARY TIME LIMITS

Extension of limitation period in case of disability

28.—(1) Subject to the following provisions of this section, if on the date when any right of action accrued for which a period of limitation is prescribed by this Act, the person to whom it accrued was under a disability, the action may be brought at any time before the expiration of six years from the date when he ceased to be under a disability or died (whichever first occurred) notwithstanding that the period of limitation has expired.

(2) This section shall not affect any case where the right of action first accrued to some person (not under a disability) through whom the person under a disability claims.

(3) When a right of action which has accrued to a person under a disability accrues, on the death of that person while still under a disability, to another person under a disability, no further extension of time shall be allowed by reason of the disability of the second person.

(4) No action to recover land or money charged on land shall be brought by virtue of this section by any person after the expiration of thirty years from the date on which the right of action accrued to that person or some person through whom he claims.

(4A) If the action is one to which section 4A of this Act applies, subsection (1) above shall have effect as if for the words from "at any time" to "occurred)" there were substituted the words "by him at any time before the expiration of three years from the date when he ceased to be under a disability."

(5) If the action is one to which section 10 of this Act applies, subsection (1) above shall have effect as if for the words "six years" there were substituted the words "two years".

(6) If the action is one to which section 11 or 12(2) of this Act applies, subsection (1) above shall have effect as if for the words "six years" there were substituted the words "three years".

(7) If the action is one to which section 11A of this Act applies or one by virtue of section 6(1)(a) of the Consumer Protection Act 1987 (death caused by defective product), subsection (1) above—

> (a) shall not apply to the time limit prescribed by subsection (3) of the said section 11A or to that time limit as applied by virtue of section 12(1) of this Act; and
>
> (b) in relation to any other time limit prescribed by this Act shall have effect as if for the words "six years" there were substituted the words "three years".

Subs. (4A) added by Administration of Justice Act 1985, s.57 and subs. (7) added by Consumer Protection Act 1987, Sched. 1.

Extension for cases where the limitation period is the period under section 14A(4)(b)

28A.—(1) Subject to subsection (2) below, if in the case of any action for which a period of limitation is prescribed by section 14A of this Act—

> (a) the period applicable in accordance with subsection (4) of that section is the period mentioned in paragraph (b) of that subsection;
>
> (b) on the date which is for the purposes of that section the starting date for reckoning that period the person by reference to whose knowledge that date fell to be determined under subsection (5) of that section was under a disability; and
>
> (c) section 28 of this Act does not apply to the action;

the action may be brought at any time before the expiration of three years from the date when he ceased to be under a disability or died (whichever first occurred) notwithstanding that the period mentioned above has expired.

(2) An action may not be brought by virtue of subsection (1) above after the end of the period of limitation prescribed by section 14B of this Act.

Added by Consumer Protection Act 1987, Sched. 1.

Fresh accrual of action on acknowledgment or part payment

29.—(1) Subsections (2) and (3) below apply where any right of action (including a foreclosure action) to recover land or an advowson or any right of a mortgagee of personal property to bring a foreclosure action in respect of the property has accrued.

(2) If the person in possession of the land, benefice or personal property in question acknowledges the title of the person to whom the right of action has accrued—

  (a) the right shall be treated as having accrued on and not before the date of the acknowledgment; and
  (b) in the case of a right of action to recover land which has accrued to a person entitled to an estate or interest taking effect on the determination of an entailed interest against whom time is running under section 27 of this Act, section 27 shall thereupon cease to apply to the land.

(3) In the case of a foreclosure or other action by a mortgagee, if the person in possession of the land, benefice or personal property in question or the person liable for the mortgage debt makes any payment in respect of the debt (whether of principal or interest) the right shall be treated as having accrued on and not before the date of the payment.

(4) Where a mortgagee is by virtue of the mortgage in possession of any mortgaged land and either—

  (a) receives any sum in respect of the principal or interest of the mortgage debt; or
  (b) acknowledges the title of the mortgagor, or his equity of redemption;

an action to redeem the land in his possession may be brought at any time before the expiration of twelve years from the date of the payment or acknowledgment.

(5) Subject to subsection (6) below, where any right of action has accrued to recover—

  (a) any debt or other liquidated pecuniary claim; or
  (b) any claim to the personal estate of a deceased person or to any share or interest in any such estate;

and the person liable or accountable for the claim acknowledges the claim or makes any payment in respect of it the right shall be treated as having accrued on and not before the date of the acknowledgment or payment.

(6) A payment of a part of the rent or interest due at any time shall not extend the period for claiming the remainder then due, but any payment of interest shall be treated as a payment in respect of the principal debt.

(7) Subject to subsection (6) above, a current period of limitation may be repeatedly extended under this section by further acknowledgments or payments, but a right of action, once barred by this Act, shall not be revived by any subsequent acknowledgment or payment.

Formal provisions as to acknowledgments and part payments

30.—(1) To be effective for the purposes of section 29 of this Act, an acknowledgment must be in writing and signed by the person making it.

(2) For the purposes of section 29, any acknowledgment or payment—

(a) may be made by the agent of the person by whom it is required to be made under that section; and

(b) shall be made to the person, or to an agent of the person, whose title or claim is being acknowledged or, as the case may be, in respect of whose claim the payment is being made.

Effect of acknowledgment or part payment on persons other than the maker or recipient

31.—(1) An acknowledgment of the title to any land, benefice, or mortgaged personalty by any person in possession of it shall bind all other persons in possession during the ensuing period of limitation.

(2) A payment in respect of a mortgage debt by the mortgagor or any other person liable for the debt, or by any person in possession of the mortgaged property, shall, so far as any right of the mortgagee to foreclose or otherwise to recover the property is concerned, bind all other persons in possession of the mortgaged property during the ensuing period of limitation.

(3) Where two or more mortgagees are by virtue of the mortgage in possession of the mortgaged land, an acknowledgment of the mortgagor's title or of his equity of redemption by one of the mortgagees shall only bind him and his successors and shall not bind any other mortgagee or his successors.

(4) Where in a case within subsection (3) above the mortgagee by whom the acknowledgment is given is entitled to a part of the mortgaged land and not to any ascertained part of the mortgage debt the mortgagor shall be entitled to redeem that part of the land on payment, with interest, of the part of the mortgage debt which bears the same proportion to the whole of the debt as the value of the part of the land bears to the whole of the mortgaged land.

(5) Where there are two or more mortgagors, and the title or equity of redemption of one of the mortgagors is acknowledged as mentioned above in this section, the acknowledgment shall be treated as having been made to all the mortgagors.

(6) An acknowledgment of any debt or other liquidated pecuniary claim shall bind the acknowledgor and his successors but not any other person.

(7) A payment made in respect of any debt or other liquidated pecuniary claim shall bind all persons liable in respect of the debt or claim.

(8) An acknowledgment by one of several personal representatives of any claim to the personal estate of a deceased person or to any share or interest in any such estate, or a payment by one of several representatives in respect of any such claim shall bind the estate of the deceased person.

(9) In this section "successor", in relation to any mortgagee or person liable in respect of any debt or claim, means his personal representatives and any other person on whom the rights under the mortgage or, as the case may be, the liability in respect of the debt or claim devolve (whether on death or bankruptcy or the disposition of property or the determination of a limited estate or interest in settled property or otherwise).

Postponement of limitation period in case of fraud, concealment or mistake

32.—(1) Subject to subsections (3) and (4A) below, where in the case of any action for which a period of limitation is prescribed by this Act, either—

> (*a*) the action is based upon the fraud of the defendant; or
> (*b*) any fact relevant to the plaintiff's right of action has been deliberately concealed from him by the defendant; or
> (*c*) the action is for relief from the consequences of a mistake;

the period of limitation shall not begin to run until the plaintiff has discovered the fraud, concealment or mistake (as the case may be) or could with reasonable diligence have discovered it.

References in this subsection to the defendant include references to the defendant's agent and to any person through whom the defendant claims and his agent.

(2) For the purposes of subsection (1) above, deliberate commission of a breach of duty in circumstances in which it is unlikely to be discovered for some time amounts to deliberate concealment of the facts involved in that breach of duty.

(3) Nothing in this section shall enable any action—

> (*a*) to recover, or recover the value of, any property; or
> (*b*) to enforce any charge against, or set aside any transaction affecting, any property;

to be brought against the purchaser of the property or any person claiming through him in any case where the property has been purchased for valuable consideration by an innocent third party since the fraud or concealment or (as the case may be) the transaction in which the mistake was made took place.

(4) A purchaser is an innocent third party for the purposes of this section—

> (*a*) in the case of fraud or concealment of any fact relevant to the plaintiff's right of action, if he was not a party to the fraud or (as the case may be) to the concealment of that fact and did not at the time of the purchase know or have reason to believe that the fraud or concealment had taken place; and
> (*b*) in the case of mistake, if he did not at the time of the purchase know or have reason to believe that the mistake had been made.

(4A) Subsection (1) above shall not apply in relation to the time limit prescribed by section 11A(3) of this Act or in relation to that time limit as applied by virtue of section 12(1) of this Act.

(5) Sections 14A and 14B of this Act shall not apply to any action to which subsection (1)(*b*) above applies (and accordingly the period of limitation referred to in that subsection, in any case to which either of those sections would otherwise apply, is the period applicable under section 2 of this Act).

Subs. (4A) added by Consumer Protection Act 1987, Sched. 1 and subs. (5) added by Latent Damage Act 1986, s.2.

Discretionary extension of time limit for actions for libel or slander

32A. Where a person to whom a cause of action for libel or slander has accrued has not brought such an action within the period of three years mentioned in section 4A of this Act (or, where applicable, the period allowed by section 28(1) as modified by section 28(4A)) because all or any of the facts relevant to that cause of action did not become known to him until after the expiration of that period, such an action—

    (*a*) may be brought by him at any time before the expiration of one year from the earliest date on which he knew all the facts relevant to that cause of action; but

    (*b*) shall not be so brought without the leave of the High Court.

Added by Administration of Justice Act 1985, s.57.

Discretionary exclusion of time for actions in respect of personal injuries or death

33.—(1) If it appears to the court that it would be equitable to allow an action to proceed having regard to the degree to which—

    (*a*) the provisions of section 11 or 12 of this Act prejudice the plaintiff or any person whom he represents; and

    (*b*) any decision of the court under this subsection would prejudice the defendant or any person whom he represents;

the court may direct that those provisions shall not apply to the action, or shall not apply to any specified cause of action to which the action relates.

(1A) The court shall not under this section disapply—

    (*a*) subsection (3) of section 11A; or

    (*b*) where the damages claimed by the plaintiff are confined to damages for loss of or damage to any property, any other provision in its application to an action by virtue of Part I of the Consumer Protection Act 1987.

(2) The court shall not under this section disapply section 12(1) except where the reason why the person injured could no longer maintain an action was because of the time limit in section 11.

If, for example, the person injured could at his death no longer maintain an action under the Fatal Accidents Act 1976 because of the time limit in Article 29 in Schedule 1 to the Carriage by Air Act 1961, the court has no power to direct that section 12(1) shall not apply.

(3) In acting under this section the court shall have regard to all the circumstances of the case and in particular to—

    (a) the length of, and the reasons for, the delay on the part of the plaintiff;

    (b) the extent to which, having regard to the delay, the evidence adduced or likely to be adduced by the plaintiff or the defendant is or is likely to be less cogent than if the action had been brought within the time allowed by section 11 or (as the case may be) by section 12;

    (c) the conduct of the defendant after the cause of action arose, including the extent (if any) to which he responded to requests reasonably made by the plaintiff for information or inspection for the purpose of ascertaining facts which were or might be relevant to the plaintiff's cause of action against the defendant;

    (d) the duration of any disability of the plaintiff arising after the date of the accrual of the cause of action;

    (e) the extent to which the plaintiff acted promptly and reasonably once he knew whether or not the act or omission of the defendant, to which the injury was attributable, might be capable at that time of giving rise to an action for damages;

    (f) the steps, if any, taken by the plaintiff to obtain medical, legal or other expert advice and the nature of any such advice he may have received.

(4) In a case where the person injured died when, because of section 11, he could no longer maintain an action and recover damages in respect of the injury, the court shall have regard in particular to the length of, and the reasons for, the delay on the part of the deceased.

(5) In a case under subsection (4) above, or any other case where the time limit, or one of the time limits, depends on the date of knowledge of a person other than the plaintiff, subsection (3) above shall have effect with appropriate modifications, and shall have effect in particular as if references to the plaintiff included references to any person whose date of knowledge is or was relevant in determining a time limit.

(6) A direction by the court disapplying the provisions of section 12(1) shall operate to disapply the provisions to the same effect in section 1(1) of the Fatal Accidents Act 1976.

(7) In this section "the court" means the court in which the action has been brought.

(8) References in this section to section 11 include references to that section as extended by any of the preceding provisions of this Part of this Act or by any provision of Part III of this Act.

Subs. (1A) added by Consumer Protection Act 1987, Sched. 1.

PART III
MISCELLANEOUS AND GENERAL

Application of Act and other limitation enactments to arbitrations

34.—(1) This Act and any other limitation enactment shall apply to arbitrations as they apply to actions in the High Court.

(2) Notwithstanding any term in an arbitration agreement to the effect that no cause of action shall accrue in respect of any matter required by the agreement to be referred until an award is made under the agreement, the cause of action shall, for the purpose of this Act and any other limitation enactment (whether in their application to arbitrations or to other proceedings), be deemed to have accrued in respect of any such matter at the time when it would have accrued but for that term in the agreement.

(3) For the purposes of this Act and of any other limitation enactment an arbitration shall be treated as being commenced—

(a) when one party to the arbitration serves on the other party or parties a notice requiring him or them to appoint an arbitrator or to agree to the appointment of an arbitrator; or

(b) where the arbitration agreement provides that the reference shall be to a person named or designated in the agreement, when one party to the arbitration serves on the other party or parties a notice requiring him or them to submit the dispute to the person so named or designated.

(4) Any such notice may be served either—

(a) by delivering it to the person on whom it is to be served; or

(b) by leaving it at the usual or last-known place of abode in England and Wales of that person; or

(c) by sending it by post in a registered letter addressed to that person at his usual or last-known place of abode in England and Wales;

as well as in any other manner provided in the arbitration agreement.

(5) Where the High Court—

(a) orders that an award be set aside; or

(b) orders, after the commencement of an arbitration, that the arbitration agreement shall cease to have effect with respect to the dispute referred;

the court may further order that the period between the commencement of the arbitration and the date of the order of the court shall be excluded in computing the time prescribed by this Act or by any other limitation enactment for the commencement of proceedings (including arbitration) with respect to the dispute referred.

(6) This section shall apply to an arbitration under an Act of Parliament as well as to an arbitration pursuant to an arbitration agreement.

Subsections (3) and (4) above shall have effect, in relation to an arbitration under an Act, as if for the references to the arbitration agreement there were substituted references to such of the provisions of the Act or of any order, scheme, rules, regulations or byelaws made under the Act as relate to the arbitration.

(7) In this section—

    (*a*) "arbitration", "arbitration agreement" and "award" have the same meanings as in Part I of the Arbitration Act 1950; and

    (*b*) references to any other limitation enactment are references to any other enactment relating to the limitation of actions, whether passed before or after the passing of this Act.

New claims in pending actions: rules of court

35.—(1) For the purposes of this Act, any new claim made in the course of any action shall be deemed to be a separate action and to have been commenced—

    (*a*) in the case of a new claim made in or by way of third party proceedings, on the date on which those proceedings were commenced; and

    (*b*) in the case of any other new claim, on the same date as the original action.

(2) In this section a new claim means any claim by way of set-off or counterclaim, and any claim involving either—

    (*a*) the addition or substitution of a new cause of action; or

    (*b*) the addition or substitution of a new party;

and "third party proceedings" means any proceedings brought in the course of any action by any party to the action against a person not previously a party to the action, other than proceedings brought by joining any such person as defendant to any claim already made in the original action by the party bringing the proceedings.

(3) Except as provided by section 33 of this Act or by rules of court, neither the High Court nor any county court shall allow a new claim within subsection (1)(*b*) above, other than an original set-off or counterclaim, to be made in the course of any action after the expiry of any time limit under this Act which would affect a new action to enforce that claim.

For the purposes of this subsection, a claim is an original set-off or an original counterclaim if it is a claim made by way of set-off or (as the case may be) by way of counterclaim by a party who has not previously made any claim in the action.

(4) Rules of court may provide for allowing a new claim to which subsection (3) above applies to be made as there mentioned, but only if the conditions specified in subsection (5) below are satisfied, and subject to any further restrictions the rules may impose.

(5) The conditions referred to in subsection (4) above are the following—

    (*a*) in the case of a claim involving a new cause of action, if the new cause of action arises out of the same facts or substantially the same facts as are already in issue on any claim previously made in the original action; and

    (*b*) in the case of a claim involving a new party, if the addition or substitution of the new party is necessary for the determination of the original action.

(6) The addition or substitution of a new party shall not be regarded for the purposes of subsection (5)(*b*) above as necessary for the determination of the original action unless either—

   (*a*) the new party is substituted for a party whose name was given in any claim made in the original action in mistake for the new party's name; or

   (*b*) any claim already made in the original action cannot be maintained by or against an existing party unless the new party is joined or substituted as plaintiff or defendant in that action.

(7) Subject to subsection (4) above, rules of court may provide for allowing a party to any action to claim relief in a new capacity in respect of a new cause of action notwithstanding that he had no title to make that claim at the date of the commencement of the action.

This subsection shall not be taken as prejudicing the power of rules of court to provide for allowing a party to claim relief in a new capacity without adding or substituting a new cause of action.

(8) Subsections (3) to (7) above shall apply in relation to a new claim made in the course of third party proceedings as if those proceedings were the original action, and subject to such other modifications as may be prescribed by rules of court in any case or class of case.

(9) [*Repealed by Supreme Court Act 1981, Sched. 7.*]

Equitable jurisdiction and remedies

36.—(1) The following time limits under this Act, that is to say—

   (*a*)   the time limit under section 2 for actions founded on tort;

   (*aa*) the time limit under section 4A for actions for libel or slander;

   (*b*)   the time limit under section 5 for actions founded on simple contract;

   (*c*)   the time limit under section 7 for actions to enforce awards where the submission is not by an instrument under seal;

   (*d*)   the time limit under section 8 for actions on a specialty;

   (*e*)   the time limit under section 9 for actions to recover a sum recoverable by virtue of any enactment; and

   (*f*)   the time limit under section 24 for actions to enforce a judgment;

shall not apply to any claim for specific performance of a contract or for an injunction or for other equitable relief, except in so far as any such time limit may be applied by the court by analogy in like manner as the corresponding time limit under any enactment repealed by the Limitation Act 1939 was applied before 1st July 1940.

(2) Nothing in this Act shall affect any equitable jurisdiction to refuse relief on the ground of acquiescence or otherwise.

Subs. (*aa*) added by Administration of Justice Act 1985, s.57.

Application to the Crown and the Duke of Cornwall

37.—(1) Except as otherwise expressly provided in this Act, and without prejudice to section 39, this Act shall apply to proceedings by or against the Crown in like manner as it applies to proceedings between subjects.

(2) Notwithstanding subsection (1) above, this Act shall not apply to—

(a) any proceedings by the Crown for the recovery of any tax or duty or interest on any tax or duty;

(b) any forfeiture proceedings under the customs and excise Acts (within the meaning of the Customs and Excise Management Act 1979); or

(c) any proceedings in respect of the forfeiture of a ship.

In this subsection "duty" includes any debt due to Her Majesty under section 16 of the Tithe Act 1936, and "ship" includes every description of vessel used in navigation not propelled by oars.

(3) For the purposes of this section, proceedings by or against the Crown include—

(a) proceedings by or against Her Majesty in right of the Duchy of Lancaster;

(b) proceedings by or against any Government department or any officer of the Crown as such or any person acting on behalf of the Crown; and

(c) proceedings by or against the Duke of Cornwall.

(4) For the purpose of the provisions of this Act relating to actions for the recovery of land and advowsons, references to the Crown shall include references to Her Majesty in right of the Duchy of Lancaster; and those provisions shall apply to lands and advowsons forming part of the possessions of the Duchy of Cornwall as if for the references to the Crown there were substituted references to the Duke of Cornwall as defined in the Duchy of Cornwall Management Act 1863.

(5) For the purposes of this Act a proceeding by petition of right (in any case where any such proceeding lies, by virtue of any saving in section 40 of the Crown Proceedings Act 1947, notwithstanding the general abolition by that Act of proceedings by way of petition of right) shall be treated as being commenced on the date on which the petition is presented.

(6) Nothing in this Act shall affect the prerogative right of Her Majesty (whether in right of the Crown or of the Duchy of Lancaster) or of the Duke of Cornwall to any gold or silver mine.

Interpretation

38.—(1) In this Act, unless the context otherwise requires—

"action" includes any proceedings in a court of law, including an ecclesiastical court;

"land" includes corporeal hereditaments, tithes and rentcharges and any legal or equitable estate or interest therein, including an interest in the proceeds of the sale of land held upon trust for sale, but except as provided above in this definition does not include any incorporeal hereditament;

"personal estate" and "personal property" do not include chattels real;

"personal injuries" includes any disease and any impairment of a person's physical or mental condition, and "injury" and cognate expressions shall be construed accordingly;

"rent" includes a rentcharge and a rentservice;

"rentcharge" means any annuity or periodical sum of money charged upon or payable out of land, except a rent service or interest on a mortgage on land;

"settled land", "statutory owner" and "tenant for life" have the same meanings respectively as in the Settled Land Act 1925;

"trust" and "trustee" have the same meanings respectively as in the Trustee Act 1925; and

"trust for sale" has the same meaning as in the Law of Property Act 1925.

(2) For the purposes of this Act a person shall be treated as under a disability while he is an infant, or of unsound mind.

(3) For the purposes of subsection (2) above a person is of unsound mind if he is a person who, by reason of mental disorder within the meaning of the Mental Health Act 1983, is incapable of managing and administering his property and affairs.

(4) Without prejudice to the generality of subsection (3) above, a person shall be conclusively presumed for the purposes of subsection (2) above to be of unsound mind—

(a) while he is liable to be detained or subject to guardianship under the Mental Health Act 1983 (otherwise than by virtue of section 35 or 89); and

(b) while he is receiving treatment as an in-patient in any hospital within the meaning of the Mental Health Act 1983 or mental nursing home within the meaning of the Nursing Homes Act 1975 without being liable to be detained under the said Act of 1983 (otherwise than by virtue of section 35 or 89), being treatment which follows without any interval a period during which he was liable to be detained or subject to guardianship under the Mental Health Act 1959, or the said Act of 1983 (otherwise than by virtue of section 35 or 89) or by virtue of any enactment repealed or excluded by the Mental Health Act 1959.

(5) Subject to subsection (6) below, a person shall be treated as claiming through another person if he became entitled by, through, under, or by the act of that other person to the right claimed, and any person whose estate or interest might have been barred by a person entitled to an entailed interest in possession shall be treated as claiming through the person so entitled.

(6) A person becoming entitled to any estate or interest by virtue of a special power of appointment shall not be treated as claiming through the appointor.

(7) References in this Act to a right of action to recover land shall include references to a right to enter into possession of the land or, in the case of rentcharges and tithes, to distrain for arrears of rent or tithe, and references to the bringing of such an action shall include references to the making of such an entry or distress.

(8) References in this Act to the possession of land shall, in the case of tithes and rentcharges, be construed as references to the receipt of the tithe or rent, and references to the date of dispossession or discontinuance of possession of land shall, in the case of rentcharges, be construed as references to the date of the last receipt of rent.

(9) References in Part II of this Act to a right of action shall include references to—

(a) a cause of action;

(b) a right to receive money secured by a mortgage or charge on any property;

(c) a right to recover proceeds of the sale of land; and

(d) a right to receive a share or interest in the personal estate of a deceased person.

(10) References in Part II to the date of the accrual of a right of action shall be construed—

(a) in the case of an action upon a judgment, as references to the date on which the judgment became enforceable; and

(b) in the case of an action to recover arrears of rent or interest, or damages in respect of arrears of rent or interest, as references to the date on which the rent or interest became due.

Subs. (4)(a) and (b) amended by the Mental Health (Amendment) Act 1982, Sched. 3. Subs. (3), (4)(a) amended and subs. (4)(b) substituted by Mental Health Act 1983.

Saving for other limitation enactments

39.—This Act shall not apply to any action or arbitration for which a period of limitation is prescribed by or under any other enactment (whether passed before or after the passing of this Act) or to any action or arbitration to which the Crown is a party and for which, if it were between subjects, a period of limitation would be prescribed by or under any such other enactment.

Transitional provisions, amendments and repeals

40.—(1) Schedule 2 to this Act, which contains transitional provisions, shall have effect.

(2) The enactment specified in Schedule 3 to this Act shall have effect subject to the amendments specified in that Schedule, being amendments consequential on the provisions of this Act; but the amendment of any enactment by that Schedule shall not be taken as prejudicing the operation of section 17(2) of the Interpretation Act 1978 (effect of repeals).

(3) The enactments specified in Schedule 4 to this Act are hereby repealed to the extent specified in column 3 of that Schedule.

Short title, commencement and extent

41.—(1) This Act may be cited as the Limitation Act 1980.

(2) This Act, except section 35, shall come into force on 1st May 1981.

(3) Section 35 of this Act shall come into force on 1st May 1981 to the extent (if any) that the section substituted for section 28 of the Limitation Act 1939 by section 8 of the Limitation Amendment Act 1980 is in force immediately before that date; but otherwise section 35 shall come into force on such day as the Lord Chancellor may by order made by statutory instrument appoint, and different days may be appointed for different purposes of that section (including its application in relation to different courts or proceedings).

(4) The repeal by this Act of section 14(1) of the Limitation Act 1963 and the corresponding saving in paragraph 2 of Schedule 2 to this Act shall extend to Northern Ireland, but otherwise this Act does not extend to Scotland or to Northern Ireland.

SCHEDULES   Section 15(6), (7)

Schedule 1: Provisions with Respect to Actions to Recover Land

PART I
ACCRUAL OF RIGHTS OF ACTION TO RECOVER LAND

Accrual of right of action in case of present interests in land

1. Where the person bringing an action to recover land, or some person through whom he claims, has been in possession of the land, and has while entitled to the land been dispossessed or discontinued his possession, the right of action shall be treated as having accrued on the date of the dispossession or discontinuance.

2. Where any person brings an action to recover any land of a deceased person (whether under a will or on intestacy) and the deceased person—

    (*a*)   was on the date of his death in possession of the land or, in the case of a rentcharge created by will or taking effect upon his death, in possession of the land charged; and

    (*b*)   was the last person entitled to the land to be in possession of it;

the right of action shall be treated as having accrued on the date of his death.

3. Where any person brings an action to recover land, being an estate or interest in possession assured otherwise than by will to him, or to some person through whom he claims, and—

    (*a*)   the person making the assurance was on the date when the assurance took effect in possession of the land or, in the case of a rentcharge created by the assurance, in possession of the land charged; and

    (*b*)   no person has been in possession of the land by virtue of the assurance;

the right of action shall be treated as having accrued on the date when the assurance took effect.

Accrual of right of action in case of future interests

4. The right of action to recover any land shall, in a case where—

(a) the estate or interest claimed was an estate or interest in reversion or remainder or any other future estate or interest; and

(b) no person has taken possession of the land by virtue of the estate or interest claimed;

be treated as having accrued on the date on which the estate or interest fell into possession by the determination of the preceding estate or interest.

5.—(1) Subject to sub-paragraph (2) below, a tenancy from year to year or other period, without a lease in writing, shall for the purposes of this Act be treated as being determined at the expiration of the first year or other period; and accordingly the right of action of the person entitled to the land subject to the tenancy shall be treated as having accrued at the date on which in accordance with this sub-paragraph the tenancy is determined.

(2) Where any rent has subsequently been received in respect of the tenancy, the right of action shall be treated as having accrued on the date of the last receipt of rent.

6.—(1) Where—

(a) any person is in possession of land by virtue of a lease in writing by which a rent of not less than ten pounds a year is reserved; and

(b) the rent is received by some person wrongfully claiming to be entitled to the land in reversion immediately expectant on the determination of the lease; and

(c) no rent is subsequently received by the person rightfully so entitled;

the right of action to recover the land of the person rightfully so entitled shall be treated as having accrued on the date when the rent was first received by the person wrongfully claiming to be so entitled and not on the date of the determination of the lease.

(2) Sub-paragraph (1) above shall not apply to any lease granted by the Crown.

Accrual of right of action in case of forfeiture or breach of condition

7.—(1) Subject to sub-paragraph (2) below, a right of action to recover land by virtue of a forfeiture or breach of condition shall be treated as having accrued on the date on which the forfeiture was incurred or the condition broken.

(2) If any such right has accrued to a person entitled to an estate or interest in reversion or remainder and the land was not recovered by virtue of that right, the right of action to recover the land shall not be treated as having accrued to that person until his estate or interest fell into possession, as if no such forfeiture or breach of condition had occurred.

Right of action not to accrue or continue unless there is adverse possession

8.—(1) No right of action to recover land shall be treated as accruing unless the land is in the possession of some person in whose favour the period of limitation can run (referred to below in this paragraph as "adverse possession"); and where under the preceding provisions of this Schedule any such right of action is treated as accruing on a certain date and no person is in adverse possession on that date, the right of action shall not be treated as accruing unless and until adverse possession is taken of the land.

(2) Where a right of action to recover land has accrued and after its accrual, before the right is barred, the land ceases to be in adverse possession, the right of action shall no longer be treated as having accrued and no fresh right of action shall be treated as accruing unless and until the land is again taken into adverse possession.

(3) For the purposes of this paragraph—

(a) possession of any land subject to a rentcharge by a person (other than the person entitled to the rentcharge) who does not pay the rent shall be treated as adverse possession of the rentcharge; and

(b) receipt of rent under a lease by a person wrongfully claiming to be entitled to the land in reversion immediately expectant on the determination of the lease shall be treated as adverse possession of the land.

(4) For the purpose of determining whether a person occupying any land is in adverse possession of the land it shall not be assumed by implication of law that his occupation is by permission of the person entitled to the land merely by virtue of the fact that his occupation is not inconsistent with the latter's present or future enjoyment of the land.

This provision shall not be taken as prejudicing a finding to the effect that a person's occupation of any land is by implied permission of the person entitled to the land in any case where such a finding is justified on the actual facts of the case.

Possession of beneficiary not adverse to others interested in settled land or land held on trust for sale

9. Where any settled land or any land held on trust for sale is in the possession of a person entitled to a beneficial interest in the land or in the proceeds of sale (not being a person solely or absolutely entitled to the land or the proceeds), no right of action to recover the land shall be treated for the purposes of this Act as accruing during that possession to any person in whom the land is vested as tenant for life, statutory owner or trustee, or to any other person entitled to a beneficial interest in the land or the proceeds of sale.

Part II
Modifications of Section 15 where Crown or Certain Corporations Sole are involved

10. Subject to paragraph 11 below, section 15(1) of this Act shall apply to the bringing of an action to recover any land by the Crown or by any spiritual or eleemosynary corporation sole with the substitution for the reference to twelve years of a reference to thirty years.

11.—(1) An action to recover foreshore may be brought by the Crown at any time before the expiration of sixty years from the date mentioned in section 15(1) of this Act.

(2) Where any right of action to recover land which has ceased to be foreshore but remains in the ownership of the Crown accrued when the land was foreshore, the action may be brought at any time before the expiration of—

(a) sixty years from the date of accrual of the right of action; or
(b) thirty years from the date when the land ceased to be foreshore;

whichever period first expires.

(3) In this paragraph "foreshore" means the shore and bed of the sea and of any tidal water, below the line of the medium high tide between the spring tides and the neap tides.

12. Notwithstanding section 15(1) of this Act, where in the case of any action brought by a person other than the Crown or a spiritual or eleemosynary corporation sole the right of action first accrued to the Crown or any such corporation sole through whom the person in question claims, the action may be brought at any time before the expiration of—

    (*a*)   the period during which the action could have been brought by the Crown or the corporation sole; or

    (*b*)   twelve years from the date on which the right of action accrued to some person other than the Crown or the corporation sole;

whichever period first expires.

13. Section 15(2) of this Act shall apply in any case where the Crown or a spiritual or eleemosynary corporation sole is entitled to the succeeding estate or interest with the substitution—

    (*a*)   for the reference to twelve years of a reference to thirty years; and

    (*b*)   for the reference to six years of a reference to twelve years.

*   *   *   *

Foreign Limitation Periods Act 1984

Application of foreign limitation law

1.—(1) Subject to the following provisions of this Act, where in any action or proceedings in a court in England and Wales the law of any other country falls (in accordance with rules of private international law applicable by any such court) to be taken into account in the determination of any matter—

    (*a*)   the law of that other country relating to limitation shall apply in respect of that matter for the purposes of the action or proceedings; and

    (*b*)   except where that matter falls within subsection (2) below, the law of England and Wales relating to limitation shall not so apply.

(2) A matter falls within this subsection if it is a matter in the determination of which both the law of England and Wales and the law of some other country fall to be taken into account.

(3) The law of England and Wales shall determine for the purposes of any law applicable by virtue of subsection (1)(*a*) above whether, and the time at which, proceedings have been commenced in respect of any matter, and, accordingly, section 35 of the Limitation Act 1980 (new claims in pending proceedings) shall apply in relation to time limits applicable by virtue of subsection (1)(*a*) above as it applies in relation to time limits under that Act.

(4) A court in England and Wales, in exercising in pursuance of subsection (1)(*a*) above any discretion conferred by the law of any other country, shall so far as practicable exercise that discretion in the manner in which it is exercised in comparable cases by the courts of that other country.

(5) In this section "law", in relation to any country, shall not include rules of private international law applicable by the courts of that country or, in the case of England and Wales, this Act.

Exceptions to s.1

2.—(1) In any case in which the application of section 1 above would to any extent conflict (whether under subsection (2) below or otherwise) with public policy, that section shall not apply to the extent that its application would so conflict.

(2) The application of section 1 above in relation to any action or proceedings shall conflict with public policy to the extent that its application would cause undue hardship to a person who is, or might be made, a party to the action or proceedings.

(3) Where, under a law applicable by virtue of section 1(1)(a) above for the purposes of any action or proceedings, a limitation period is or may be extended or interrupted in respect of the absence of a party to the action or proceedings from any specified jurisdiction or country, so much of that law as provides for the extension or interruption shall be disregarded for those purposes.

(4) In section 2(1) of the Limitation (Enemies and War Prisoners) Act 1945 (which in relation to cases involving enemy aliens and war prisoners extends certain limitation periods), in the definition of "statute of limitation", at the end, there shall be inserted the words—

> "and, in a case to which section 1(1) of the Foreign Limitation Periods Act 1984 applies, so much of the law of any country outside England and Wales as applies by virtue of that Act."

Foreign judgments on limitation points

3. Where a court in any country outside England and Wales has determined any matter wholly or partly by reference to the law of that or any other country (including England and Wales) relating to limitation, then, for the purposes of the law relating to the effect to be given in England and Wales to that determination, that court shall, to the extent that it has so determined the matter, be deemed to have determined it on its merits.

Meaning of law relating to limitation

4.—(1) Subject to subsection (3) below, references in this Act to the law of any country (including England and Wales) relating to limitation shall, in relation to any matter, be construed as references to so much of the relevant law of that country as (in any manner) makes provision with respect to a limitation period applicable to the bringing of proceedings in respect of that matter in the courts of that country and shall include—

> (a) references to so much of that law as relates to, and to the effect of, the application, extension, reduction or interruption of that period; and
>
> (b) a reference, where under that law there is no limitation period which is so applicable, to the rule that such proceedings may be brought within an indefinite period.

(2) In subsection (1) above "relevant law," in relation to any country, means the procedural and substantive law applicable, apart from any rules of private international law, by the courts of that country.

(3) References in this Act to the law of England and Wales relating to limitation shall not include the rules by virtue of which a court may, in the exercise of any discretion, refuse equitable relief on the grounds of acquiescence or otherwise; but, in applying those rules to a case in relation to which the law of any country outside England and Wales is applicable by virtue of section 1(1)(*a*) above (not being a law that provides for a limitation period that has expired), a court in England and Wales shall have regard, in particular, to the provisions of the law that is so applicable.

Application of Act to arbitrations

5. The references to any other limitation enactment in section 34 of the Limitation Act 1980 (application of limitation enactments to arbitration) include references to sections 1, 2 and 4 of this Act; and, accordingly, in subsection (5) of the said section 34, the reference to the time prescribed by a limitation enactment has effect for the purposes of any case to which section 1 above applies as a reference to the limitation period (if any) applicable by virtue of section 1 above.

★　　★　　★　　★

Prescription Act 1832

Claims to right of common and other profits à prendre, not to be defeated after thirty years enjoyment by merely showing the commencement; after sixty years enjoyment the right to be absolute, unless had by consent or agreement

1. No claim which may be lawfully made at the common law, by custom, prescription, or grant, to any right of common or other profit or benefit to be taken and enjoyed from or upon any land of our sovereign lord the King, or any land being parcel of the duchy of Lancaster or of the duchy of Cornwall, or of any ecclesiastical or lay person, or body corporate, except such matters and things as are herein specially provided for, and except tithes, rent, and services, shall, where such right, profit, or benefit shall have been actually taken and enjoyed by any person claiming right thereto without interruption for the full period of thirty years, be defeated or destroyed by showing only that such right, profit, or benefit was first taken or enjoyed at any time prior to such period of thirty years, but nevertheless such claim may be defeated in any other way by which the same is now liable to be defeated; and when such right, profit, or benefit shall have been so taken and enjoyed as aforesaid for the full period of sixty years, the right thereto shall be deemed absolute and indefeasible, unless it shall appear that the same was taken and enjoyed by some consent or agreement expressly made or given for that purpose by deed or writing.

In claims of right of way or other easement the periods to be twenty years and forty years

2. No claim which may be lawfully made at the common law, by custom, prescription, or grant, to any way or other easement, or to any watercourse, or the use of any water, to be enjoyed or derived upon, over, or from any land or water of our said lord the King, or being parcel of the duchy of Lancaster or of the duchy of Cornwall, or being the property of any ecclesiastical or lay person, or body corporate, when such way or other matter as herein last before mentioned shall have been actually enjoyed by any person claiming right thereto without interruption for the full period of twenty years, shall be defeated or destroyed by showing only that such way or other matter was first enjoyed at any time prior to such period of twenty years, but nevertheless such claim may be defeated in any other way by which the same is now liable to be defeated; and where such way or other matter as herein last before mentioned shall have been so enjoyed as aforesaid for the full period of forty years, the right thereto shall be deemed absolute and indefeasible, unless it shall appear that the same was enjoyed by some consent or agreement expressly given or made for that purpose by deed or writing.

Claim to the use of light enjoyed for 20 years

3. When the access and use of light to and for any dwelling house, workshop, or other building shall have been actually enjoyed therewith for the full period of twenty years without interruption, the right thereto shall be deemed absolute and indefeasible, any local usage or custom to the contrary notwithstanding, unless it shall appear that the same was enjoyed by some consent or agreement expressly made or given for that purpose by deed or writing.

Amended by Rights of Light Act 1959, ss.1 and s.4(2).

Before mentioned periods to be deemed those next before suits

4. Each of the respective periods of years herein-before mentioned shall be deemed and taken to be the period next before some suit or action wherein the claim or matter to which such period may relate shall have been or shall be brought into question and that no act or other matter shall be deemed to be an interruption, within the meaning of this statute, unless the same shall have been or shall be submitted to or acquiesced in for one year after the party interrupted shall have had or shall have notice thereof, and of the person making or authorizing the same to be made.

Amended by Rights of Light Act 1959, s.3(6) and Commons Registration Act 1965, s.16(2).

In actions on the case, the claimant may allege his right generally, as at present. In pleas to trespass and certain other pleadings, the period mentioned in this Act may be alleged. Exceptions, &c. to be replied to specially

5. In all actions upon the case and other pleadings, wherein the party claiming may now by law allege his right generally, without averring the existence of such right from time immemorial, such general allegation shall still be deemed sufficient, and if the same shall be denied, all and every the matters in this Act mentioned and provided, which shall be applicable to the case, shall be admissible in evidence to sustain or rebut such allegation; and that in all pleadings to actions of trespass, and in all other pleadings wherein before the passing of this Act it would have been necessary to allege the right to have existed from time immemorial, it shall be sufficient to allege the enjoyment thereof as of right by the occupiers of the tenement in respect whereof the same is claimed for and during such of the periods mentioned in this Act as may be applicable to the case, and without claiming in the name or right of the owner of the fee, as is now usually done; and if the other party shall intend to rely on any proviso, exception, incapacity, disability, contract, agreement, or other matter herein-before mentioned, or on any cause or matter of fact or of law not inconsistent with the simple fact of enjoyment, the same shall be specially alleged and set forth in answer to the allegation of the party claiming, and shall not be received in evidence on any general traverse or denial of such allegation.

Presumption to be allowed in claims herein provided for

6. In the several cases mentioned in and provided for by this Act, no presumption shall be allowed or made in favour or support of any claim, upon proof of the exercise or enjoyment of the right or matter claimed for any less period of time or number of years than for such period or number mentioned in this Act as may be applicable to the case and to the nature of the claim.

Amended by Rights of Light Act 1959, s.1.

Proviso for infants, &c.

7. Provided also, that the time during which any person otherwise capable of resisting any claim to any of the matters before mentioned shall have been or shall be an infant, idiot, non compos mentis, feme covert, or tenant for life, or during which any action or suit shall have been pending, and which shall have been diligently prosecuted, until abated by the death of any party or parties thereto, shall be excluded in the computation of the periods herein-before mentioned, except only in cases where the right or claim is hereby declared to be absolute and indefeasible.

What time to be excluded in computing the term of forty years appointed by this Act

8. Provided always, that when any land or water upon, over, or from which any such way or other convenient watercourse or use of water shall have been or shall be enjoyed or derived hath been or shall be held under or by virtue of any term of life, or any term of years exceeding three years from the granting thereof, the time of the enjoyment of any such way or other matter as herein last before mentioned, during the continuance of such term, shall be excluded in the computation of the said period of forty years, in case the claim shall within three years next after the end or sooner determination of such term be resisted by any person entitled to any reversion expectant on the determination thereof.

Limitation

9. This Act shall not extend to Scotland . . .

Remainder of section repealed by Statute Law Revision Act 1874.

10. [*Repealed by Statute Law Revision Act 1874.*]

11. [*Repealed by Statute Law Revision Act 1874.*]

INDEX

Accrual of the Cause of Action,
8–10
adverse possession, 95–97
arbitral awards, 10
company, dissolution of, 8
contract, 9, 33–36
of loan, 37–41
defendant capable of being
sued, 8
negligence. *See* Negligence.
patents, 9
personal injury actions, 67
exclusion of time limit, 9
property damage. *See* Property,
Damage To.
retrospective effect of decisions,
9–10
tort. *See* Tort.
writ, issue of, 10
Administrative Law, England,
judicial review, 108–109
Adverse Possession,
accrual of the cause of action,
95–97
acknowledgment of owner's
title, 96
leases, 97
tenancy agreement, 96, 97
discontinuance, 95
dispossession, 95
animus possidendi. See intention
of possessor *below.*
future interests, 86–87
general principles of, 87–88
implied licence, 93–94
intention
of owner, 95
of possessor (*animus
possidendi*)
exclusion of all others, 95
fences, relevance of, 94
nature of intention, 94–95
possession by child, 95
limitation and prescription,
distinguished, 86
tenancy agreements, 92–93, 96,
97
time, expiry of
damages, recovery of, 98
leasehold land, 98
covenants running with
land, 99
privity of estate, 99
registered, 98–99
unregistered, 98

Adverse Possession—*cont.*
time, expiry of—*cont.*
registered land, 97–98
rent, recovery of, 98
unregistered land, 97
title
acquisition of by limitation,
requirements of
acquisition of possession,
88
discontinuance, 88–89
definition, 88
nature of the property,
88
dispossession, 89–90
definition, 88
future development, 89
relevance of squatter's
intention, 89–90
factual possession
nature of the land, 90
shared driveways, 91
trivial acts, 91
waste land, 90
lawful
permission of the owner,
91–92
express revocation of, 92
Agent,
defendant's, act of, 26–29
definition, 27
plaintiff's, acts of, 27
construction cases, 28

Company Law Cases, 32–33
Concealment,
Consumer Protection Act 1987,
62
conversion and, 61
defendant's agent, act of, 27–29
deliberate, 22–24
conscious decision, 22
plaintiff's knowledge, 23
witnesses
application of estoppel, 23
duty to trace, 23
postponement and, 21
reasonable diligence, 25–26
third parties and postponement
of limitations, 29–30
Conflict of Laws,
arbitrations, 7
contracts, 7
double actionability, 7

Conflict of Laws—*cont.*
 limitation, 6
 prescription, 5–6
 public policy, 6
 renvoi, 6
 undue hardship, 6, 7
Contract,
 accrual of the cause of action,
  33–36
  breach
   anticipatory, 34
   continuing, 34–36
    building cases, 35
    continuing duty of care,
     establishing, 36
    duty after completion,
     35
   date of, 34
  action for money had and
   received, 37
  carriage, of, 41–42
   by air, 42
   by rail, 42
   by road, 42
   by sea, 41–42
  company law cases, 32–33
  concurrent action in tort and,
   availability of, 36–37, 49
  conflict of laws and, 7
  failing to materialise, 37
  insurance, 41
  Latent Damage Act 1986 and,
   42–43
  loan, of, 37–41
   accrual of the cause of action,
    37–38
    date for repayment, 38
    demand, 38
   acknowledgment and part
    payment of debt, 38–39
   quantum meruit claim, 39
   assignment of debt, 39
   guarantee, contracts of, 39
   indemnity, contracts of,
    39–41
    joinder of third parties, 40
    "pay to be paid" clauses,
     40
    statutory indemnity, 40–41
  sale of goods, 34
  simple, 31
   specialties and,
    distinguished, 32
  specialties, 31–38
   exceptions to 12-year rule, 33
   non-pecuniary right, 33
   rent and mortgage interest,
    33
   simple contracts and,
    distinguished, 32
   statutes as, 31–32
    money due under, 33

Contribution, 17
Conversion, 3, 21–22, 58–61
 concealment and, 61
 definition, 58
 extinction of title, 59
 fraud and deliberate
  concealment, 61
 subsequent, 59
 theft, 59–60
  conversion followed by theft,
   60
  right to recover goods, 60
  subsequent purchaser in good
   faith, 60
Counter-Claims/Set-Off, 17–18
Cross-Claim, Defence and,
 Distinguished, 17

Death, 116–119
 caused by defendant, 117–118
  action on behalf of
   dependants, 117
  action on behalf of estate,
   117–118
  damages for personal
   injuries, 117–118
  disability and, 117
  knowledge of, 118
 claiming personal estate of
  deceased person, 118–119
  personal representative,
   action against by
   creditors, 119
  trustee, 118–119
 of defendant, 118
 of plaintiff, 118
Defamation, 56–58
 discretionary extension, 57
Disability, 19–20
 death caused by defendant, 117
 mental illness, 20
 minors, 20
 plaintiff, of
  arising after date of the
   accrual, duration of, 83
  legal disability, 83
  mental ill-health, 83
Documents, Negligent Execution
 Of. *See* Negligence.

Easement, 4
 acquisition of, 100
 user
  against whom?, 103
  "as of right", 101–103
  by whom?, 103
  consistent with
   presumption of grant,
   101

Easement—*cont.*
  acquisition of—*cont.*
    user—*cont.*
      continuity of, 101
      force and, 102
      forty-year period, 106
      nature of right acquired
        repairs, 103
        right of way, 103
      permission and, 102–103
      secrecy and, 102
      twenty-year period, 105,
        106
  creation of, 100
  interruption of use and, 105,
    106
  light, right to. *See* Light, Right
    To.
  nuisance, committing, 100
  Prescription Act 1832, 104–107
Equity,
  acquiescence, 114
  analogy with other limitation
    period, 114–115
  laches, 114
  statutory limitation periods, 114
Estoppel, Doctrine Of, 23
European Community,
  calculation of time, 112–113
  complaint of failure to act,
    109–110
  contractual and tortious liability
    of, 110
  time limits, nature and policy
    of, 110–112

False Imprisonment, 56
Final Judgment or Order,
    determination of, 11
Fraud,
  action based on, 21–22
  Consumer Protection Act 1987,
    62
  conversion and, 61
  defendant's agent, act of, 27–29
  postponement and, 21
  reasonable diligence, 25–26
  third parties and postponement
    of limitations, 29–30

Interlocutory Judgment or Order,
    determination of, 11

Judicial Discretion,
  Birkett v. *James*, principles in,
    77–78
  Court of Appeal, intervention
    by, 76
  defendant
    conduct of after cause of
      action arose, 82
    solicitors and insurers, 82
    prejudice to, 75, 78
      relevance of negotiations,
        78
  guidance on exercise of, 76
  multi-partite claims, 84–85
    Opren litigation, 84–85
  plaintiff
    delay by
      cogency of evidence and,
        81
      length of and reasons for,
        80
    disability, duration of, arising
      after date of the accrual,
        83
      legal disability, 83
      mental ill-health, 83
    expert advice, 84
    prejudice to, 75, 76, 79–80
    prompt and reasonable action
      by, 83–84
    relevance of relationship
      with defendant, 83
  unfettered, 75, 80
Judicial Review, 108–109
Judiciary, Attitudes to Limitation
    Periods, 2

Laches, 3, 114
Light, Right To, 4, 100–101,
    106–107
  amount of light taken, 107
  sensitive plaintiff, 107
  time immemorial and, 104
Lost Modern Grant, Doctrine Of,
    104

Mental Illness, Disability And, 20
Minors, Disability And, 20
Mistake, 24–25
  Consumer Protection Act 1987,
    62
  defendant's agent, act of, 27–29
  postponement and, 21
  professional negligence and, 25
  reasonable diligence, 25–26
  third parties and postponement
    of limitations, 29–30

Negligence, 30, 36–37
 accrual of the cause of action,
  44–45
  Latent Damage Act 1986, 53
 negligent execution of
  documents, 49–52
  concurrent action in
   contract and tort, 49
  contract, drafting of, 50–51
  damage
   definition of, 49–50
   "actual", 50
  encumbrance of interests
   in land, 50
  insurance policy, non-
   disclosure of material
   facts in, 51
  loss of interest in
   matrimonial home, 50
Nuisance, 58

Opren Litigation, 84–85

Personal Injury Actions,
 calculation of time, 10
 carriage statutes and, 63
 claims, exclusion of limitation
  period, 16
 criminal injuries compensation,
  74
 cumulative injury, 65
 damages, 2
  death caused by defendant,
   117–118
 definition of personal injury,
  64–65
 direct claims for compensation,
  66
 employers and defective
  machinery, 66
 mental distress, 65
  personal injury and,
   distinguished, 65–66
 running of time
  accrual of the cause of action,
   67
  knowledge, 67–69
   attributable, 69
   constructive, 72–73
    failure to seek medical
     advice, 72–73
   date of, defining, 67–68
   definition of, 68
    belief not sufficient, 68
   identity of the defendant,
    71–72
    corporate groups, 71–72
    harmful drugs, 71
    hit and run accidents, 71

Personal Injury Actions—cont.
 running of time—cont.
  knowledge—cont.
   legal advice, 73–74
   medical advice, 74
   of particular act or
    omission, 69–70
   significance of the injury,
    71
Pleadings, Amendment Of, 13–15
Prescription, 2–3
 common law, 104
  time immemorial test, 104
 easement acquired by. See
  Easement.
 lost modern grant, doctrine of,
  104
 Prescription Act 1832, 104–107
Property, Damage To,
 accrual of the cause of action,
  45–49
  economic loss, 46
   followed by physical
    damage, 47
  emergence of previously
   latent defect, 46
  result of, 46–47
 carriage statutes and, 63

Quantum Meruit Claim, 39

Sale of Goods, Contract For, 34
Set-Off/Counter-Claims, 17–18
Specialties. See Contract.
Striking Out, Power To, 11

Tenancy Agreements, 92–93, 96,
 97
Third Parties,
 innocent, definition, 29
 joinder of in contract of loan,
  40
 postponement of limitations,
  29–30
  innocent purchasers, 29
 proceedings, 16
Time Immemorial, 104
Tort,
 accrual of the cause of action, 9
 Latent Damage Act 1986,
  52–56
  damage
   damages and,
    distinguished, 55
   when reasonable person
    would consider
    sufficient, 54–55

Tort—*cont.*
  accrual of the cause of action—
      cont.
    Latent Damage Act 1986—
        cont.
      facts ascertainable with
          expert advice, 56
      knowledge
        date of reasonable
            discoverability,
            55–56
        definition of, 53
        "material facts", 54
        negligence, 53
        surveyors and, 54
  negligence. *See* Negligence.
  property damage. *See*
      Property, Damage To.
  carriage statutes, 63
  concurrent action in contract
      and, availability of, 36–37,
      49
  Consumer Protection Act 1987,
      61–62
  fraud, concealment and
      mistake, 62
  knowledge, date of, 62
  conversion. *See* Conversion.
  defamation, 56–58
    discretionary extension, 57
  Defective Premises Act, 61
  false imprisonment, 56
  nuisance, 58
  trespass, 56
Trustee,
  action for proceeds in
      possession of, 116

Trustee—*cont.*
  beneficiaries
    time-barred, 116
    unidentified, 116
  fraud and, 115–116
  meaning of, 115
  personal representative, as,
      118–119

Writ,
  amendment of, 13–15
    addition of new cause of
        action, 14
    addition of new party, 16
    alteration of capacity of
        party, 14
    claims for negligent
        misstatement, 15
    correction of name of party,
        13–14
    retrospective, 15
    significant change in nature
        of proceedings, 14–15
  dismissal for want of
      prosecution, 18–19
    delay prior to expiry, 19
  expiry of, burden on plaintiff,
      11
  extension of, 12–13
    showing good cause, 12–13
  limitation period, expiry of
      prior to issue, 11
  period of validity of,
      calculating, 12
  third party proceedings, 16